Doing Second Language Research

Also published in
Oxford Handbooks for Language Teachers

Doing Second Language Research

James Dean Brown and
Theodore S. Rodgers

UNIVERSITY PRESS

OXFORD
UNIVERSITY PRESS

Great Clarendon Street, Oxford OX2 6DP

Oxford University Press is a department of the University of Oxford.
It furthers the University's objective of excellence in research, scholarship,
and education by publishing worldwide in

Oxford New York

Auckland Cape Town Dar es Salaam Hong Kong Karachi
Kuala Lumpur Madrid Melbourne Mexico City Nairobi
New Delhi Shanghai Taipei Toronto

With offices in

Argentina Austria Brazil Chile Czech Republic France Greece
Guatemala Hungary Italy Japan Poland Portugal Singapore
South Korea Switzerland Thailand Turkey Ukraine Vietnam

OXFORD and OXFORD ENGLISH are registered trade marks of
Oxford University Press in the UK and in certain other countries

ISBN: 978 0 19 437174 2

Printed in China

This book is printed on paper from certified and well-managed sources.

CONTENTS

ACKNOWLEDGMENTS

We would like to thank Henry Widdowson, Julia Sallabank, Simon Murison-Bowie, and the anonymous readers who gave us valuable feedback at various stages of this project. We would especially like to thank Adrian Palmer for piloting our materials with his students and giving us excellent feedback and encouragement. We must also recognize and thank the hundreds of graduate students who have tolerated our in-class experimentation with the various incarnations of these materials and in the process encouraged, critiqued, and improved our efforts.

The authors and publisher are grateful to those who have given permission to reproduce the following extracts and adaptations of copyright material:

The American Psychological Association for an extract from *American Psychologist* 1975, 30 © American Psychological Association 1975.

Cambridge University Press for extracts from *Using Surveys in Language Programs* by James D. Brown (2001); *The Learner-Centered Curriculum* by David Nunan (1991); J.C. Alderson and A. Beretta (eds.): *Evaluating Second Language Education* (1992); and R. K. Johnson (ed.): *The Second Language Curriculum* (1989).

CULI International Conference for an extract from A. Wongsothorn, A. Maurice, K. Prapphal and B. Kenny (eds.): *Trends in Language Programme Evaluation* (1986).

The Estate of James Joyce for an extract from *Ulysses*, Episode 18, Penelope.

Hodder and Stoughton Limited for extracts from *The Story of My Life* by Helen Keller.

The Institute of Mathematical Statistics for an extract from *Annals of Mathematical Statistics*, Vol. 20 (1949).

JALT for an extract from D. Nunan and D. Griffee (eds.): *Classroom Teachers and Classroom Research*.

Norazida Johar for an extract from *Reading Strategies Used by Good and Poor Readers in Narrative Texts: An Exploratory Study* (1996).

Lim Wai Lee for an extract from *An Analysis of Students' Dyadic Interaction on a Dictogloss Task* (2000).

Susan Lytle for an extract from 'Merging Assessment and Instruction: Protocols in the Classroom' by Carol S. Brown and Susan L. Lytle, in Glazer, Susan Mandel et al. (eds): *Reexamining Reading Diagnosis: New Trends and Procedures.*

The MIT Press for extracts from Thomas Sebeok (ed.): *Style in Language;* and K. A. Ericsson and H. A. Simon (eds.): *Protocol Analysis.*

Multilingual Matters Ltd. for extracts from Claus Færch and Gabriele Kasper (eds.): *Introspection in Second Language Research;* and A. Cummings and R. Berwick (eds.): *Validation in Language Testing.*

Pearson Education Limited for extracts from *The Classroom and the Language Learner* by L. van Lier © Longman Group UK Limited 1988; *Observation in the Language Classroom* by Dick Allwright; and *Statistical Tables for Biological, Agricultural and Medical Research* © 1963 by R.A. Fisher and F. Yates.

Richard Schmidt for an extract from R. Day (ed.): *Talking to Learn: Conversation in Second Language Acquisition* (Newbury House).

Richard J. Shavelson for an extract from 'Research on Teachers' Pedagogical Thoughts, Judgments, Decisions, and Behaviour' by Richard J. Shavelson and Paula Stern, published in the *Review of Educational Research* 51 (4).

Catherine Snow for an extract from E. Hatch (ed.) *Second Language Acquisition* (Newbury House).

Merrill Swain for an extract from Cook and Seidlhofer (eds.): *Principle and Practice in Applied Linguistics* (Oxford University Press).

TESOL for an extract from *The Place of Research Within the TESOL Organization* by J.D. Brown, M. Knowles, D. Murray, J. Neu, and E. Violand-Hainer.

Times Books International, an imprint of Times Media Pte, for an extract from *The Serpent's Tooth* by Catherine Lim.

Ken Willing for an extract from D. Nunan (ed.): *Learning Styles in Adult Migrant Education* (National Curriculum Resource Centre Adult Migrant Education Program 1988).

Henning Wode for an extract from E. Hatch (ed.): *Second Language Acquisition* (Newbury House).

Serap Yucel for an extract from S. Tuzel-Koyman and E. Kortan (eds.): *Interaction on the Threshold of a New Millennium* (Ankara: Middle Eastern Technical University).

Illustrations by Richard Duszczak © Oxford University Press.

PREFACE

The last two decades have seen growing importance placed on research in second and foreign language teaching and learning. Researchers see their work as important, of great relevance to practice. Yet to teachers their research often seems to be remote from the practical world of teaching; research is done by people called researchers, teaching done by people called teachers. But most researchers do teach and most teachers can, and we maintain should, also be researchers. Teachers need to be participants in the process, not merely consumers. This book sets out to provide the means by which they can achieve this as well as to answer the question of why it is important that they should.

The books on second language research methods that have been published over the last twenty years do one of three things: they help classroom teachers to become better consumers of research studies relevant to their own teaching (Brown 1988); or they train teachers to set up and conduct research studies at their own institutions (Butler 1985; Woods, Fletcher, and Hughes 1986; Seliger and Shohamy 1989; Bailey and Allwright 1991; Johnson 1992; Nunan 1992; and Freeman 1998); or they both show how to do research and also provide analyses of exemplary studies of particular design types (Hatch and Farhady 1982; Hatch and Lazaraton 1991).

None of these books, however, put readers *inside* the research process as subjects or data analysts or research reporters. The book we have written here, *Doing Second Language Research*, assumes it is both possible and desirable to do just that—to give readers an intimate sense of research processes by involving them in the tasks that all research participants experience.

To that general end, this book has the following more specific goals:

1 *To familiarize readers with the basic types of research design used in second language studies.* To do so, we explain the characteristics of various design types, the logic underlying design selection, the steps typical of each type of research design, and the purposes of such designs. All necessary research terms are systematically introduced in the contexts in which they are typically used.
2 *To provide a* feel *for what research activities are like in second language studies by engaging the reader in several roles within a variety of mini-studies.* The reader's roles include that of research subject, research organizer, research data collector, research data analyst, and research reporter. For

the most part, we assume that these roles are preliminary to becoming a research designer. The book covers some of the fundamental roles in designing research studies but does not assume that this alone is adequate preparation for independent design of such research studies. In formal quantitative research analysis, most researchers will input their data into one of the computer-based statistics programs such as SPSS, SAS, MINITAB, etc. In keeping with the underlying philosophy of this book, we have asked you to hand tabulate most measures required. We find that our own students are much clearer as to how such measures work and what they are for when they have had hands-on experience with their calculation. However, to avoid possible errors due to copying, we have provided a downloadable version of many of the statistical tables and photocopiable worksheets in Microsoft Excel format on the Oxford Teachers' Club website, www.oup.com/elt/teacher/L2research. Spreadsheet programs such as Excel can also be used to manipulate data and perform calculations. Tables reproduced on the Website are marked 'www' after the caption.

3 *To offer an introduction to some of the classic research studies into second language learning and teaching by engaging readers in thinking about and discussing these studies as well as participating as subjects in adapted versions of some of these studies.* Each section provides background information and critical dimensions for these classic studies as well as a list of key references related to the studies.

The audience for this book

We have both been teaching the concepts of language research for years at the University of Hawai'i at Manoa, Temple University in Japan, Columbia University in Japan, Bilkent University in Turkey, and elsewhere. The book we have written is aimed at just the kinds of students we have been teaching in these institutions, typically graduate student-teachers, whose first language is not necessarily English. We firmly believe, however, that what we present here will be of general interest to all teaching practitioners who want a more systematic way of developing their own skills in, and understanding of, the process of teaching, as well as consumers of research who need to be able to form a judgement as to the validity of research reports.

In our teaching we have long felt a strong need for a book that puts readers inside the research process so they can experience what it is like to be the subjects of research, to compile their own data, to analyze those data, and to report the results in a systematic, organized, and understandable way. Readers also need to be able to design their own research, interpret their results and the results of other studies, understand the significance of each research type, and reflect on what their research means. We have found that teachers are much more curious to find out what research data mean when the data are their own. They are intrigued to see how their responses compare with those of their peers. And, we find that student-teachers will much more readily commit themselves to the sometimes demanding processes of research analysis, interpretation, and reporting when the data originate from themselves and their colleagues. In short, we feel that it is important for language teachers to learn more than the facts of research and how it is conducted; they need also to acquire an intimate sense of the excitement and fun of research processes. We help them do so in this book by involving them from a number of perspectives in all facets of seven types of research.

Organization of this book

We have written *Doing Second Language Research* to bridge the gap between theory and practice in second language research. The coverage of the book is comprehensive in the sense that it includes technical as well as real-world issues related to the concerns of language teachers as consumers of research and language researchers as conductors of research. At the same time, the approach used to explain all definitions and concepts is straightforward and easy to assimilate—neither too complex nor too simplistic. We address a variety of language research issues that will prove useful to language teaching professionals in various institutions. Each chapter is organized into the following sections:

1 Introducing the research type
2 Experiencing the research type
3 Compiling the data generated by the research type
4 Analyzing the data generated by the research type
5 Designing the research type
6 Interpreting the research type
7 Significance of the research type
8 Reflecting on the research experience

Chapters 2 and 8 also have sections on reporting research results.

We have attempted to insure that *Doing Second Language Research* provides realistic and useful language research tools that will assist language teachers as researchers in doing their jobs. All explanations are designed to be accessible to classroom language teachers, but also to those graduate students who are preparing to become language-teaching professionals. As such, we define and explain the theoretical and practical issues of language research in digestible chunks. The statistical concepts are covered in a step-by-step recipe book manner with many examples and exercises throughout the discussions. In addition, key terms are clearly highlighted IN SMALL CAPITAL LETTERS throughout the text with definitions found nearby in the text and collected together at the end of the book in a glossary. Finally, each chapter contains a succinct summary for review purposes.

Using this book

We have designed this book so that readers can work in class groups to generate their own data under teacher supervision, or can work on their own as individuals adding their data to data we will sometimes provide. While the general design of the book is for use in a formal learning environment, individual users will find comments directed at how they can adapt the various exercises to their purposes. We would strongly suggest that all users of the book (whether working as part of a group or as individuals) buy a notebook (possibly one with graph paper in it) so they can keep track of all the exercises and notes they make during the process of experiencing research.

In addition, we have consciously provided far more exercises than will be practical to cover during class time in a normal semester-length course (with a view to providing teachers with a certain amount of flexibility). This will present no problem for individual readers because they can cover all the exercises in their own time or pick and choose as they see fit. However, teacher-educators trying to fit this material into a normal semester-length course (of say 45 contact hours) will need to select those exercises that seem best for their students and decide in advance which should be handled as in-class activities and which should be done as homework.

In summary, we have taken a very new approach to the issues involved in doing second language research. For the first time, one book focuses on helping language teachers appreciate and reflect on what it feels like to be inside the research process, how to actually conduct, compile, and analyze research data, and how to interpret and report the findings so they can be used by their language teaching colleagues.

Note
In Hawaii the politically correct spelling is Hawai'i (as on page xii) with an 'okina' representing the glottal stop in Hawaiian. We use the more common dictionary spelling of Hawaii in the remainder of the text.

PART ONE

Introduction

1 THE NATURE OF RESEARCH

Introducing research

Consider the following quotations:

> *Research is the process of going up alleys to see if they are blind.*
> MARSTON BATES, 1906–1974
> American writer

> *Research is what I'm doing when I don't know what I'm doing.*
> WERNHER MAGNUS MAXIMILIAN VON BRAUN, 1912–1977
> German-born American rocket engineer

> *If you steal from one author, it's plagiarism; if you steal from many, it's research.*
> WILSON MIZNER, 1876–1933
> American dramatist and wit

A consensus of sorts but hardly concrete definitions. In this chapter, we will explore the meaning of 'research' as used in the language teaching profession. More particularly, we will seek to help you towards a definition most suitable to you and your work and in so doing introduce many of the concepts that will permeate the rest of the book.

Experiencing research

Research is an exploration of experience of one kind or another, sometimes formal and technical, but not necessarily so. A good way of understanding the nature of research is to first experience it by doing it, initially in a simple and elementary way.

Sigmund Freud introduced a method of psychological research called 'free association'. In one form of free association, the researcher repeats a word and subjects are asked to say the immediate response that comes to mind each time the word is said. One subject's free associations to the cue word 'money' were the following:

Researcher		Subject
1	Money	green
2	Money	rich
3	Money	gold
4	Money	dirty
5	Money	car
6	Money	Fred
7	Money	ten
8	Money	cash
9	Money	banker
10	Money	coins

Exercise 1.1

Now you try some free associations to the word 'research'. With a partner, have the partner say the word 'research', while you, the subject, say the first thing that comes to mind. The cue word 'research' should be repeated after each response. If you are working alone, simply write your free associations in the spaces provided.

Collect ten free associations to the word 'research'. Remember, these responses should be the first ideas that leap to mind.

	Cue Word	Response
1	Research	
2	Research	
3	Research	
4	Research	
5	Research	
6	Research	
7	Research	
8	Research	
9	Research	
10	Research	

Students at the beginning of our language research courses are often asked to write down some of their associations to the concept of research. Here are some of the responses from one such group at the University of Hawaii:

endless	sometimes painful
convincing	experiment
findings	consistent
unpredictable	analysis
publish	statistics
never perfect	boring
time consuming	experts
implications	

Exercise 1.2

Compare your list of associations with the list of associations from the University of Hawaii group. What similarities and differences do you observe between the two lists? Can you see any way of beginning to classify these associations? Make a note of similarities and differences and some possible classifications of responses.

These exercises have three messages that you should remember: first, people can both agree or disagree in their views of what research is; second, research is often about comparing people or groups of people, documents or groups of documents, test scores or groups of test scores, and so forth (in this case, you were comparing the characteristics of research in two lists); and third, in doing research of any kind, both similarities and differences may turn out to be interesting.

Exercise 1.3

Reflecting on your own associations and those from the University of Hawaii group, compose a short definition of research and keep a record of it.

As you will see later, a very similar open-ended question was asked in a survey of English as a foreign or second language teachers sampled in a fairly large-scale research project based on the membership of the International TESOL organization. Later in the chapter, you will be able to compare your answer in Exercise 1.3 to the answers of a number of respondents in that survey.

Compiling research data

Before anything useful can be done with research data, you will need to compile the data. Compiling data means putting all the data together in one place in such a way that you can more easily analyze and interpret them. This might mean putting numerical data in rows and columns on graphing paper or in a spreadsheet, or it might mean transcribing taped interviews, or coding activities observed in a classroom. The exercises in this section will introduce you to this concept of compiling data. You will do it in many different ways as you progress through the book.

Exercise 1.4

Previously we asked you to think about some ways to classify the association responses that you and the University of Hawaii group made. Classifying is a central activity in compiling data.

  1   Form several broad columns on a piece of paper and put what you see as similar associations in one column. Are there *synonym-like* responses, *attitude* responses, *sub-component* responses, *result* responses? You may also need a *miscellaneous* column where you put responses that don't seem to group with any other responses.

  2   Label each column with what you consider to be a descriptive cover term.

Analyzing research data

As reported in Brown (1992b), during 1991, the TESOL Research Task Force formed by the executive board of TESOL (an ESL/EFL teacher organization called Teachers of English to Speakers of Other Languages) sent out a questionnaire to 1000 TESOL members randomly selected from the General Membership of TESOL, and 200 each from four interest sections: Applied Linguistics, Higher Education, Research, and Teacher Education. The overall return rate was 33.4 percent. One question on the questionnaire was 'How would you define research?'

Some of the anonymous respondents defined research as follows:

  1 Finding the source or cause of something.
  2 It is peeling away the layers of onion so as to see how and why something works or doesn't work or where it fits in the grander scheme with increased understanding.
  3 Investigation into how and why things work or don't work.

4 Finding answers to questions.
5 Exploring the mundane to find new depths and connections.
6 Discovery of new knowledge.
7 Controlled investigation of a theory.
8 Careful, thorough study.
9 Rigorous inquiry into theoretical or practical issues.
10 The necessary underpinnings to advancement of the profession—without it, we are in danger of uttering unsubstantiated jabberwocky and not doing our students justice.
11 The search for the truth.
12 Use of scientific method to test a theory.
13 Working consciously and critically (but not necessarily objectively) at important problems in human endeavor.

There are a number of ways that we could sort through those definitions in an effort to find interesting patterns. For instance, one way to search for patterns would be to simply reorganize the definitions from the shortest to the longest as follows.

Exercise 1.5

Arrange the above definitions from shortest to longest and see whether it helps you to find anything of interest.

You probably found that Exercise 1.5 helped you in a general way to sort the definitions from the simplest, most direct definitions to the longest, most complicated definitions. But it probably didn't help you to see any other interesting patterns.

The majority of the definitions of research offered by the respondents to the TESOL Research Task Force questionnaire were of the long complicated type, so some other method of analysis was clearly necessary in the original research project. A sample of those long responses follows:

1 In its widest sense, to seek new ways to improve language education and intercultural communication training.
2 An investigation of a particular topic, or problem, through a document search and/or empirical study (the conducting of experiments) and analysis.
3 (a) stating a hypothesis; (b) designing a means of testing it; (c) gathering necessary data; (d) analyzing data; (e) interpreting data; (f) publishing conclusions, if of interest.
4 Investigation of how language is learned and the most effective means of teaching it.

5   Investigation through the reading of literature, experimentation, and/or any other type of data gathering to aid in formulating/proving theories or to aid in the practical application of theory.

6   Looking around to see what everyone else is doing and justifying my assumptions and validating my beliefs.

7   Searching for information on how students process information, internalize data and retain it for communicative purposes.

8   Something that profs at universities that grant *advanced* degrees do because they don't teach and need to publish.

9   Stating a hypothesis; gathering data; testing the hypothesis; relating the conclusions to issues at hand.

10 Systematic inquiry which 1) generates heuristics for future research; yields questions 2) builds theory 3) tests theory 4) provides guidance to practice 5) aids general understanding of an endeavor.

11 Working toward truth, proving theories, trying out new approaches— and then compiling results, analyzing results and sharing with colleagues.

12 Two kinds: library (on already written projects), 'laboratory' (new research with subjects, etc.).

13 The search for information that will help practitioners (in this case, teachers) better carry out their jobs. Unfortunately, research often seems to lack practical applications.

14 Systematic study of language issues and use in order to improve delivery of services to our students.

Exercise 1.6

Look at the ways the above definitions are worded. Notice that some of the definitions start with gerunds, indicating that they are probably about processes, while others begin with noun phrases indicating that they may be more about the products of research. Using that strategy or similar ones, list whatever categories of definitions you see in the list of 14 definitions given above. Then write the definition numbers of at least some examples that fit each of your categories next to your category labels.

Brown (1992b) divided the 14 definitions above into five categories (which may or may not be similar to yours). His categories were as follows: (a) the *types* of research, (b) the *topics* of research, (c) the *purposes* of research, (d) the *processes* of research, and (e) just plain *cynical* answers.

Exercise 1.7

Write down the numbers of the three definitions that best fit each of Brown's five categories. Include both short (S) and long (L) sets of definitions.

Such definitions of research could also have been categorized according to the characteristics of different groups participating in the survey, like the definitions of males versus those of females, or differences in definitions for respondents holding different levels of degrees (BA, MA, PhD, etc.), or for groups working at different levels of education (elementary, secondary, undergraduate, graduate), or any number of other ways of categorizing the people who responded to the questionnaire. However, Brown (1992b) chose instead to look at the differences in responses for different interest sections. Here is an extract from the report:

> Interestingly, the people in the general membership primarily focused on experimental research and the scientific method, while respondents in the Applied Linguistics and Research interest sections tended to be very sensitive to the differences between quantitative and qualitative research:
>
> 1 Qualitative, quantitative, or evaluative investigations including purely theoretical and community-based scholar/practitioner topics.
> 2 Research attempts to explain issues, analysis methods and attitudes using numbers and 'sense'. Qualitative and quantitative means.
>
> Some of the Research interest section members were careful to mention the importance of linking theory and practice:
>
> 1 The search for answers to interesting/useful questions, with the understanding that posing the question is an important (crucial) part of the research. Under this definition, any teacher worth his/her name is a researcher.
> 2 Research should be useful to practitioners but grounded in theory.
> 3 Classroom/teaching applications of testing hypotheses;
> practice ⟷ theory
> (Brown 1992b: 10)

(There are some technical terms used here such as 'qualitative' and 'quantitative'. We will be looking more closely at these in the next section of this chapter.)

Given that you have now seen ways to sort data by length, analyze data into categories of definition types, and categorize data by the groups of people producing it, you are now ready to analyze your own data. You have also looked at how a number of people, including yourself, have defined research. Starting with one or two word associations, you then looked at examples of more elaborated definitions of research and looked at ways in which definitions of have been categorized.

Exercise 1.8

How would you categorize your own definitional statement of research?

1   In which of Brown's five categories would you place your own definition? Explain why you think your definition belongs in this category.

2   Which of the definitions given by Brown's respondents comes closest in meaning to your own?

3   Is there a definition in Brown's examples which you particularly favor, that you might like to adopt as your own? If so, why?

Designing research

In this section, we will explore two issues central to designing good research studies: research traditions available to second language scholars and contextual factors that must be considered in designing second language research.

Research traditions available to second language scholars

Language researchers draw on many traditions in doing their work. Figure 1.1 attempts to sort out the relationships among those traditions, starting with two basic categories: secondary and primary research.

SECONDARY RESEARCH includes any research based on secondary sources, especially other researchers' books and articles. Secondary research is further subdivided into LIBRARY RESEARCH (which includes any research done for a school or university course, usually in the form of a term paper) and LITERATURE REVIEWS (which include any research based on the literature that adds to the common body of human knowledge).

PRIMARY RESEARCH includes any research based on primary, or original, data (for example, students' test scores, classroom observations of their language learning behaviors, questionnaire responses, etc.). Primary research is further divided into qualitative, survey, and statistical research.

Figure 1.1 Broad categories of research

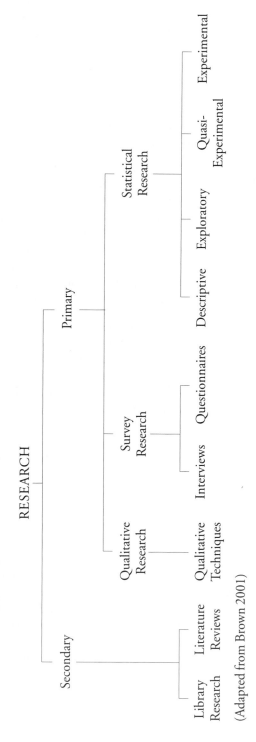

RESEARCH

Secondary

Primary

Library
Research

Literature
Reviews

Qualitative
Research

Survey
Research

Statistical
Research

Qualitative
Techniques

Interviews

Questionnaires

Descriptive

Exploratory

Quasi-
Experimental

Experimental

(Adapted from Brown 2001)

A closer look at QUALITATIVE RESEARCH, which is based predominantly on non-numerical data, reveals that it can be subdivided into various different non-numerical QUALITATIVE RESEARCH TECHNIQUES for gathering data (for example, observations/field notes, case studies, diaries, etc.). Sometimes, qualitative research also uses the interviews and questionnaires that we have chosen here to categorize as survey research techniques.

SURVEY RESEARCH is subdivided into INTERVIEW research (i.e. face-to-face data gathering using question-and-answer formats) and questionnaire research (i.e. studies employing paper-and-pencil or computer-delivered question-and-answer formats for data collection).

STATISTICAL RESEARCH, which is based predominantly on numerical data and consequently often referred to as *quantitative* as opposed to *qualitative*, includes DESCRIPTIVE RESEARCH (i.e. studies that describe a sample in numerical terms), EXPLORATORY RESEARCH (i.e. studies that, in one way or another, examine correlations among variables), QUASI-EXPERIMENTAL research (i.e. studies that compare group behavior in PROBABILISTIC terms under controlled conditions using INTACT GROUPS), and EXPERIMENTAL RESEARCH (i.e. studies that compare group behavior in probabilistic terms under controlled conditions using RANDOM ASSIGNMENT to groups).

Given all the research traditions shown in Figure 1.1, the overall concept of language learning and teaching research will clearly have to be defined fairly broadly. For the purposes of this book let us define research 'as any systematic and principled inquiry in language learning and teaching'. And of course, one of your first steps in designing any research project will be to decide what type, or types, of research you are doing.

Contextual factors in second language research

In the preface to this book we noted that our intention is to give users of the text 'a *feel* for what research activity is like in second language studies by engaging the reader in several roles within a variety of mini-studies'. We have also undertaken to 'familiarize readers with the basic research design types used in second language studies'.

There are two senses of context implied in these statements of intention. One of these senses deals with the various functional contexts in which individuals participate within the sphere of research activities. Designers, analysts, critics, reporters, philosophers, those being studied, each have different contexts of participation in the research enterprise. One goal of this book is to give readers some sense of each of these individual contexts of research activity.

A second sense deals with the context of the particular design or framework within which a research study is undertaken. We shall look at seven such design frameworks across the continuum, which we have labeled, with some caution, qualitative to quantitative research. The choice of a research design type turns on research purpose, research climate, institutional preference, intended audience, and researcher personality and inclination.

There are a number of other senses—some obvious, some not so obvious— in which context is a critical determinant in the way research is undertaken and the way research results are disseminated. We will outline a few of these other contexts and suggest you consider how these contexts may influence your own research possibilities.

1   *The international and national contexts* International and national organizations sponsor much academic research and set political priorities for such research. The U.S. second language teaching community profited hugely by the surge of educational concern following the Soviet launching of Sputnik, in that a number of U.S. government-financed educational research and development activities suddenly became fundable. UNESCO and other United Nations agencies have set development targets in, for example, life-long learning and have provided research and development funds for projects that qualify within these areas. Bilingual education, universal literacy, consumer education, and critical thinking are other areas that have received bureaucratic blessing and abundant funding. It obviously makes some sense to get an idea of these larger (and changing) priorities in thinking about likely sources of encouragement and support for your own research.

2   *The professional context* Enthusiasms for particular kinds of research wax and wane within the field of second language studies. A quick examination of the table of contents of some of the major research journals in the field over a number of years will clearly show how the popularity of various research topics and styles cluster over time. A look at the latest of these journals will suggest what kinds of research are presently being pursued most enthusiastically and published most regularly.

3   *The institutional context* Institutional settings as vast as the Los Angeles public school system and as intimate as one-on-one tutoring have been the contexts for various kinds of second language acquisition (SLA) research. The size, institutional priorities, available support structures, past experience, and administrator personalities will shape what kinds of research can best be carried out within the institutional boundaries. Institutions are often in implicit competition with similar institutions and often develop or respond to research agendas accordingly. Researchers may find that educating the decision-makers within their working territory is a necessary part of their research design.

4 *The local context* We use local context to refer to the actual situation in which researchers and those being researched meet. This local context may be a classroom, or a private home, or a laboratory, or an Internet bulletin board. Here the physical context (for example, classroom size and shape), chronological context (for example, time in the academic year), social context (for example, degree of homogeneity/heterogeneity among students), pedagogical context (for example, class learning/teaching styles), and psychological context (for example, comfort level of participants in regard to research study participation) all will shape research possibilities (and impossibilities).

5 *The personal context* You, as a reader of this book, have come with certain presuppositions about research and your own possible role as researcher. We trust that your reading and engagement with the ideas presented here will enlarge your view of what research is and expand your own sense of capability to undertake research of a variety of types. But you will always have an individual view about what you do best, like best, and believe most valuable. (One can hope these intersect.) It is well to be able to expand your capacity to undertake and to learn from various kinds of research studies. It is also good to do periodic self-checks to evaluate your own growth and to assess your own beliefs, your own sense of competency, and your own sense of priorities. These are the ultimate contextual factors that will determine your success as a researcher in the exciting field in which you are now an apprentice.

Exercise 1.9

We are, in one sense, all *experts* in some local context. We all have spent a lot of time in schools and in study and have our biases towards which elements of local context best support or discourage learning.

Review the elements discussed under *the local context*. Sketch out the contextual elements that you feel would be optimal in undertaking a research study you might imagine doing in some local situation.

Exercise 1.10

We have discussed a number of different senses in which *context* plays a critical role in second language research. All of these contextual considerations are important in deciding what research to do and how to do it. Some of these contexts may be more personally meaningful to you than others.

Consider two or three of the contexts of research that seem particularly important to you and make a list of 3 to 5 reasons why you feel these are important.

Interpreting definitions of research

So far in this chapter, we have attempted to define what we mean by research, we have done a small piece of research, and we have looked at the different ways in which research can be done. In the last section, we touched on a number of contextual factors which may influence the kind of research which you may do. The way you think about research, even the way you feel about different types of research, will influence the way you do research, especially how you interpret your results.

Consider for instance the dichotomy that is often mentioned between QUALITATIVE (typically the label for non-numerical research) and QUANTI-TATIVE (numerical) RESEARCH. They refer to broad categories of research types, but one needs to be wary of oversimplification. Both qualitative and quantitative research come in many types, and the line dividing the two categories is not at all clear. Let's consider each of those issues separately.

First, a close look at *qualitative research* reveals that it can easily be sub-divided into the various *qualitative research approaches*. For instance, case studies (Chapter 2), introspection research (Chapter 3), classroom research (Chapter 4), and others have all been referred to as qualitative research approaches. For more on this topic, see Lazaraton (1995). Similarly, *quantitative research* can easily be subdivided into different approaches including descriptive (Chapter 5), exploratory (Chapter 6), quasi-experimental (Chapter 7), and true-experimental (also discussed in Chapter 7) techniques. For more on this topic, see Brown (1988) and Hatch and Lazaraton (1991). So, neither qualitative nor quantitative research can be considered a single research type.

Second, the line dividing qualitative and quantitative research types is not all that clear. Grotjahn (1987) argued that the qualitative/quantitative distinction is an oversimplification. His analysis took into consideration the data collection method (i.e. experimental or non-experimental), the type of data that resulted (i.e. qualitative or quantitative), and the type of analysis conducted on the data (statistical or interpretive). He argued that these three factors could be combined in eight different ways to create a wide variety of research types.

Sometimes, predominantly qualitative research also uses numbers and some quantitative studies may use non-numerical data. In addition, you may have noticed that survey research was put between qualitative and statistical research in Figure 1.1. We did this because survey research includes interviews and questionnaires. Since interviews and questionnaires can pose open-response questions to gather non-numerical data or closed-response questions to gather numerical (or at least quantifiable) data, these survey techniques are used in both qualitative and quantitative studies. Thus survey research provides some common ground between the qualitative and quantitative approaches. (See Brown 2001 for more on survey research.)

Exercise 1.11

Throughout this chapter, you have seen that there are a number of different ways to classify definitions of research. Briefly review what those ways were, then interpret those results by answering the following questions:

1   What are the different ways of classifying definitions of research in second language teaching?

2   What does the diversity of categories tell you about research in second language teaching?

3   Which category (or categories) do you find the most useful for defining and thinking about research in second language teaching?

Significance of defining research

Why does it matter how you think about research? First, because doing any type of research involves a great investment in learning how that type of research is done. Second, because the way you set about doing a research study, including the conventions of data gathering, compiling, analyzing, and interpreting the results can and will shape what you learn from the study. Madigan, Johnson, and Linton (1995) argue, for example, that the language of psychology and indeed the very conventions of the *Publication Manual of the American Psychological Association* (American Psychological Association 1994) shape the ways students and professionals in psychology think about and do research. Changes made in the fourth edition of the *Manual* (1994) included gender neutral language, the use of 'gender' for 'sex', of 'participants' for 'subjects' in a study, and much else. These changes materially affected the nature of research undertaken and researchers' attitudes.

The actual terminology used to define research projects can have an effect on one's attitudes to and the results obtained from the research. In Chapter 8 we will look at different terminologies for quantitative and qualitative research and see that terms traditionally used for quantitative research can actually mislead one when carrying out qualitative studies.

Clearly then, how you think about research in general and what your preferences are for working within the general qualitative or quantitative approaches can affect the very terminology that you use to plan and think about your research, and of course, will also affect how you compile, analyze, and interpret the data.

Exercise 1.12

Look back at the list of characteristics and definitions of research that you and others have produced and examined in previous exercises.

1   Think about all that you have experienced in this chapter with a special focus on the various types of research and research approaches you now know about.

2   Think of something you would like to do research about and consider what type of research would produce the most useful results.

3   Write a definition for the type of research you might choose and jot down some characteristics of that type of research.

4   How do the characteristics and definition of research that you wrote down here compare to what you first wrote in Exercises 1.1 and 1.3?

Reflecting on research definitions

A number of other questions may help you to reflect on why it is important as a language teaching professional for you to think about the meaning of research. Such questions can be directly related to what you have experienced and learned in this chapter.

Exercise 1.13

Consider and respond to the following questions:

1   In experiencing research, what did you find out about how people think about definitions of research? About the characteristics of research?

2   To what degree did compiling the research data for your whole class help you to understand the diversity of views you and your colleagues hold about the nature of research?

3   How did analyzing those compiled data help you to understand some of the patterns in the ways you and your colleagues define research, and some of the patterns in the different kinds of research that are done? How did analyzing those data for patterns help you to understand the importance of finding patterns in the confusion of our experiences in the world? How might finding such patterns in the research of language teaching and language learning prove helpful to us as language teachers?

4   What are the different types of research? What are the differences between primary and secondary research? Library research and literature review? Qualitative and statistical? How can survey research

be both qualitative and quantitative? What is the distinction between interviews and questionnaires in survey research?

5   What are some examples of how functional contexts and design contexts might affect your choices in doing your research? How might international, national, professional, institutional, local, and personal contexts shape your research in a given study and even your research agenda over a professional lifetime?

By now, based on what you have experienced in this chapter, you may have decided that you prefer one type of research or another. As we suggested above, one potential problem with deciding too far in advance is that your choice may limit your ways of thinking about and studying a particular problem or issue. Indeed, the strongest researchers may be those who remain flexible, that is, researchers who are not bound by artificial distinctions like qualitative versus quantitative, ones who will be able to adapt their research methods to the issues they are trying to learn about, and to the places their research leads them.

Summary

In this chapter, you found that 'research' has many definitions. You yourself explored the characteristics of research and tried your hand at defining the concept. After compiling a few definitions, you examined some data from the TESOL survey project and tried analyzing those data into five different categories of response: types, topics, purposes, processes, and cynical answers.

You also examined the research traditions available to you as a language teaching professional and considered the contextual factors that need to be considered in doing research (including international, national, professional, institutional, local, and personal contexts). Then you examined the continuum bridging qualitative and quantitative research noting that both research approaches come in many types and that there is no clear line dividing them. Finally, you reflected on the various aspects of research covered in this chapter.

PART TWO

Qualitative research

2 CASE STUDY RESEARCH: DEVELOPMENTAL RESEARCH

Introducing case study research

Circumstances alter cases.
THOMAS CHANDLER HALIBURTON, aka 'Sam Slick', 1796–1865
Canadian lawyer, politician, judge, and writer
The Old Judge, Chapter 15

But misery still delights to trace
Its semblance in another case.
WILLIAM COWPER, 1731–1800
English poet

One of the principal ways in which researchers have tried to gain insight into the processes underlying language learning has been through careful study of the cases of individuals learning a language. CASE STUDIES, themselves, have had a long history and have played major roles in a number of different disciplines. Sigmund Freud's psychoanalytic theories and Jean Piaget's studies of children's mental and social development were founded on the *cases* of particular individuals.

In language education research, case studies often involve following the development of the language competence of an individual or small group of individuals. Many case studies are thus DEVELOPMENTAL STUDIES as well as case studies. In brief,

1 Case study research comprises an intensive study of the background, current status, and environmental interactions of a given social unit: an individual, a group, an institution, or a community, while
2 Developmental research comprises an investigation of patterns and sequences of growth and change as a function of time.

In this chapter, you will be undertaking a developmental case study of a rather exceptional deaf and blind child learning English, the mother tongue of her parents. After having looked at some data from her early letter writing, you will prepare some tables and accompanying text as a means of both analyzing and displaying your developmental findings. You will be introduced to the standard form used in reporting research findings, in particular to the use of tables, to the ABSTRACT and to the LITERATURE REVIEW. Throughout the chapter, some of the relationships between first and second language acquisition in developmental case study research will be considered. Finally, you will also have an opportunity to conduct a small case study of *yourself* and look at some of the criteria for interpreting and critiquing case studies as reported in the literature.

Experiencing case study research

Observing the progress of their children in learning to speak their mother tongue (and in some cases, a second language) is a popular pastime for many parents. Parents who are also linguists have often published their observations in the professional literature. Typically, these publications have appeared as case studies based on regular observation and recording of a child's verbal behavior in learning a first or second language. These studies have raised important questions about the degree to which patterns of first and second language development are similar or dissimilar. In comparing first language (L1) and second language (L2) acquisition data, Ellis notes 'some striking similarities have been found in syntactic structures such as negatives, but there are also some differences' (Ellis 1994: 110).

The hypothesis of a common 'natural order' in shaping both first and second language learning has also been very influential in language acquisition studies. Lightbown and Spada (1999) provide a clear overview of research built around this natural order hypothesis.

Exercise 2.1

(Warm-up)

Below are some samples put together from several L1 diary studies of the stages that most children pass through in mastering the adult forms for *negation* in English. There are four samples given for each of five stages. The blocks of samples are not given in chronological order of development but in random order. Your task is to

1   re-sort the blocks of samples into probable chronological order,

2   state what you think the characteristics of negative sentences are at each stage,

3   make up a new sentence to add to each block indicating how you think negation is expressed at that stage, and

4   discuss your analysis with a partner.

Sample A
I don't can explain.
He don't will like it.
Don't have any monies.
I don't see nothing mop.

Sample D
You no sit there.
He no bite.
There no squirrels.
They no have water.

Sample B
No go.
No mitten.
No fall.
No stop there.

Sample E
They don't want it.
You can't tell her.
He's not coming in.
It's not danger.

Sample C
Do not tell her.
We don't like him.
He doesn't laugh like us.
She didn't believe me.

You can see obvious changes in grammar, and speech segments clearly get longer as children get older. What are some of the other signals of advancing linguistic maturity?

Use Table 2.1 to record your answers.

Table 2.1 Phases of language development for English negation (www)

Phases	Language examples	Comments

Photocopiable © Oxford University Press

We now turn to our principal study in this section, which also focuses on language samples taken over a period of time. We can clearly see linguistic development in these samples, although simple length of sample is not as clear a cue as it was in the previous exercise.

In this section, you will examine some samples of personal letters written by a deaf and blind child, Helen Keller, between her seventh and eight birthdays. The early letters of Helen Keller provide authentic, naturalistic, and interesting indicators of language development collected as *written* L1 case study data. In addition, they offer evidence for some of the well-attested stages of language development as they appear in both first and second language learners of English.

One reason we have used these Keller letter data is that they are clear and distinctive. Helen herself had a careful and easily readable, if unusual, style of printing, and her letters are quite easy to interpret. Authentic developmental case study language data are rarely this uncluttered, but the central issues of analysis and plotting of linguistic development will provide sufficient challenges for you as research analyst.

A question that we will return to throughout the chapter is the degree to which the processes and sequencing of L1 and L2 development are similar. A widely-cited researcher (Ervin-Tripp 1974) holds that 'in broad outline, the conclusion is tenable that first and second language learning is similar in natural situations'. We have noted the Ellis summary comment that 'the similarities between L1 and L2 acquisition are strongest in syntactical structures such as negatives…' (Ellis 1994: 110). The development of syntactic structures and negation are central foci in this chapter.

This provides the second reason for the use of these data. Helen was learning basic English at the same time as she was learning how to write. We feel the data shed light on both L1 and L2 development as well as on the techniques used to collect and analyze such developmental data in various language learning situations.

Helen Keller was born without sight or hearing. With the help of her tutor, Anne Sullivan, she learned finger spelling. However, it was not until April 5, 1887, when she was six years old, that Helen learned that the finger spelling of the letters 'w-a-t-e-r' spelled out the word 'water', and that 'water' was the name for the liquid that flowed over her hand from the garden pump. Instantly, Helen realized 'that everything has a name, and that the manual (finger) alphabet is the key to everything that she wants to know'. (Keller 1954)

> So. Boston,
> May 1, 1891.
> My dear Mr. Brooks;
>   Helen
> sends you a loving greet
> ing this bright May-day.
> My teacher has just told
> me that you have been
> made a bishop, and that
> your friends everywhere
> are rejoicing because
> one whom they love
> has been greatly honor-
> ed.

Once Helen understood that letters spelled words and that words named things, her progress in language development was phenomenal. Within three months after her discovery at the pump and by the time she had turned seven years old, Anne Sullivan had taught Helen to read Braille and to write her first letters. She wrote in square-hand letters, similar to the sample on the previous page.

Exercise 2.2

Below are *randomly ordered samples* of Helen's actual letters to her friends, all written between her seventh and eighth birthdays (June 1, 1887 to February 24, 1888). Her language development is amazingly fast. Helen was both learning English and the conventions of writing during this period, and the samples demonstrate developmental stages in these processes. For the purposes of the exercise, the samples are presented in random order.

1   Read the letter excerpts noting their linguistic features. Rank order the excerpts from *earliest* to *latest*.

2   Identify and discuss new language features in each letter; for example, a new verb tense, a new sentence pattern, a new pronoun, a new phrase pattern, new patterns of writing mechanics.

Letter excerpts from Helen Keller *(in random time order)*

A   I am happy to write to you this morning. I hope Mr. Anagnos is coming to see me soon. I will go to Boston in June and I will buy father gloves, and James nice collar, and Simpson cuffs. I saw Miss Betty and her scholars. They had a pretty Christmas-tree, and there were many pretty presents on it for little children.

B   Helen will write mother letter papa did give helen medicine mildred will sit in swing mildred did kiss helen teacher did give helen peach george is sick in bed george arm is hurt anna give helen lemonade dog did stand up.

C   I will write you a letter I thank you for pretty desk I did write to mother in memphis on it mother and mildred came home wednesday mother brought me a pretty new dress and hat papa did go to huntsville he brought me apples and candy.

D   helen write anna george will give helen apple simpson will shoot bird jack will give helen stick of candy doctor will give mildred medicine mother will make mildred new dress

E   This morning Lucien Thompson sent me a beautiful bouquet of violets and crocuses and jonquils. Sunday Adeline Moses brought me a lovely doll. It came from New York. Her name is Adeline Keller. She can shut her eyes and bend her arms and sit down and stand up straight. She has on a pretty red dress. She is Nancy's sister and I am their mother.

F   Helen will go to school with blind girls Helen can read and count and
spell and write like blind girls mildred will not go to boston Mildred does
cry prince and jumbo will go to boston papa does shoot ducks with gun
and ducks do fall in water and jumbo and mamie do swim in water and
bring ducks out in mouth to papa.

(Keller 1954)

Compiling case study data

Exercise 2.3

Using whatever strategy works best for you as a group, prepare a table that
combines data from the group in the form shown in Table 2.2. When you are
done, your table should look similar to the one shown in Table 2.3. Be sure to add
up the totals for each row in the column furthest to the right in order to crosscheck that your data make sense and that there is nothing missing. Discuss any
disagreements that show up in the table and decide as a class what the most likely
chronological order must be. Record the identifying letters for those ranking in
the bottom row of your table. (Again, see example in Table 2.3.) For those readers
who are working alone, you can adapt this exercise by combining your personal
data with the example data in Table 2.3. Then decide what you think the correct
rank order ought to be.

The letter samples show evidence of a variety of linguistic and letter format
changes as Helen matures and her language capability increases. Linguists
typically categorize language changes and language foci in terms of:

PHONOLOGY: the study of language sounds
MORPHOLOGY: the study of word structure
SYNTAX: the study of sentence grammar
DISCOURSE: the study of the organization of longer spoken and
written texts

Table 2.2 Form for compiling results for Helen Keller letter chronological ordering (www)

Time Order Sample	First	Second	Third	Fourth	Fifth	Sixth	Totals
A							
B							
C							
D							
E							
F							
Ranking							

Table 2.3 Example compilation for Helen Keller letter chronological ordering

Time Order Sample	First	Second	Third	Fourth	Fifth	Sixth	Total number of partici-pants
A					///// ///// //	///	15
B			///// ///// ///	//			15
C		///// ///// /	////				15
D	///// ///// /////						15
E						///// ///// /////	15
F		//		///// ///// ///			15
Ranking	D	C	B	F	A	E	

Exercise 2.4

Since the data here are letters, we have no data on the phonology of Helen's spoken language. We do have evidence of morphological, syntactic, and discourse development as evidenced by her early letters. Given your understanding of the above terms, list, impressionistically, some of the changes you find in the letters in the following three categories:

    I   Morphological/Word changes

    2   Syntactical/Sentence changes

    3   Discourse/Text structure changes

Analyzing case study data

You now need to undertake more detailed linguistic analyses of the language of Helen's letters, noting changes in vocabulary, grammar, punctuation, capitalization, letter format, reference, and cohesion. You should then organize these changes in the form of a table. As you will see, tables are often used not only to organize data analysis, but also in research reports as a way of presenting results in a final form.

Exercise 2.5

Consider the data dealing with noun changes in Helen's letters. There are several sub-categories of nouns. See if you can think of what these might be before looking at the categories of nouns in Table 2.4.

Then do the following:

    I   Look at Table 2.4. Make a copy of this table, in which to record your noun data.

    2   Re-examine the letter samples in their chronological order. Fill in as many of the cells in Table 2.4 as you can, using all of the noun data from the chronologically ordered letter samples.

    3   Your completed Table 2.4 should look something like the results shown in the Answer key for this exercise on page 257. Note any differences between your table and the answer key and discuss as a group until you can agree on your choices.

    4   Track the entries from the sample letters to the cells in the table. Are there any additional data samples that you could put in the cells from the letter data? What are some of these?

Table 2.4 Chart for recording noun data in the Helen Keller letters (www)

	Proper Nouns	Simple Nouns	Plural Nouns	Compound Nouns	Pronouns	Noun Phrases
Letter 1						
Letter 2						
Letter 3						
Letter 4						
Letter 5						
Letter 6						

Exercise 2.6

Now that you have looked at an example display for some of the letter data, prepare a similar table for some other key feature in the Helen Keller data. Verbs and verb phrases might be a good choice. The rows will be the same, representing the six letter samples. Examine the data and see what likely verb phrase categories should constitute the column labels. Then examine the letters for examples to fill the cells of the table.

Exercise 2.7

Earlier we mentioned changes in Helen's letters with respect to

vocabulary
grammar
punctuation
capitalization
letter form
reference
cohesion

1   What changes have you noted in any of these that could be put in table form? Discuss.

2   Make a table focusing on one of these other elements in which you show key changes in Helen Keller's mastery of language and writing conventions during the period for which data were collected. If you keep the rows as representing the letter samples, how might the columns be labeled?

If you have done this exercise as a class, individual students should compare their data tables with at least one other student.

Reporting your results

In previous exercises, you organized your data analysis in tables and rough notes. We will come back to the use of tables in the next section. However, for the moment, let's consider the overall organization of your research. The ultimate goal of your research is to report your findings to the world and hopefully to help re-shape that world in some small measure as a result of your study. You will therefore need to know how you will eventually turn your data analyses into research reports, journal articles, and books. Keeping that final result in mind can help you to analyze your results, especially in a way that will be easily reportable.

First of all, when reporting the results of such analyses, you need to be aware of the *standard form* typical of such reports. Presentation of studies in standard form makes it easier for interested readers to know where to look for findings or procedures of relevance to their own interests. It also helps assure you, as a researcher, that you haven't forgotten important information or analyses in your study.

The STANDARD FORM for research reports typically contains some or all of the sections in the following outline:

Abstract
  I   **Introduction***
          A Literature review
          B Purpose (including research questions or hypotheses)
  II   **Methods***
          A Participants*
          B Materials*
          C Procedures*
  III   **Results***
  IV   **Discussion**
  V   **Conclusions**
References
Appendices
Tables

First, notice in the outline that major headings/sections have Roman numerals and subheadings/subsections have capital letters. Second, the asterisks(*) mark those sections that are more or less essential for most studies. Finally, the Abstract, References, Appendices, and Tables are not included as part of the body of the report. They support the main argument as set out in the main body of the report and they may vary considerably in format, placement, and importance from study to study.

Longer research reports, theses, etc. will typically have all of these elements, though they may not always be labeled as such and are sometimes combined with other elements. Shorter pieces, such as short journal articles, may have only the asterisked elements.

Why do we bring up the overall organization of your research report this early in our book? We feel that it is important for you to keep that overall picture in mind from the very beginning of the project so you do not end up with missing pieces when the time comes to write up that report. Consider for instance the *Participants* section. If you do not realize that you will need to describe the participants in some detail in the final report, you might overlook the need to gather information about their age, gender, educational background, language proficiency, years studying the language, and any other characteristics that you feel may shape your data or affect your results. Thus, knowing where you are headed in the reporting process can help you efficiently gather all necessary information while the study is going on.

Using tables in research reporting

Let us now return to the specific point of using tables. As noted above, tables are used not only in the process of analyzing your original data but also in organizing and reporting the results. Below is an excerpt from a research report by Henning Wode as it appeared in a book of readings edited by Hatch (1978). Wode's paper was part of a larger series of research studies aimed at examining the development of certain English structures by both first language (L1) native English-speaking children and by German-speaking children acquiring English as a second language (L2). Earlier, in the first exercise of this chapter, we looked at some data focused on children's development of negative structures in English. Wode has a related focus in this study, in that he is particularly interested in comparing the development of negatives between groups of young L1 and L2 learners of English. Among the research questions addressed by Wode's studies were the following:

1 Is L2 acquired in a developmental sequence?
2 Is there an ordered sequence of stages?
3 Are the developmental sequences the same for L1 and L2?
4 To what extent does the L2 child rely on prior L1 knowledge?
5 Under what circumstances and in what situations does L1 knowledge influence L2 acquisition?

In comparing developmental sequences for negatives in L1 English children and in L2 English (L1 German) children, Wode reports as follows:

> These data support the view that L2 acquisition follows developmental sequences, and that these sequences are ordered. They disconfirm the idea that L2 and L1 acquisition are wholly parallel. Apparently, there may be parallels, like, for instance, I-IIb and IV of Table 7-4; but there may also be differences, as in III of Table 7-4. Differences of this sort, I think, are due to the structure of L1, i.e. the child's prior linguistic knowledge. What is fascinating about this insight is not that L2 children should rely on prior L1 knowledge, but that, apparently, they do so in highly restricted ways, i.e. only at specific points in their development are they liable to fall back on L1. (Wode 1978: 110–111)

Wode's table is shown as Table 2.5.

Table 2.5 Developmental Sequences for L1 English vs. L2 English/L1 German

L1 English			L2 English/L1 German		
I		no	I-II	a	no
					no, you
II	a	no, Mom			
II	b	no close	II	b	no play baseball
		'don't close the door'			'let's not play baseball'
III		Katheryn no like celery	III	a	1) that's no good
		Katheryn not quite through			2) lunch is no ready
		I can't open it			3) I got nothing shoe
					4) John go not to the school
					5) I can no play with Kenny
					6) I cannot hit the ball
				b	I didn't see
				c	I didn't can close it
IV	a	you don't want some supper	IV	a	don't say something
	b	I am not scared of nothing		b	don't tell nobody

(Wode 1978: 111)

Several things are worth noting in Wode's text and table:

1 The table and text are interlocked. A table appears with accompanying text explaining the table and highlighting points in that table the author wants the reader to focus on.
2 The author compromised here with transcription of the language data. He was not concerned with pronunciation, so instead of phonetic transcription, he used *modified* written text (i.e. no sentence capitalization and no sentence punctuation) to report his data. The author decided on what data reporting form best suited his purpose.
3 The number of the participants was not reported. Wode was trying to show some general trends over a large number of mixed participants with mixed data. He was not reporting on any specific child or larger group of children.

Exercise 2.8

Consider each of Wode's original research questions listed again below. Write notes for the answers we now have, based on the extract from Wode's article and Table 2.5.

1   Is L2 acquired in a developmental sequence?

2   Is there an ordered sequence of stages?

3   Are the developmental sequences the same for L1 and L2?

4   To what extent does the L2 child rely on prior L1 knowledge?

5   Under what circumstances and in what situations does L1 knowledge influence L2 acquisition?

Note that a good combination of text and table can not only summarize data efficiently but can also help the reader anticipate what will be discussed next. Based on what you know from Table 2.5 and the accompanying text, what do you think Wode will discuss next in his paper?

Exercise 2.9

Consider one of the tables you have prepared during your data analysis of the Helen Keller letters summarizing some feature of language development in the sequence of letters. Write a paragraph directing a reader to one or more aspects of the table that you think are of particular note. You can write this as if you were in the middle of an article reporting on your study of the letters, assuming prior knowledge on the part of the reader as to what has come before. The easiest way to start is to write something like, 'You will note in Table X, that…'. But you may have a more imaginative way to focus the reader's attention on matters of interest within your table.

Designing case study research

The importance of a thorough literature review

We turn now to another important element in STANDARD FORM reporting that we discussed previously: the LITERATURE REVIEW.

Any research study typically stands on the shoulders of studies that preceded it. In order to acknowledge that debt to previous studies and show where the new study fits into the field, the study often begins with a literature review. This not only summarizes what related studies have been done in the past and what they have shown, but, as importantly, it discusses what *hasn't* been done and what *hasn't* been shown. A good literature review provides both the context and the justification for the new study. It shows why there is a need for the study about to be reported.

In a longer report, such as an MA thesis, the literature review forms an entire chapter and is a crucial introduction to the reported study. Even in shorter reports, such as journal articles, it needs to be clear and comprehensive. In any case, carrying out a thorough review of the literature is an important part of designing your research project because:

1 you don't want to re-invent an existing wheel that is already in the literature;
2 you want to learn from any mistakes that were made in the previous research so you do not repeat them; and
3 you want your research to fit with and add to the research that has preceded it.

Consider the following short literature review from a research article (adapted from Snow and Hoefnagel-Hohle 1978: 335). The article, for which this is the abstract, also focuses on a central theme of this chapter—the similarities and differences between first and second language acquisition.

> Various researchers have recently stressed the similarities between first and second language acquisition (Corder 1974; Hansen-Bede 1975; Holley and King 1971; McNamara 1973), pointing out that errors typical of first language acquisition, such as overgeneralization, also occur in second language acquisition (Ravem 1974; Richards 1974), and that interference is of limited importance (Buteau 1970; Wardhaugh 1974). These conclusions disagree with the traditional view based on contrastive analysis, concerning the prevalence of interference errors. (Fries 1957; Lado 1957; Stockwell, Bowen and Martin 1965). One possible explanation for the disagreement is that interference errors may be more typical of those who have gone through second language training, whereas those who learn a second language in an unstructured, 'picking-it-up' situation may use strategies more similar to those of the first language learner.

Exercise 2.10

Read the literature review above and answer the following questions:

　1　What is the topic being considered in this article?
　2　What two positions are being contrasted?
　3　What question(s) do you think this report will direct itself to?

A good literature review provides you with a sound basis for your research and will help convince the reader that your findings are valid and interesting. Some questions, then, to get you started:

1 How does one set up a literature review and create the *categories* for the review?
2 How does one decide what *issues* to examine within the categories?
3 How does one go about finding relevant *research* on these issues?

Let us consider the first topic: determining the categories for a particular literature review.

In preparing a literature review for the Helen Keller study, what categories and issues might be relevant? Well, users of this text might want to know something about data from both *L1* learners and *L2* learners. We would probably want to know something about both *oral* and *written* language development in children. And we would probably need to look at differences, if any, between the language development of *average* children and those, like Helen, who are *sense-impaired.*

These interrelating categories are shown in Figure 2.1. This diagram has eight cells, one of which cannot be seen. Those that can be seen are numbered for reference 1–6 and 8. The data in our central study came from the written language of a sense-impaired seven-year-old L1 learner .

This information would be coded as belonging in cell 8. In our literature review, we might want to check for the existence of other cell 8-type information, for example, information about the *L1 written* language of *sense-impaired* children, that might give us a context for considering Helen's letters. If we wanted to check on how Helen's written data compared with average L2 learners, we would look for literature relevant to cell 4. Other research in any of the eight cells *might* be relevant to include in the literature review for your study of Helen Keller's letters. Naturally, you would have to do a search and see what you could find and how relevant whatever you find seems.

Exercise 2.11

Consider the following questions:

    1   What kind of research studies may be found in cell 7?

    2   In which cell(s) would the data from Exercise 2.1, on the development of children's use of the negative, be found?

    3   In which cell(s) would Henning Wode's study (Exercise 2.8) be found?

4   From your own point of view, rank the cells from 1–8 in terms of how
     central to a literature review accompanying the Helen Keller study you
     think each of these categories might be.

5   What additional cells might you add to develop a research review for the
     Helen Keller study?

*Figure 2.1 Language acquisition literature review categories for Helen Heller
research study*

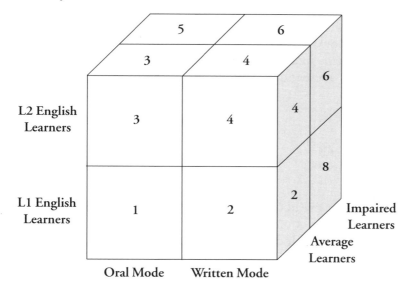

Twenty-four hour self-case study

We are going to ask you to make a twenty-four hour case study of yourself,
reporting all the language you use and can identify during this period. First,
however, we need to introduce some descriptive terms which will help you in
this process.

The use of language is often seen as the defining characteristic of the human
animal. Our interactions, our thoughts, even our dreams, are surrounded by
and steeped in language. Sometimes the language is pretty much one-way as
when we listen to radio or recorded material, watch television, daydream, or
get (or give) a scolding. At other times, however, it is two-way, three-way, or
many-way.

One way to analyze, simplify, and organize the purposes of language use is in
terms of a model of *language functions.* A variety of models have been proposed;

they all attempt to categorize what language is used for—its functions—rather than how language is grammatically structured—its forms. For example, we usually think that the *function* of questioning is most often expressed by the *form* of the interrogative. Similarly, the statement *function* is most often expressed by the declarative sentence *form*, and the command *function* by the imperative *form*. However, it is not always the case that functions and forms are matched in this way. For example, the utterance 'Will you just shut up?' may be interrogative in form but is functionally more likely to be intended (and hopefully interpreted) as a command than as a question.

One of the more widely cited models of language functions is the one proposed by Roman Jakobson (1960). Jakobson held that there are six necessary elements in any communicative act. Using rather simpler labels, these elements are: Sender, Content, Code, Composition, Contact, and Receiver.

Jakobson further maintained that associated with each of these elements there was a 'core function'. That is, if the focus was predominantly on the *sender*, the functional focus was likely to be a personal/emotive one—the *how-I-feel* function. If the focus was primarily on the *content*, the function was *referential*. If the focus was primarily on the social *contact* rather than on content, Jakobson named this function the *phatic* function. These terms and the others below will become clearer by reference to the examples which follow.

The diagram below shows how Jakobson represented the six core language functions as they were associated with the six basic communication elements.

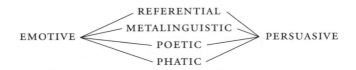

Extrapolation from the Jakobson model yields typical kinds of genres and pre-packaged phrases which might be associated with each of these functions. A representation of the model of language functions in communication (Rodgers 1989 after Jakobson 1960) and some sample genres and phrases of high utility in expressing the associated functions are shown below:

EMOTIVE *(Focus on the feelings of the sender)*
 GENRES: Valentines, graffiti, love/hate notes
 I like/enjoy ... (a lot).
 I'd like to ....
 I feel (pretty/sort of) bad/good/stupid/dumb/pleased about ....
 I hate/love it when that happens.
 Don't you hate/love it when ... .
 I'm so ... (emotional adjective).
 I could ...(verb (+ personal pronoun)).

REFERENTIAL *(Focus on the message content)*
 GENRES : Textbooks, recipes, encyclopedias
 Where is it going to be?
 How far is it to ...?
 What time is it going to get started?
 What part of the ...?
 The X is the most/least important part of (the) Y.
 Let X stand for Y.

METALINGUISTIC *(Focus on linguistic code)*
 GENRES : Grammars, dictionaries, thesauri
 How do you say/spell ...?
 What do you mean by that?
 Why do you always say that ...?
 I can't ever find the right word(s)/way to say what I mean.
 In other words ....
 It's like ....

POETIC *(Focus on well-made message composition)*
 GENRES : Novels, short stories, poems
 Once upon a time, ...
 Once there was a X who lived in Y and who had a very (adjective + noun).
 It was a dark, cold, rainy night. ...
 It's really just kind of a moon-June sort of piece/poem/song.
 Colorless green ideas sleep furiously.

PHATIC *(Focus on the social contact)*
 GENRES : Small talk, vows, sports cheers
 How are you (doing)?
 What's happening?
 Have you heard anything from ...?
 Let's (try to) get together next (time target).
 I, Joe, do take thee, Marilyn ...

PERSUASIVE *(Focus on influencing the receiver)*
    GENRES : Advertisements, sermons, infomercials
    Why don't you give it/him/her a try/go/chance.
    Would you be willing to try it for a (time span)*?*
    And if ye heed not the Word, then shall ye …!
    (Is there any way you)/Could (you)(possibly) help me (verb + complement)*?*
    No obligation. No salesman will call.

We will now look at making a twenty-four hour case study of your own language use. The aim of this is to give you a sense of how a case study works in practice.

Exercise 2.12

To prepare yourself for your case study, think back on the language you used in the last twenty-four hours. The data for the start of your day might look something like this:

Language & Description Event	Function(s)	Time
1 Lay in bed thinking what I would say to Sam about what he did at the party	Referential/Emotive	20 mins.
2 Watched TV news	Referential	30 mins.
3 Breakfast with mother	Phatic	35 mins.
4 Chatted at bus stop with somebody	Phatic	5 mins.
5 Asked bus driver to wake me up at U.	Persuasive	1 min.
6 Read local section of newspaper	Referential	15 mins.
7 Started crossword puzzle	Metalinguistic	10 mins.

etc.

Starting with when you wake up tomorrow, keep a running record of your *functional* language uses for the day. Prepare a data sheet similar to the example above. Then, answer the following questions:

    1   What percentage of your day involved using language of some form?

    2   What language functions did you use most and least during the day?

    3   Was a great deal of your language use multi-functional, that is, involving more than one function at the same time?

4 Do you think this was a *typical* language day for you? In what ways was it not typical? Was there anything that surprised you?

5 Compare your data analysis with a partner. How was your case study like your partner's and how was it different?

Exercise 2.13

This exercise is in the form of preparing an abstract, one of the basic elements we listed earlier as part of the standard form of research reporting.

Read the following fictional abstract of a twenty-four hour self-case study noting the types of information that are included and how they are organized. Then, using this as a model, write up an abstract (as if for an article in which you are reporting the results of your case study) and which highlights the key data from your study.

A Day in the Language Life of Myrtle Yamamoto (Abstract)
The aim of this study was to track the amount and kind of language use experienced by one native speaker of English during a 24-hour (working day) period in local setting. This was an observer-participant study in which the subject/analyst was a 45-year-old, native English-speaking, female language teacher living in Boston, Massachusetts. The type of language use (conversation, lecture listening, daydreaming, etc.) was labeled impressionistically, while the functional classification for language use (emotive, referential, persuasive, etc.) was coded using the six-function system developed by Jakobson (1960). Times for each language use event were recorded in minutes to the nearest minute. Data were tallied in a notebook carried for the purpose either immediately following the use event or retrospectively within two hours of the use event when immediate record keeping was impractical. Results showed that the types of language use were quite broad (31 types noted) while the functional language use was largely restricted to two functions—phatic and referential. A further study is planned in which periods of silent language use (dreaming, thinking, under-breath cursing, etc.) are reported and analyzed in greater detail.

Interpreting case study research

As with any research model, there are strengths and weaknesses to the case study. Bailey (1991) provides a good summary of the strengths and weaknesses for one type of case study in her article entitled 'Diary Studies of Classroom Language Learning: The Doubting and Believing Game'. For Bailey, the 'doubting and believing game' refers to two stances towards research—one, critical and skeptical in questioning the author's position, and the other adopting the author's position uncritically and seeking those insights which could possibly be gained by taking a fully positive stance. We will adopt Bailey's *game* model in our discussion for this section.

The doubting game

A number of authors have noted that the key threats to the usefulness of case study research are the threats to internal and external validity. (We will consider these important themes in more detail in subsequent chapters, notably in Chapters 4 and 8.)

INTERNAL VALIDITY. Here the question is whether the researchers have really observed what they set out to observe and have reported all the critical observational data, or just samples that most strongly support their hypotheses. Since the reader of the developmental/case study does not typically have access to the original participants or the original data, this is often hard to determine. Good questions to ask are:

1 Do you feel you get an accurate and comprehensive picture of the participants and the situations in which the study took place?
2 Do you get a clear understanding of the concepts and the hypotheses the researcher is trying to investigate?
3 Does the researcher seem to be thorough in collecting and coding the data presented?
4 In any studies of human participants, particularly case studies, there are data which seem confusing and out of pattern. Does the researcher report not only hypothesis-confirming data but disconfirming or puzzling data as well?

Exercise 2.14

Consider the Helen Keller study you have completed earlier. What additional data would be useful to have in order to insure internal validity of this study? Possibilities might be:

1   Additional letters.
2   Speech samples in conversations with those to whom she has written letters, samples of language input to Helen. (Did she read Braille books at this point in her life? She obviously received letters. What were they like? How were they communicated to her?)
3   Any language instruction given to Helen by her tutor, Annie Sullivan, especially with regard to the mechanics of writing and forms of personal letters.
4   Comments about Helen's language development by her parents, her tutor, her friends, etc.

Choose one of these possibilities (or nominate another of your own) and explain why you think this particular type of additional data would be your first preference.

EXTERNAL VALIDITY. Here the question is whether the researcher can legitimately generalize from the case study participant(s) and situation to other people and situations. It is difficult to generalize from a sample of one. However, Best and Kahn wrote of case study research:

> The element of typicalness, rather than uniqueness, is the focus of attention, for an emphasis upon uniqueness would preclude scientific abstraction and generalization of findings. As Bromley notes, 'A "case" is not only about a "person" but also about the "kind of person". A case is an exemplar of, perhaps, even a prototype for, a category of individuals.' Thus, the selection of the subject of the case study needs to be done carefully in order to assure that he or she is typical of those about whom we wish to generalize. (Best and Kahn 1989: 92)

Exercise 2.15

Consider the Helen Keller study. Now make two columns, one with the word *typical* at the top, and the other with the word *unique* at the top. In these columns, list the ways in which Helen might be considered *typical* and the ways she might be viewed as *unique*. How might the data collected from the Helen Keller study be tested to see how generalizable it might be to other people and to other situations?

Potential problems with case studies

In her discussion of the 'doubting game' Bailey (1991: 70) notes that most of the potential shortcomings of case studies revolve about issues of generalizability, or issues regarding external validity. She notes that these concerns can be divided into three main categories:
(a) problems regarding the participants,
(b) problems in data collection, and
(c) problems in data analysis.

Exercise 2.16

What questions might arise about the following areas of case study concern?

  1   The participant (for example: Is the participant also the researcher?)
  2   The data collection (for example: How was data recorded and transcribed?)
  3   The data analysis (for example: Were statistical measures used?)

The believing game

Despite the concerns raised above about generalizability, case studies offer a variety of potential benefits. Bailey (1991: 90) lists these potential benefits under the categories of
(a) Benefits for language teachers
(b) Benefits for language learners
(c) Benefits for language learning research

Exercise 2.17

Consider either the Helen Keller study or your own twenty-four hour self-study. What benefits might you derive from studies of this sort that would fall within Bailey's categories? Can you think of other kinds of benefit that might flow from such studies?

One characteristic of case and developmental research seems particularly important to us. That characteristic is candor. If the researcher is straight-forward with us, discusses problems in carrying out the research, acknowledges confusion about some analyses, and does not try to make the study seem overly important, then we feel we are closer to the actual case situation. We may even feel that we are being given a personal introduction to the participant(s) as well as an honest look at both the methodology and the results of the study. Case study research is often written up in a more conversational style than is quantitative research. A non-pretentious tone is easy to relate to and, again, gives us more of an *insider* sense of what is going on.

Leopold's monumental study of his daughter Hildegard provides an engaging example of a very scholarly study presented in a conversational style, with lots of insights and memorable anecdotes for the reader. We will close this section with a quotation from Leopold's study in demonstration of the above remarks:

[Hildegard Age 5] has a desire to learn German, because she would like to be taken along to Germany some time. Once she offered me her entire wealth of ten cents to enable me to pay for the journey... Favorite prices for her are $3.00 and 10 cents; they have no particular individual value. The other day she measured herself with a ruler and declared that she weighed sixty pounds... Footnote: This item drives home to me the value of the daily diary. In my memory the incident had become transformed thus: she looked at a thermometer and said that she weighed $60.00. This version improves the story, which I have told many times when I did not feel the weight of scientific responsibility. (Leopold 1978: 24)

Significance of case study research

In order to understand something of the significance of case studies it is worth spending some time on looking at the meaning and derivation of the word 'case'. 'Case' is used in a number of different disciplines including law, medicine, sociology, and, indeed, linguistics. Etymologically related to *chance*, its ancient adjectival form is *casual*, one of the definitions of which is 'happening or coming to pass without design, and without being foreseen or expected'. In case studies, unlike experiments, we have little or no control over how the form or content of the data will appear. In this sense, there is *chance* involved in what we will find and what the relevance of the findings might be. Most researchers who undertake *case studies* assume, however, that there is going to be *a design* in their case study and that they are going to discover and present to the world some heretofore unrecognized insights in connection with that design. Nevertheless, there is always something *chancy* about case studies. The researcher may pick an unfortunate case to study; or the researcher may not be around to observe when the really interesting patterns emerge; or it may be that no one sees any relevance in the results obtained to the larger world of research concerns.

As we have noted, a number of case studies have been done by language scholars observing the first language or second language development of their own children. Michael Halliday (1975), Werner Leopold (1939–1949), Ruth Weir (1962) are among the many linguists who have published studies of the language development of their own offspring. Both the research techniques and the findings of these studies of children's language acquisition have been adopted and adapted by SLA researchers in their studies of the development of second languages by adults.

In recent years, there have been a number of candid *self*-case studies by established applied linguists analyzing and reporting on their own learning, in adulthood, of a second language. John and Francine Schuman (1977),

Wilga Rivers (1979), Kathleen Bailey (1983), and Richard Schmidt (with Sylvia Frota) (1986) have all published self-studies widely quoted in the applied linguistics literature. Here is a sample from Schmidt's diary entry of an early experience in his Portuguese language learning, undertaken while he was living in Brazil.

> I ... went to the new class, which was already in session ... a drill was in progress. SER again, which must be every teacher's lesson one. Teacher (L) asks, student responds: 'Voce e americana?' ('Are you an American?'); 'Sou, sim' ('I am, yes'). When it was my turn the question was 'Voce e casado?' ('Are you married?'); so I said 'Nao'. L corrected me: 'Sou, sim'. I objected: 'Eu nao sou casado'. L said (in English), 'We are practicing affirmative answers'. I objected again, 'I'm not married', and L said, 'These questions have nothing to do with real life'. My blood was boiling, but I shut up...What a sour start! But I think I will stick with it. (Schmidt and Frota 1986: 244)

Exercise 2.18

1   What was it that Schmidt didn't like about the language class? What was it that the language teacher didn't like about Schmidt?

2   Recall a time in your own previous language learning (or teaching) experience when learner and teacher didn't see eye to eye on what should be happening in the class.

Most developmental case studies involve a researcher studying the language development of one (or more) learner(s) who are not offspring or themselves. Roger Brown (1973) set many of the ground markers for studies conducted over a relatively long period of time, or longitudinal studies, in his study of the first language acquisition of Adam, Eve, and Sarah. Another landmark case study—in this case of Wes, a Japanese L1 adult learning English as a second language—was reported by Schmidt (1983). Rubin (1975), Naiman, Fröhlich, Stern, and Todesco (1978), Rubin and Thompson (1983) and others contributing to the so-called *good language learner* studies, relied on summarizing individual cases as the central tool in carrying out their research. Results of these studies (and others using alternative methodologies) stimulated much of the current interest in language-learner strategies and strategy training such as that reported in Oxford (1990) as well as O'Malley and Chamot (1990).

The following list contains a summary of those factors that Nunan examined in a follow-up to the Rubin and Thompson (1983) case study summaries of good language learners. Nunan (1991: 152–3) looked at the top ten preferences for learning strategy use in response to four categorical questions submitted to 44 *good-language-learning* language teachers.

> **Category One:** When you learned English, which of the following ways of learning did you like?
>
> **Category Two:** When you learned English, which of the following ways of learning did you find most helpful?
>
> **Category Three:** If you were going to learn another language, which of the following ways of learning would you use?
>
> **Category Four:** Think of the learners you are currently teaching: how do you think they would respond?

The items reported by participants in Category Three were the following (note that these are in alphabetical order, not in the order of participants' preferences):

Having a coursebook	Small group work
In-class conversation	Talking to friends
Learning by doing	Talking to L1 speakers
Learning by hearing	Watching television
Pictures, films, videos	Practicing out of class

Exercise 2.19

Now do each of the following steps:

1   Read through Nunan's list and think about each item in terms of your own second language learning experience. Jot down what your preferences might be in learning a new second language.

2   Now rank the ten items (given above) in order of what you feel would be the most important strategies for you in learning a new language. (This doesn't mean that you would actually *follow* these strategies all the time.).

3   Compare your list with that compiled by Nunan (or by a fellow student), and discuss where your lists are similar and different in order.

(The rank that Nunan's *good-language-learning* language teachers gave him is shown in the Answer Key on page 258 for comparison.)

Reflecting on case study research

Van Lier has proposed a taxonomy of educational research design types built around the two axes of *intervention* and *selectivity* (see Figure 2.2). Research can vary along the axis of intervention from formal laboratory experimentation (high intervention) to informal classroom observation (non-intervention).

Similarly, the researchers can be *very selective* in the types of data they want to focus on, for example, obligatory use of the definite article by immigrant ten-year-old boys, or *very non-selective*, for example, all behavior observed of all participants.

Van Lier identifies four territories bounded by the crossroads of selectivity and intervention. He identifies these as *watching*, in which both intervention and selectivity are low; *measuring*, in which intervention is minimal but the data focus is highly restricted; *asking/doing*, in which the researcher might intervene to ask participants to talk about what they are thinking; and *controlling*, in which the researcher conducts an experiment restricted both in participants and content focus. Each of these territories is marked by different research *types* and different potential audience *inhabitants*.

Figure 2.2 Parameters of educational research design

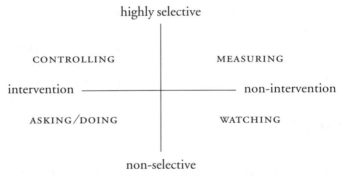

(van Lier 1988)

Exercise 2.20

Consider where in the van Lier schema you would place the Helen Keller study.

1   Write a short paragraph defining the kind of research type you feel the Helen Keller study is (according to the van Lier description) and why you classify it as you do.

2   How would you classify your own twenty-four hour case study?

3   In a sentence or two describe a research study which you feel might stand as a prototype for each of the quadrants. (Hint: The research types explored in this book represent the full range of research types proposed by van Lier).

4   At this point in your study of second language learning research, where do you think your own interests lie? In which of van Lier's quadrants would you place your preference for research?

Summary

In this chapter, we have examined the design, execution, and reporting of developmental case study research as it has been carried out in L1 and L2 studies. We focused primarily on single-participant case study research as it has been used in the study of language development. We suggested that case study research is one of the most attractive styles of research for the first-time researcher, in that organizational and reporting style tend to be less formal than in other kinds of study, and case study researchers always have ready participants in themselves, their children, and their friends. A major caution in both design and interpretation of case study research involves the generalizability of such research. Case study researchers need to assure their audience that the study has been thoroughly and accurately documented and that implications of the study are clearly drawn, and not overstated.

3 INTROSPECTIVE RESEARCH: VERBAL PROTOCOLS

Introducing introspective research

The eye of man hath not heard, the ear of man hath not seen, man's hand is not able to taste, his tongue to conceive, nor his heart to report, what my dream was.
WILLIAM SHAKESPEARE, 1564–1616
A Midsummer Night's Dream, Act 4, scene 1

This somewhat jumbled recount by Bottom in *A Midsummer Night's Dream* indicates Shakespeare's skepticism about the possibility of the tongue conceiving or the heart reporting what a dream was. But getting reports about what the brain conceives or the heart feels has been a central challenge for human beings (and for psychologists sent to represent human beings formally). Psychology has wrestled (and continues to wrestle) with the issue of defining and analyzing human emotional/mental states throughout its short history as a discipline. The most obvious (and most controversial) way of doing research on, say, mental states is by asking those people who claim to have on-going mental states what is going on as they mentalize. Asking participants to delve into their own states of consciousness and verbally report on cognitive, affective, or social aspects of that consciousness is the technique used in introspective studies.

The researcher using introspective techniques usually sets a task and then asks participants to report on what their brains (or hearts) are processing as they carry out the task. A number of people—you probably know some—seem to mutter their way through life. However, there are a number of life's tasks that almost all of us *talk through* as we do them. An example of this *talking through* process familiar to most people is that of doing mental (or even written) arithmetic.

Exercise 3.1

(Warm-up)

Consider the following multiplication problem and how you go about solving it. To learn more about that process, write down the (mental) words you say to yourself as you go through the process of solving the problem.

$$45$$
$$\times \underline{52}$$

Most people seem to talk—either aloud or sub-vocally—their way through solution of such problems: 'Two times five is ten, put down zero, carry the one; two times four is eight, plus one is nine…' If you were to carry out the steps of solving an arithmetic problem fully aloud and if you or an observer/listener were to record and transcribe what you are reporting aloud, this would be the beginning of an introspective study.

In this chapter, you will have roles as participant and researcher as you carry out and collect data on some tasks involving introspective reporting. You will also have a chance to examine in some detail some of the options that are available to you as a researcher as you go about coding the data that you collect and analyze.

An excellent overview of the several ways in which introspective research has been used in second language studies is provided by Færch and Kasper's book *Introspection in Second Language Research* (1987). The text covers introspective studies in test-taking and validation, translation, reading, problem-solving, error analysis, motivation, etc.

Introspective studies had a period of centrality in psychological studies in the early twentieth century. Such studies had the blessing of such psychological giants as William James: 'Introspective observation is what we have to rely on first and foremost and always. The word introspection need hardly be defined—it means, of course, the looking into our own minds and reporting what we there discover' (James 1890: 185). Following James, introspective notions were early underwritten by extensive laboratory studies, particularly those conducted by Titchener (1912). These formal introspective explorations seemed fashionably linked to the introspective and stream-of-consciousness writing styles of leading contemporary literary figures such as James Joyce, Marcel Proust, and Virginia Woolf.

Yet within a few years, introspective studies of the Titchener type were under strong attack by those like 'Watson (1913) who argues, with evidence, that the introspective verbal report is untrustworthy for scientific purposes'

(Ericsson and Simon 1993: 58). With the rise of behaviorism in psychological studies, introspection came under further attack. For almost fifty years introspective studies of any sort were virtually abandoned.

It was Ericsson and Simon's now already classic work, *Verbal Protocols* (1984, 1993), which, in large measure, was responsible for reviving interest and which showed the way past the criticisms that had been raised against such studies in their earlier form. Ericsson and Simon argued that psychological studies of any sort needed to be designed in respect to a model of mental processes, and they formulated such a model on the basis of information processing theory. The critical feature of this theory is that it assumes a multiple memory model comprising both short-term and long-term memory stores and presumed mechanisms by which they are activated.

As a result of decisions based on the model and experimental work that followed from it, several principles for introspective studies were formulated. These included the dictums that

1 time intervening between mental operations and report is critical and should be minimized as much as possible;
2 verbalization places additional cognitive demands on mental processing that requires care in order to achieve insightful results;
3 verbal reports of mental processes should avoid the usual social conventions of talking to someone;
4 there is a lot of information in introspective reports aside from the words themselves. Researchers need to be aware of these parallel signal systems and be prepared to include them in their analyses;
5 verbal reports of automatic processes are not possible. Such processes include visual and motor processes and low-attention, automatized linguistic processes such as the social chat of native speakers; and
6 research should be based on a model of mental processes that allows predictions about how mental operations will be organized under various conditions.

As a partial consequence of these dictums, Ericsson and Simon distinguished three levels of verbal report.

1 TALK-ALOUDS where the report is concurrent with a given mental task and for which the information is already linguistically encoded and can be directly stated. An example would be talking aloud while thinking how to spell a word.

2 THINK-ALOUDS where the report is concurrent with a given mental task but where the heeded information is not already linguistically encoded and thus requires linguistic encoding for verbalization. Describing what a corkscrew looks like would be an example.

3 RETROSPECTIVE STUDIES where the report is subsequent to a given mental task and where information consists of selected foci, descriptions, explanations and interpretations. Reporting on the route by which you arrived at your present location would be an example.

Whether you are working alone or working in a class situation, you should be aware that many of the most valued introspective studies are of the solo or self-report type, where one person is both participant-subject and analyst. Diary studies, which we discussed in Chapter 2, are an obvious type of self-reporting and self-analysis. Some contemporary second-language course instructors have learners keep some sort of introspective record of their language learning impressions as a component of the language learning course. In these cases, students are acting both as language-learning participant-subjects and second-language acquisition researchers.

All researchers working in the introspective tradition emphasize the importance of recording—both audio and video where possible—participant responses for later analysis. If you are working on your own, you will definitely need to record your introspective verbalizations on audio tape for later analysis. In some class situations, we acknowledge that having enough tape recorders to share between every two students in the class as well as having noise-restricted, non-distractive areas within your study areas for tape recording may not be realistic expectations. Alternative approaches could include working in pairs and having one member of the pair take notes of what the other says. You may also be able to book time in a language laboratory if you are working in an institution that has one.

The following exercises are designed to give you some experience in carrying out some *classic* introspective tasks whether you are working alone or as part of a class. If you are using this text on your own, you will be wearing two hats. Where exercises are described as *pair* exercises, you will be acting as your own partner, first tape recording your introspections as *participant-subject* and then analyzing these recorded introspective records as *researcher*. Most of these pair exercises are easily interpretable as *two-hat* exercises for the solo learner. In addition, several of the activities have a game-like quality, and you may want to ask a family member or friend to act as your partner while you do the exercise.

We have tried to observe the dictums listed above (page 55) and to encourage you to do the same as you carry out the task exercises and as you analyze the results.

Experiencing introspective research

People differ greatly in their habits of *vocalizing* experience. However, we all vocalize (or sub-vocalize) some things that we do or think about.

Exercise 3.2

List as many situations as you can think of when you *talk to yourself* about something you are thinking about. Sometimes talking to yourself will be unobservable to an outside observer, sometimes you might sub-vocalize your thinking while moving your lips, and sometimes you might actually talk to yourself out loud, or maybe even shout your thoughts.

Now, decide how many of the situations you listed you would call mental/cognitive/ intellectual (like solving a mathematics problem) and how many you would say are emotional/affective/social (like talking to yourself about how you are feeling when you get up in the morning or about someone's behavior in class, at a party, while driving a car, etc.).

Perhaps an over-riding consideration, if not principle, is that the introspective tasks should be within the linguistic and cognitive capabilities of the participant subjects. This is particularly true when working with second language subjects. Some practice exchanges will indicate at what level of conceptual language participant subjects are competent.

Now let's consider a few of the general principles that apply to this type of introspective research:

Principle one *Always use a tape recorder or other recording device such as a computer or mini-disk recorder.*

Even though you will be making transcriptions and notes, words could be lost if they come too fast and furiously for you to write them all down. You will need your tape recordings to make accurate transcriptions and to check your notes. The tape recorder should be inconspicuous but still allow you to get reasonably clear recordings.

Principle two *Think aloud. Don't talk.*

Most of the time when we talk out loud we are talking to someone. We are explaining, defending, persuading, or whatever. It is hard to get out of these verbal behaviors when we are trying to *talk aloud* or *think aloud*. To encourage the participants not to engage in social conversation but rather to report what is going on directly in their mental processing, it is helpful if researchers sit behind the participant during verbal reporting. In this position, the researcher can give directions, encourage, remind participants who have been quiet for several seconds to keep verbalizing, and discourage participants from *talking to* the researcher rather than *talking to* themselves.

Principle three *Do not be too directive in instructions to participants.*

Participants need to be clear about what the task they are undertaking is and in what form and with what frequency they are expected to respond. But you do not want to shape participant responses. You want to know what the participants are thinking not what they think about what you are thinking.

Ericsson and Simon (1984, 1993) is the source most frequently cited in introspective studies. It deals both with the modeling of the mental processes said to be tapped by introspective reports as well as the appropriate procedural detail said to maximize the veridicality of verbal reports of mental processes and to minimize extraneous factors. Ericsson and Simon elaborate a set of instructions and warm-up exercises said to optimize the usefulness of introspective reporting. These instructions are quoted below. Follow these as you read through them.

> *Ericsson and Simon Instructions for Talk Aloud*
> In this experiment we are interested in what you say to yourself as you perform some task that we give you. In order to do this we will ask you to talk aloud as you work on the problems. What I mean by talk aloud is that I want you to say out loud *everything* that you say to yourself silently. Just act as if you are alone in the room speaking to yourself. If you are silent for any length of time I will remind you to keep talking aloud. Do you understand what I want you to do?
> Good, before we turn to the real experiment, we will start with a couple of practice problems. I want you to talk aloud while you do these problems. First, I will ask you to multiply two numbers in your head. So talk aloud while you multiply 24 times 34!
> Good!
> Now I would like you to solve an anagram. I will show you a card with scrambled letters. It is your task to find an English word that consists of all the presented letters. For example, if the scrambled letters are KORO, you may see that these letters spell the word ROOK. Any questions? Please *talk aloud* while you solve the following anagram!
> <NPEPHA >   (Answer: HAPPEN)
> Good!

(Ericsson and Simon 1993: 376)

In the exercises which follow you will have an opportunity to take part in some of the better-known types of verbal reporting of mental processes. You will alternate the roles of participant (*p*) and researcher (*r*). Instructions will indicate when in the exercise you are to switch roles.

Exercise 3.3

Answer the following questions:

1 What are the two kinds of warm-up exercises that the Ericsson and Simon instructions dictate?

2 Why do you suppose these particular two exercises were selected?

3 What three features of the instructions strike you as most important for collecting useful introspective reports?

4 What features of the instructions satisfy the criteria we have outlined earlier in this section?

As we indicated previously, solving an arithmetic problem often involves *thinking aloud* while solving the problem. Ericsson and Simon suggest this as an initial practice activity for introspective studies.

Exercise 3.4

Working in pairs, decide who is the *participant* and who is the *researcher*. Then do the following:

1 The researcher makes up a two-by-two number multiplication problem for the participant to solve (for example, 54 x 39).

2 The participant *talks aloud* while multiplying the number in her head. The researcher records or writes down what the participant says as she solves the problem.
Many participants find the task of multiplying the numbers in their heads too difficult and frustrating. (This includes the two authors of this text.) If so, do the multiplication on a piece of paper. The talking aloud requirement doesn't change.

3 When you have finished, reverse roles, and follow the same procedures and repeat steps 1 and 2.

4 Then both partners should work together in answering the following questions:
   a Did both participants keep talking while solving the problem?
   b Was there any difference between the kinds of talk of the two participants?
   c Was there any difference in the strategies that the two participants used in solving the problem?
   d What changes would you make in the procedure to make the exercise more useful, less confusing?

Anagram puzzles have long been popular in a variety of alphabetic languages. An anagram is a spelling out of a word from another word or a collection of letters. Thus, 'arts' is an anagram of 'tsar' or of 'star'. Scrabble is essentially an anagram game. A number of texts also include anagrams as second language learning exercises as well. People go about solving (or creating) anagrams in a variety of different ways. Anagrams thus provide a good basis for certain kinds of introspective linguistic studies and/or as warm-ups for other kinds of studies.

Exercise 3.5

Working in pairs, begin by deciding who is the *participant* and who is *researcher*. Then do the following:

1 The *researcher* gives the *participant* a six-letter anagram to solve. In this case, the anagram is LIPYMS.

2 The participant works on solving the anagram (paper and pencil are OK) all the while *talking aloud* about what he is doing. Remember the primary point of the exercise is recording the thought processes, *not* solving the puzzle.

3 The researcher records or writes down what the participant says while he is solving the anagram.

4 When you have finished, reverse roles, and follow the same procedures using a different six-letter anagram and repeat steps 1, 2, and 3.

5 Both partners should work together in answering the following questions:
a Were there any problems in solving the anagrams?
b Were the problems clear from the *talk aloud* procedures?
c Did the two *participants* use different strategies in solving the anagram puzzles?
d Would either participant like to try using some of the strategies their partners used in solving a new anagram? For example, some participants find that organizing letters in a circle rather than in a line allows them to see patterns more quickly.

Two of the areas in which introspective studies have proved most fruitful have been in the investigation of the processes involved in reading comprehension and written composition. These are obviously areas of keen interest to language researchers and language teachers. One of the frequently used formats for studying reading processes involves the use of *sign-posted* reading texts. The reading text is prepared in such a way that there are periodic markers in the text signaling the reader to momentarily stop and report what she is thinking about the text at this point. The researcher records or writes down these comments and then analyzes them, looking for patterns and strategies the participant uses in reading the text.

Exercise 3.6

Working in pairs, begin by deciding who is *participant* and who is *researcher*. Then do the following:

I The researcher reads the instructions for the task to the participant, then gives the reading text to the participant. (The text and the instructions are in Appendix 3.1 on page 264.)

2 The participant reads the text, stopping at the *signposts* (small boxes) to say what he is thinking right then. Researcher records (and/or takes quick notes about) the participant's commentary.

3 When you have finished, reverse roles, and follow the same procedures and repeat steps 1 and 2 using the same text.

4 Then both partners should work together in answering the following questions:

 a Did both participants keep talking while solving the problem?

 b Was there any difference between the kinds of talk of the two participants?

 c What changes would you make in the procedure to make the exercise more useful, less confusing?

Compiling introspective data

As we have noted, most introspective/retrospective data are recorded on a tape recorder. In addition, the researcher may have made notes and/or have done partial transcriptions. A first task will be to transcribe the target data from the tape recordings and figure how to integrate any notes or transcriptions you, as researcher, made at the time of data collection. A task often done concurrently is *segmenting* the transcription so that each segment represents an apparent short thought unit. These segmented units will be what you will code and analyze, and what will become the heart of your research report. So you need to consider carefully what the segments should be and how you will explain what a segment is in your write-up.

Exercise 3.7

Take the data from one of the anagrams you solved in Exercise 3.5, then transcribe and segment them. You should take data that have at least five steps to find the solution so you will have enough data to work with. You will probably find it most useful to put the data in list form, with each spoken segment representing one item on the list.

What form do transcriptions take? Typically, you might want to note three kinds of information (if it is not obvious from the participant's spoken data):

   I   What is the participant focusing on? What is the immediate target of the participant's introspective comment, if this can be determined?

   2   What exactly is the participant saying during the focus period?

   3   What other observations did the researcher make during this focus period?

One well-known language researcher reminds us that 'We communicate so much information non-verbally in conversations that often the verbal aspect of the conversation is negligible' (H. D. Brown 1994). Another researcher said that only 1% of the meaning in speech involves language. He identified rhythm, speed, pitch, intonation, timbre, and hesitation phenomena as the more important meaning bearers in speech (Lotz 1963). The importance of this non-verbal data is the principal reason why researchers use audio and video recordings where possible. This enables them also to record pauses, changes of reporting speed, loudness or tone, what else the participant was doing during introspective speech (gestures, eye movement, body shifts, etc.).

Exercise 3.8

This exercise will focus on a few kinds of non-verbal data.

   I   Many different kinds of communication signal are sent and received in normal face-to-face conversation. List as many of them as you can.

   2   Working in pairs, decide who will be the researcher and who the participant. The researcher's task is to take note of as many different kinds of communication signal that the participant produces while doing this task. These signals may include language signals, like words, repetitions, loudness, speed, pauses, etc. They may include gestures, facial expressions, eye movements, body movements, etc. Be ready to note as many of these response signals as you can.

3   The researcher says the following to the participant: 'How would you describe a corkscrew?'

4   Now, reverse roles. The new researcher says the following to the new participant: 'Think of five people you know whose first names begin with the letter *T*.'

5   Both partners in their role as researcher should now make an abbreviated transcription, noting particularly non-word kinds of signal that the participants were producing while carrying out their tasks.

6   How many and what kind of non-word signals did each of you note? Work together to classify these non-word signals and make a combined list.

Most researchers would probably agree that taking note of non-verbal as well as verbal information is useful in collecting *rich response* data. Færch and Kasper (1987: 8) point out that analysis of participants' oral production is typically highly limited in its scope, in that the 'text is cleansed from most of the performance features such as … slips of the tongue, self-corrections, supra-segmentals and temporal variables (pauses, speed, rate and manner of articulation.' This comment remains true of most introspective studies, in part because it is hard to determine:

1   how much and what kinds of response data should be recorded,
2   how these data should be noted and coded, and
3   how such data should be interpreted in terms of participants' mental states.

In your own introspective studies, you need to consider if such non-verbal data will be critical to your coding and analysis, and determine a method for transcribing such data.

Analyzing introspective data

Coding of language data

Coding data is a critical task in almost all forms of both social and physical research. It is first necessary to mark what you have collected for what it is: in geology a rock type, in musicology a folk-song type, in hydrology a water sample, in verbal protocol studies an introspective commentary. Some kinds of coding are fairly straightforward. If it is necessary to code some sample for color, a color chart will provide a code. If it is necessary to code samples for size, a clock or a ruler or a weighing scale or a loudness indicator will often indicate on its own scale face what an appropriate code would be. However, when we are talking about the *meaning* or *use* of a sample of *language*, coding is usually not so straightforward. A host of codes for language grammatical types, sound types, function types have been proposed, but none of these can be considered standard in the same sense that a meter (or yard) stick is an agreed-upon standard.

Consider the coding systems used by researchers examining the strategies that readers bring to bear in the understanding of a new piece of text. The coding systems proposed for analyzing reading comprehension verbal protocols include highly detailed and complex models such as that proposed by Pressley and Afflerbach (1995) whose comprehensive model of 'constructively responsive reading' attempts to integrate the full range of reading processes included in the coding scheme. In contrast, systems containing only two elements have been proposed in which all reading responses are coded as being either *reflexive* or *extensive*. REFLEXIVE RESPONSES are those in which readers direct comments away from the text and towards their own thoughts and feelings, usually in the first or second person, whereas EXTENSIVE RESPONSES are those in which readers attempt to deal with the message conveyed by the author, usually in the third person, rather than relating the texts to themselves (Block 1986).

Critical questions in interpretation of verbal protocol data involve the coding system used:

1 Are the code categories clear and unambiguous?
2 Is the coding scheme reliable? Will alternative analysts code data in the same way?
3 Do the results of coding lead to useful analyses?

Analysis of verbal protocols

We have thus far sampled just a few of the many applications for verbal protocol research.

Within each of the introspective study applications, a variety of task types is possible. Obviously, the type of analysis the researcher performs will vary with application and task type. For example, within the application type we have labeled 'Solving Anagrams' there are at least four task types:

1 Task Type A: How can all the given letters be arranged to form a single word? (NPEHPA = HAPPEN)
2 Task Type B: How many different words of three letters or more can be formed from the letters in a given word? (ALPHABET = BET, BEAT, TAB, PEAL, TABLE, etc.)
3 Task Type C: What longer word might all of these words have been made from? (TEAR, SUN, TRUANT, RESTART = RESTAURANT).

4 Task Type D: What letter might you add to the word below to make a new anagram meaning *begin*? [RATS + (?) (word meaning *begin*) = RATS + (T) (word meaning *begin*) = START]

For each of these different task types, somewhat different data analysis procedures might be necessary. However, some general procedures may be typical of protocol analysis in general and may, in one form or another, occur in almost all forms of protocol analysis. Typical steps in protocol analysis include the following:

1 Responses are transcribed, segmented, and arrayed in the order produced.
2 These are roughly overviewed and patterns looked for in the responses.
3 Codes are devised (or borrowed) in order to label kinds of observed response.
4 Codes are assigned to response segments.
5 Code sequences and combinations are examined for patterns.
6 Coding combinations are compared to see if larger classification of code types seems possible and, if so, how codes will be so classified.
7 Combinations of codes and coding classes are examined to see if types of participant *strategies* can be identified.
8 Other protocols of similar task types are studied to see if the coding, classification and strategy assumptions prove adequate for analysis of these new protocols. If not, steps 2–8 are repeated to reconcile the analytical scheme to all of the available protocol data.

The first part of any data analysis is to determine what kind of data you have, how they link to what you are trying to find out, and what is customary in analyzing data of the type you have collected. Obviously, you would like to know what kind of data you are likely to finish with before you start. This is a little tricky, in part because you never really know what participants (even yourselves) are likely to say and thus cannot fully anticipate what kind of data you might wind up with. Another problem is that introspective studies, especially in second language acquisition, are relatively new, and the determination of what is most and least critical in this kind of research is still in the midst of formative discussion. Another consequence of the newness of the field is that alternative coding systems are constantly emerging and you will have to decide which system or kind of system you are going to use to analyze your data.

It is tempting to take one of the existing coding systems developed for a previous study and employ it in your own study. The *advantages* of this are:

1 The coding system already exists, is documented, and has the prestige of published acceptance.
2 Your study becomes part of a set which uses a common coding system and for which data comparisons can readily be made.

The *disadvantages* of this choice are:

1 The coding system may imperfectly fit your data which come, of course, from an original and unique study.
2 You will not experience the excitement that accompanies making up a brand-new coding system.

The temperate advice is probably 'Try employing a coding system which already exists and adapt it as necessary'. Go for an original system only if the borrowed one proves clearly inadequate for your purposes. You may also find it necessary to change the data analysis/coding system after you have already committed yourself to one particular model.

An example of a simple coding scheme for anagram solution verbal protocols is given by Ericsson and Simon. In this scheme, all participant responses are coded as one of two response types—constraint type or alternative type.

CONSTRAINT TYPE (or C-type) RESPONSES are those in which the participant uses her knowledge of possible letter sequences in English as a guide for constructing longer sequences, for rejecting a test sequence as 'un-English' or as a search probe to try to think of words in lexical memory that contain such sequences. C-type responses often appear as a 'spelling out' of possible letter sequences and letter positions.

ALTERNATIVE TYPE (or A-type) RESPONSES are those in which the participant pronounces a sequence (or some letter combination similar to the sequence) in an attempt to find a sound match in lexical memory. A-type responses often appear as 'sounding out' of possible syllables or words. An example of the Ericsson and Simon C-type and A-type coding is shown in Table 3.1.

Exercise 3.9

Look at the Ericsson and Simon coding in Table 3.1 and answer the following questions:

1 What convention did the researcher use to distinguish pronunciation tries from spelling tries?

2 Were there any responses that weren't coded? Why do you think that was so?

3 What code(s) might you add for responses like these?

Table 3.1 Coding example: analysis of a think-aloud protocol from participant solving the anagram NPEHPA

N-P, neph, neph	
Probably PH goes together	C: PH
Phan	A: phan
Phanny	A: phanny
I get phan-ep	A: phan-ep
no. Nap-	A: nap
Phep-an, no	A: phep-an
E is a the end	C: E(end)
Phap-en	A: phap-en
People, I think of.	A: people
Try PH after the other letters	C: PH(end)
Naph, no	A: naph
I thought of paper again	A: paper
E and A sound alike, couldn't go together	
without a consonant	
Try double P	C: PP
Happy	A: happy
Oh, Happen	A: happen

(Ericsson and Simon 1987: 49)

Exercise 3.10

Table 3.2 shows one participant's (George's) responses to the anagram ROHMET (the required anagram word is MOTHER). Look at the data in Table 3.2 and code George's responses as C-type or A-type in the table.

Exercise 3.11

Find the anagram data from Exercise 3.7 and do the following:

1   Segment it as shown in the exercises above if you have not already done so.
2   Code the segments using the A-type and C-type system practiced above.
3   Answer the following questions:
   a   Does the coding work for your data?
   b   Were there any questionable cases?
   c   What were they?
   d   Do you find you need additional codes or a different coding system?

Table 3.2 Think-aloud protocol from participant (George) solving the anagram ROHMET

Response	Code (C or A)
1 Let's see rohmet	
2 Or maybe metroh	
3 t-r could be first	
4 trohem	
5 t-h-r?	
6 throme	
7 throw me?	
8 r-m at the end?	
9 Something orm?	
10 h-e-r goes together? her	
11 moth?	
12 Oh, stupid me! mother	

A variety of schemes have been proposed for coding data by subjects as they make introspective comments on a reading text. Table 3.3 shows such a coding scheme as developed by Brown and Lytle for coding exhibited reading strategies in reading think-alouds.

A verbal protocol taken from a second language learner of English as he introspected on the text 'The Lady of the Moon' is shown in Appendix 3.2, page 266. (This was the reading focus for Exercise 3.6.)

Exercise 3.12

Look at the verbal protocol in Appendix 3.2 and do the following:

  1 Code the protocol according to Brown and Lytle's coding system.

  2 Answer these questions:

   a What problems, if any, did you have in applying the coding scheme to the data?

   b Were there ambiguous cases where you wanted to apply more than one code? Is multiple coding a useful solution?

   c Were there instances where you felt none of the code categories applied to the data sample?

   d Could you create a new code in the same coding format to cover such a case?

Table 3.3 Coding scheme for reading verbal protocols (letters in parentheses are the codes)

1 *Monitoring* (M): 'I don't understand.' 'This doesn't make sense.'
   Manifested in statements or questions indicating the reader doubts his/her understanding (including conflicts).

2 *Signaling* (S): 'What do I understand?'
   Manifested in statements in which the reader signals his/her current understanding of the text's meaning (agrees, paraphrases, summarizes).

3 *Analyzing* (A): 'How does this text work?'
   Manifested in statements in which the reader, viewing the text as an object, notices, describes, or comments on the features of text (e.g. words, sentences, text structure, style). Thus, for the purpose of observing a reader's sense of text structure, we would expect to see this move occur within the think aloud process.

4 *Elaborating* (E): 'What does this make me think of?'
   Manifested in statements describing the ways the reader is responding to or experiencing the text such as imagery, recalling prior knowledge, liking/disliking.

5 *Judging* (J): 'How good is this?'
   Manifested in statements indicating the reader is evaluating the text (ideas or text features).

6 *Reasoning* (R): 'How can I figure this out?' 'What might X mean?'
   Manifested in statements or questions indicating the reader is trying to resolve doubts and interpret the text (e.g. hypothesis, prediction, question, use of evidence).

(Brown and Lytle 1988)

Designing your own introspective research study

You have seen that most introspective research studies have the following characteristics:

1 they ask for reasonably free-form responses (i.e. they are usually not pre-formatted);
2 they are given orally by the participant (i.e. they are usually not written);
3 they elicit cognitive processes (i.e. they usually deal with thinking rather than, say, motor activity);
4 they involve carrying out a specific task (i.e. they usually involve a given task rather than a generic life activity);

5 they take place within particular dimensions and are of limited duration (i.e. they are usually accomplished within very limited space and time constraints); and

6 they are produced during or shortly following carrying out of the task (i.e. responses are usually given at the time of the activity, not hours, days, or weeks afterwards).

So you might want to design your own study within these dimensions.

At the beginning of this chapter we saw that Ericsson and Simon have described three general types of introspective studies: 'talk-alouds', 'think-alouds', and 'retrospective studies'.

Exercise 3.13

Review how talk-alouds, think-alouds, and retrospective studies were described on pages 55–6, then do the following:

1   Restate the differences between these three research study types in your own words.

2   From the mini-studies you have done or read about, give an example of a talk-aloud, a think-aloud, and a retrospective study.

3   *Think aloud* what you feel to be the pros and cons of each of these three types of introspective studies from your own personal point of view. Don't think about and then discuss. Talk about what you are thinking. Now!

A first consideration involves choosing an area to study. We have mentioned some of the areas in which introspective studies have been done and results found fruitful. Here is a list of some such areas:

1 Solving logic problems
2 Solving physics problems
3 Solving mathematics problems
4 Test-taking
5 Reacting to classroom instruction
6 Determining chess moves
7 Solving a maze
8 Selecting a computer/hand calculator
9 Solving anagrams
10 Crossword puzzle working
11 Making word associations
12 Describing an abstract picture
13 Memorizing nonsense syllables
14 Translating
15 Recalling L2 vocabulary
16 Outlining a composition
17 Writing text to cues
18 Peer editing
19 Reading comprehension
20 Interpreting poetry
21 Creating titles for text samples
22 Completing cloze-type passages
23 Ordering scrambled sentences/paragraphs

Exercise 3.14

Read through the above list and then answer the following questions:

  I   Which of these areas strike you as most interesting from the point of view of second language research?

  2   Are there other areas of potential introspective study research you can think of that are not included in the above sample? What are they?

  3   Pick one of the areas you listed in numbers I or 2 as a tentative one for your own study.

You should now have the beginnings of a profile for your study. The profile should define your choices in respect to the following areas of information:

1 Talk-aloud, think-aloud, or retrospective study
2 Topical area and task type(s)
3 Rationale: Why are you personally interested in doing a study of the kind you are outlining?
4 Coding and analysis: You really won't know fully how to code and analyze your data until you have the data. However, it is always advisable to speculate first as to what you think the data will look like and what kind of coding and analytical system is likely to work best for the type of data you foresee.

Exercise 3.15

Write a one-paragraph research proposal that includes the information you have assembled above. The proposal should give a name to the study, state a major question (or questions) which the study is intended to answer, outline the methodology of the study (based on the information you compiled above) including who the participants will be, and suggest how the data will be analyzed, for example, what type of coding will most likely be involved.

Interpreting introspective research

There have been a number of objections raised with respect to the gathering and interpretation of mentalistic data. Ericsson and Simon have cataloged these objections and have made suggestions as to how the shortcomings of previous introspective studies can be overcome. We have referred to these suggestions previously. In interpreting introspective studies, whether done by you or other researchers, it would be wise to:

1 review these objections to introspective studies;
2 check if the researcher has recognized the potential problems of such studies; and
3 see if the researcher has tried to minimize the impact of these problems.

Here, we will review some of these potential problems and suggest how their impact can be minimized.

Objection A *Introspection on thinking processes of any type is either impossible or unfeasible.* Several investigators have held that it is very difficult for participants to report on the processes of their own thinking. In the heyday of introspection studies of the early 20th century, researchers felt it was necessary to give lots of practice in introspection before you got to the *real* experience. Titchener, a leader in introspective studies of this period, gave each of his participants 10,000 practice trials before he recorded trial 10,001 as the *real thing* (Boring 1953).

Even more cautious researchers believe that the self-reporting of thinking processes is impossible, however well participants are trained. In a widely cited paper, Nisbett and Wilson (1977: 233) held that, 'People often cannot report accurately on the effects of particular stimuli on higher order, inference-based responses ... and sometimes cannot even report that an inferential process of any kind has occurred.'

As Ericsson and Simon note, the key words here are *often, sometimes,* and *higher order, inference-based* responses. Proper procedural cautions (particularly in respect to researcher instructions and participant training), say Ericsson and Simon, can reduce *often* and *sometimes* to *rarely*. We know that 'the more automatized a skill is, the less its underlying cognitive processes are available for introspection' (Lennon 1989: 377). Therefore, researchers need to exercise care in choosing introspective tasks that do not require participants to deal with introspection of higher order, highly automatized linguistic processes.

We should note that a number of the activities of most interest to language educators are not higher order or automatized linguistic processes. Some of these are deliberate undertakings; language users are aware of and can report about these in terms of options considered and choices made. For example: (a) trying to remember a word or name (in any language), (b) conscious efforts to produce utterances that are logically coherent, situationally appropriate, and grammatically correct in a language being learned, (c) trying to make sense of a difficult reading passage, (d) determining how to organize a written piece for optimal reception, and (e) translating a text from L1 to L2 or vice versa.

In examining a report of an introspective study, you need to ask yourself if the language activity being studied is of the type about which we can reasonably ask people to report on their mental processes. If the process is quite deliberate (such as those mentioned above), then these may be language use tasks which are deliberate enough and conscious enough for reporting the steps of mental processing to be realistic.

Objection B *Even if introspection on mental states is possible and even if it involves some processes of interest to language educators, introspective reports are bound to be unreliable.* To some extent most of the criticisms leveled at introspective studies deal in one way or another with issues of RELIABILITY. Key questions are:

1 Does the participant have access to the mental processes that he/she is trying to articulate?
2 Do the researcher's instructions, examples, or training bias the participant to report what the researcher is looking for rather than what the participant is experiencing?
3 Does the verbal reporting get in the way of the mental processing and cause it to be something other than what it would be if there was no requirement to verbalize involved?

Advocates of introspective studies have acknowledged the potential problems of reliability of verbal reports of mental processes. However, despite significant recent advances in the use of MRI (magnetic resonance imager) scans to correlate particular language tasks and brain locations, the nature of brain processing in carrying out these tasks is still little understood. The claim of introspective researchers is that, until such time as brain readouts are possible, introspective reports are the best evidence we have of human mental processes. With all their flaws, verbal protocols collected with proper care provide the most reliable evidence as to what goes on in the brain when we undertake certain mental tasks, such as learning a second language. (For more on this, see the second edition of Ericsson and Simon (1993). The authors suggest a variety of strategies to increase reliability of verbal reporting of mental processes.)

Exercise 3.16

From the cautions listed above as well as cautions from previous sections, make a draft checklist for critiquing introspective studies. A beginning for such a checklist is shown in Appendix 3.3 (pages 267–8).

Exercise 3.17

Use the checklist you developed in Exercise 3.16 to critique a short extract from an introspective study such as quoted in Swain (1995) shown as Appendix 3.4 (pages 269–70).

Significance of introspection as a scholarly focus

Introspection has always been with us, even before rush-hour driving. Plato and Aristotle are usually cited as early practitioners in the formal use of introspection to explore reasoning, thought, and *truth*. At the opening of this chapter, we quoted William James, the father of modern psychology, as saying: 'Introspective observation is what we have to rely on first and foremost and always. The word introspection need hardly be defined—it means, of course, the looking into our own minds and reporting what we there discover' (James 1890: 185). Indeed, introspective studies played a major role in psychology in the first two decades of the twentieth century, something which was reflected in a number of seminal novels at the time.

Short segments from fictional stream-of-consciousness writing are sometimes used to preface verbal protocol elicitations to suggest to participants a particular verbal style of translating thought into language. Below is a text sample from the famous last chapter of Joyce's classic work *Ulysses*. This is comprised entirely of stream of consciousness introspections by Molly Bloom, one of the major characters in the book. Joyce writes these introspections, largely without punctuation, to indicate the continuing and linked nature of introspective thoughts. The text section we have chosen deals with Molly Bloom's introspections on an aspect of language itself. Here Molly Bloom is turning over thoughts about her last name—'Bloom'.

> … that old Bishop that spoke off the altar his long preach about womans higher functions about girls now riding the bicycle and wearing peak caps and the new woman bloomers God send him sense and me more money I suppose theyre called after him I never tho ught[1] that would be my name Bloom when I used to write it in print to see how it looked on a visiting card or practising for the butcher and oblige M Bloom youre looking blooming Josie used to say after I married him well its better than Breen or Briggs does brig or those awful names with bottom in them Mrs Ramsbottom or some other kind of a bottom …
> (Joyce 1922/1993:712)

---

[1] The word 'tho ught' is split not because of author error, but because the first edition of *Ulysses* was published in France, and the printers were working from a hand-written manuscript with little or no knowledge of English.

Exercise 3.18

Answer the following questions. (You may wish to review the suggested procedures in Exercise 3.11.)

1   If you were reading these lines aloud, how would you read them? Note volume, pitch, speed, tone, and hesitations.

2   How would you segment this passage into *thought units*?

3   What kinds of language information are missing in this written segment? If you wanted a more detailed record of how Molly might be verbalizing these thoughts, how might you signal these in the written record?

4   What are the three different thoughts that the word 'Bloom' brings to Molly's consciousness?

5   If you had to choose another last name what would it be and what thoughts might you have about that name? Try to write some of these thoughts in the stream of consciousness style of Molly Bloom.

We saw earlier that the enthusiasm for introspective studies was short-lived, held to be of doubtful validity, and overtaken by behaviorism. As recently as 1987, Cavalcanti could observe, 'Verbal protocols are never mentioned as a technique for data collection in books on research methodology' (Cavalcanti 1987). Since that time, however, introspective research projects have blossomed to such an extent that (admittedly somewhat biased) commentators presently state that verbal reports are now generally recognized as major sources of data on participants' cognitive processes in specific tasks (Ericsson and Simon 1993). We have detailed some of these tasks in various sections of this chapter.

Reflecting on introspective research

You have seen (and experienced) that introspective research studies are of a wide variety of different types. Færch and Kasper (1987) offer a comprehensive classification system for introspective/verbal protocol studies that we have adapted for this reflective overview (see Table 3.4).

In our adaptation we have assumed that any verbal protocol study can be marked as being of one type or another within each category. Considering the first category, a verbal protocol study will either involve *Cognitive* or *Affective/Social* kinds of tasks. The plus/minus marks in our adaptation indicate the more typical (+) and less typical (−) category of task in second language acquisition (SLA) introspective studies. In this case, the marking suggests that introspective studies more typically involve cognitive tasks than affective/social tasks.

Exercise 3.19

Take one of the mini-introspections you have done, and write answers to the following question:

I   Identify the study and code it using the adapted Færch and Kasper system in Table 3.4. Some of the classification categories may not be fully transparent, but do your best to interpret each of the categories, maybe through class or partner discussion.

2   Did the classification suggest any types of introspective research you might not have considered or been aware of before? What were these?

Not only is there a variety of types of introspective research, there is also a variety of different uses to which introspective research has been applied. For language teachers, there are a number of payoffs which current work has provided. These payoffs include the use of introspective techniques and findings as:

1 language teaching instructional tools, especially in the teaching of reading and writing (Lytle 1982);
2 a guide to text and materials writers with regard to readability, etc. (Jacobs 1997);
3 a source of insight into pervasive questions of discourse coding (Kasper 2000);
4 a source of a classification system of task types (Skehan 1997);
5 a guide to the classification of the subject matter of tasks (Cohen 1987);
6 an aid to the identification of learning strategies (Chamot 1999);
7 a source of insight into how the brain works (Simon 1979);
8 a guide to test design and alternative modes of evaluation and assessment (Green 1998); and
9 a catalyst for learners sharing effective ways to learn (Rodgers 2000).

Table 3.4 Classification of verbal protocol data types

+ Cognitive
(– Affective/Social task)

+ Procedural knowledge (e.g. Writing a grammatically correct sentence)
(– Declarative knowledge) (e.g. Explaining a sentence's grammar)

+ Written stimulus
(– Spoken stimulus)

+ Receptive mode (e.g. Reading)
(– Productive mode) (e.g. Writing)

+ Continuous Process (e.g. Whole reading passage)
(– Focus Element) (e.g. Focus on passive verbs only)

+ Specific Activity (e.g. Give reading passage)
(– General tendencies) (e.g. Reading in general)

+ Immediate response
(– Delayed response)

+ Participant training
(– No participant training)

+ Researcher structured
(– Unstructured)

+ Recall support
(– No recall support)

+ Self-initiated (e.g. Responses volunteered at any point)
(– Other initiated) (e.g. Responses cued at particular points)

+ S <-> R Interaction between participant and researcher
(– S <-> S Interaction between participant and participant)

+ Integration with activity
(– Non-integration with activity)

(After Færch and Kasper 1987)

Exercise 3.20

Given your now considerable familiarity with introspective research types and uses, which type of introspective research study can you imagine wanting to learn more about and, perhaps, wanting to carry out? Choose an area of focus, such as one of those given above. Write down a name for the study and indicate how it might be described by type using the Færch and Kasper system in Table 3.4.

Summary

In this chapter, you have looked at the odd history of introspective reporting from various disciplinary inquiries into the operations of the human mind. You have seen that in the twentieth century introspective studies moved from enthusiastic endorsement to abandonment to enthusiastic resurrection. This rise/fall/rise history may serve to remind us that choice of research paradigms is a matter of fashion as much as of objective analysis. Certainly introspective studies in language-related areas are at the time of writing on the rising tide of acceptance and enthusiasm.

You have also considered how current studies have tried to respond to some of the earlier criticisms of introspective studies, particularly in regard to issues of validity and reliability. A variety of cautions have been issued, and research procedures aimed at minimizing slack in such studies have been prescribed.

In sum, it is necessary to design studies based on a model of mental processes, and to incorporate proper warm-up activities, careful task instructions, and appropriate monitoring of participants' task performances in order to optimize opportunities for valid and reliable findings.

4 CLASSROOM RESEARCH: INTERACTION ANALYSIS

Introducing classroom research

Zounds! I never was so bethump'd with words,
Since first I called my brother's father dad.
WILLIAM SHAKESPEARE, 1564–1616
on his early elementary school Language Arts experience.
Re-used in *King John* Act 2, scene 1, line 466

Gladly wolde he learn and gladly teche.
GEOFFREY CHAUCER, C 1343–1400
Canterbury Tales, Prologue, line 308

One of the criticisms frequently leveled by educationalists at second language acquisition research, and educational research generally, is that research and researchers are too far removed from teachers' and learners' immediate concerns. One response to this criticism has been to try to focus research more directly on issues clearly important to teachers and learners. In particular, the ways in which teachers and learners interact in the classroom have become a major concern in the attempt to make educational research more accessible and practical.

This chapter, then, is about teachers and learners and how they interact in the broad set of contexts we have labeled *classrooms*. The cover term CLASSROOM we take to cover a wide range of learning contexts where learners and teachers meet in the context of second language acquisition—classes in schools, multi-media labs, distance learning situations, one-to-one tutoring, on the job training, computer-based instruction, and so on. Like 'classroom', the term INTERACTION is used with a variety of different senses; it has been used with respect to

1 theories of linguistic description,
2 models of second language acquisition,
3 instructional exchanges between teachers and learners,

4 task completion conversations between learners and learners, as well as
5 the internal conversations between authors and readers.

The study of classrooms and of interaction have independent and rich research histories.

We will be considering the intersection of these traditions—second language acquisition studies involving research into interactions within a classroom environment. We will be looking in particular at two issues that have been of long-term interest to classroom interaction researchers—the nature of teachers' correction of learner errors and learner-to-learner communication in task-based group work.

Experiencing classroom research

Although we have defined classrooms and interaction quite broadly, most classroom interaction research studies are done in regular school classrooms and focus on interactions between teachers and learners or between learners and learners.

Given our experiential approach to the study of second language acquisition research, our first choice would be to ask you to go out and gather some detailed data from language teaching classes. Unfortunately, we cannot require you to go and collect data from live second language classes for a variety of obvious reasons: (a) it may be a time when no classes are in session, (b) you may have difficulty gaining access to classrooms, (c) you may not fit inconspicuously into a language class, (d) it may be difficult to make high-quality recordings of class interactions, (e) the data might be such that you can't analyze them usefully because the class happens to be watching a film, and so on.

A second approach might be to use the daily doings of your own class—the class you are in using this book—as the source of interaction data. Again, there are some problems with this: (a) the class is not a language teaching class, (b) it is hard to participate in a class fully and simultaneously do all the jobs a classroom researcher has to do—one role or the other will suffer, and (c) the teacher of this class may not be keen to be a research object right now.

A third approach would be to get a film or video featuring a lot of school classroom footage and use this as the data source. There are problems with this choice as well: (a) while there are many films featuring classrooms as settings—*Blackboard Jungle, Up the Down Staircase, The Breakfast Club, Lord of the Flies, The Dead Poets' Society, Stand By Me*, for example—these are movie classrooms and not much like classrooms in real life; (b) there are not many feature films focusing on language teaching and learning; and (c) films and videos made for research purposes taken in language classes are hard to come by and often of poor technical quality.

A fourth approach is to have each of you generate some classroom interaction data in the roles of teachers and learners. While this also has its disadvantages (most of you already know the language of this class pretty thoroughly), it seems the best option. It stays with the plan of the book to have you, the readers, be the sources of the data as well as analysts of the data. If you are in a class, everyone can have access to the same data, as necessary. And we can focus on particular aspects of classroom interaction that we want to highlight by careful selection of interaction tasks.

This fourth option, then, is the one we have chosen to take in this chapter. You may want to pursue one of the other options outlined above if the local situation encourages this, or if you are working alone.

Teacher interactions with learners

What teachers do in classrooms has been the major focus of classroom interaction studies. There are over 200 classroom observation instruments that have been developed, and most of these focus on how teachers interact with learners. Over twenty observation instruments have been developed just for studying classroom interaction in second language classes. Again, most of these focus on the teacher (Long and Sato 1983). Some principal topics of interest have been:

1 Teacher questions
2 Teacher error corrections
3 Quantity of teacher speech
4 Teacher explanations
5 Teacher 'wait-time' for student responses

You are going to collect some data about one of these topics for later analysis. It is always best to tape record any kind of verbal data you are collecting; usually you can't write as fast as people can speak. Also, a taped record allows you to check your notes and add new comments such as vocal tone, pauses, loudness, etc. You may also find it useful to use video recordings so that non-verbal signals—gestures, facial expressions, body postures, participant spacings, etc.—can be available for analysis. If you have a partner to transcribe the data, some of these exercises can be done without an audio or video recorder, but they are best done with them if at all possible.

Teacher error correction

All learners make errors in learning a new language. Some commentators even feel that errors are necessary stepping-stones to acquiring a second language. But most learners and most teachers feel that it is part of the teacher's responsibility to let learners know if they have made an error and to assist them in not making a similar error again. Learners and teachers have preferences for what kinds of error correction they feel most useful and least intrusive in classroom interaction.

Exercise 4.1

Think about the following error from a beginning oral English class: *He not go home*. Now answer the following questions:

 1   How many different ways can you think of by which a language teacher might respond to this spoken error? Put a different way, how many oral error correction types can you think of? Write these down.

 2   What would be your preference of these types of error correction? Rank four of them in terms of your preference.

Nystrom (1983) looked at speech error correction behaviors of four teachers in bilingual primary school classrooms in the U.S. The kinds of error noted were classified as: PHONOLOGICAL, Lexical, MORPHOLOGICAL, SYNTACTIC, DISCOURSE, Dialect, and Content. Profiles of the kinds of errors noted by two of the coded teachers, A-1 and B-2, are shown in Table 4.1.

Exercise 4.2

Create an error that you think typical of each of the types of error listed above. Don't worry if the linguistic terms are not altogether familiar to you. Create what you think are likely interpretations of the terms and create error examples to match. Keep a copy of these error examples for later analysis.

Table 4.1 Error-type profile comparing two teachers – Teacher A-1 and Teacher B-2 (For a characterization of the teachers in the study referred to here, see Appendix 4.1 on page 271.)

Errors	No. A-1	No. B-2	% of total (A-1)	% of total (B-2)
Phonological	13	50	28.8	37
Lexical	16	17	35.6	13
Morph/Syntactic	4	10	8.9	6
Discourse	5	11	11.1	8
Dialect	3	28	6.7	21
Content	4	20	8.9	15
Total	45	136	100.0	100

(Adapted from Nystrom 1983:174, 178)

Nystrom provided further information on her four bilingual teachers' error correction styles. In Table 4.2, she compares teacher response profiles for her four teachers and identifies nine different types of teacher error correction (models correct form, repeats faulty form, etc.).

Table 4.2 Teacher response profiles in percentages (For a characterization of the teachers in the study referred to here, see Appendix 4.1 on page 271.)

Teacher corrections to errors	A-1	A-2	B-1	B-2
Models correct form	10	20	–	17
Drills correct form	6	10	–	10
Repeats faulty form	10	16	–	12
Prompts correct form	13	13	–	13
Explains correct form	3	4	–	7
(Re)states question/prompt	3	12	–	8
Tells student what to say	14	10	–	5
Reduces directions	2	–	–	–
Expands directions	3	4	–	4

Note: This table is abbreviated and omits teacher responses to correct student productions. Thus, the columns do not add up to 100%.

(Adapted from Nystrom 1983: 175)

Exercise 4.3

Create an error and an error correction for each of the nine types. Pick errors with 3rd person present tense verbs as your learner error type (for example, *Lim like to play hockey*, or *Kim want to hits him*). For each error type, write down the error example and the example of a possible teacher correction. Take the roles of both error maker and error corrector. If working with a partner, take turns in these roles. Stay with this one type of student error (3rd person singular present tense verbs) but use different vocabulary for each example. Keep your list of error and error correction examples for later data analysis. Be sure to note the error correction types you did not include in your list in the previous exercise.

Learner-to-learner interactions

In the previous section you have experienced something similar to classroom interaction research as it bears on teachers' interactions with learners. The other major type of classroom interaction is between learners and learners. In communicative methodology, increasing emphasis is placed on language learning tasks which involve pair work and group work. Given this perspective, it is obviously critical to know what goes on in these convocations of learners and how, if at all, learner-to-learner interactions contribute to language acquisition.

Since the following exercise involves two learners in an interaction situation, it would be helpful if those of you working alone could get a family member or friend to do the picture sequencing task with you. If you can't find anyone you can convince to play this game with you, you can find data for learners doing this task in Appendix 4.2 on pages 272–3.

In one area of pedagogy, interaction patterns and learning outcomes have been studied extensively over the last 40 years. This area is labeled broadly cooperative learning.

> Cooperative learning is group-learning activity organized so that learning is dependent on the socially structured exchange of information between learners in groups and in which each learner is held accountable for his or her own learning and is motivated to increase the learning of others. (Olsen and Kagan 1992:8)

> Research studies of cooperative learning in very diverse school settings and across a wide range of content areas, have revealed that students completing cooperative learning group tasks tend to have higher academic test scores, higher self-esteem, greater numbers of positive social skills, fewer stereotypes of individuals of other races or ethnic

groups, and greater comprehension of the content and skills they are studying. (Stahl 1995: 1)

In order to get a sense of how learner-to-learner interaction is studied in language learning classes, you will next take part in a cooperative classroom learning activity. You will observe two learners communicating in a cooperative picture-sequencing task, and you will code the communications using a simple coding system. The codes with examples are shown in Table 4.3. Notice that there are nine codes—three codes that could be considered positive codes, a parallel group of three negative codes, and five neutral codes as follows:

The POSITIVE CODES are
>   proposal without reasoning,
>   proposal with reasoning, and
>   support.

The NEGATIVE CODES are
>   counter-proposal without reasoning,
>   counter-proposal with reasoning, and
>   non-support.

The NEUTRAL CODES are
>   describes a picture,
>   filler,
>   doubt,
>   neutral, and
>   operational.

One of the classic activity types found in second language instructional materials is the PICTURE-SEQUENCING task. In picture sequencing a set of four or more pictures following some plot line is presented in random order. Either following teacher dictation or group discussion, learners organize the pictures in what they feel to be their correct or logical order. We have provided four picture sequences for use in this activity in Appendix 4.3 on pages 274–7. The pictures in each set are labeled alphabetically for identification. The alphabetical labeling has nothing to do with the final sequence.

Table 4.3 Interaction codes for cooperative picture ordering task

Picture Sequencer Moves	Code	Example
Describes a Picture	D	There's a clock on the wall that says '8:00'
Proposal w/o Reasoning	P–	I think picture C should go first.
Proposal w/ Reasoning	P+	I think picture C should go first because the sun is coming up
Support	S	Looks right. I agree. What's next?
Non-support	N	Nope. Unh, unh. Don't think so. Some other.
Counter-proposal w/o Reasoning	CP–	No, I think B is first.
Counter-proposal w/ Reasoning	CP+	But everybody's happy in B. I think it should go first.
Filler, Doubt, Neutral	F	Mmmm. Maybe. Let's see
Operational	O	What do we have to do? Shall I start? Are we done?

Photocopiable © Oxford University Press

Exercise 4.4

It is best to work with an enlarged A4 or letter size photocopy of the picture set (Appendix 4.3 on pages 274–7) cut into individual pictures so they can be moved around by the cooperating pair. (As always, a tape recorder is very helpful for this activity. However, if you have a secretary/recorder, the activity is designed to be feasible without a tape recorder.) Keep the coding sheets and any discussion notes for compiling and analysis.

Now, do this exercise in the following steps:

 1   Form a pair with another student and then get together with another pair so that there are four of you. (If the class size does not divide up into exact groups of four, the residual group should be more rather than fewer than four.)

 2   One pair will play the role of *picture sequencers* and the other pair, *classroom observers*. (If you are working with a single partner in this exercise, it will be necessary to tape record your interactions as *participants* doing the task and analyze the taped interactions as *observers*.)

3   The picture sequencers will be designated as A and B. The observers will each observe one picture sequencer, A or B.

4   The randomly organized picture problem sets are shown in Appendix 4.3. The task is for picture sequencers to lay out the pictures and then to organize them, *through discussion*, into what strikes them as the most *natural* sequence of pictures.

5   Using the codes in Table 4.3, observer for A will code and take shorthand notes of what A says; observer for B will code and take shorthand notes of what B says. We recommend a practice round and a for-the-record round using codes in Table 4.3.

6   In the next section, the observers will pool their codes and shorthand notes into a mini-transcription sketching the task interactions of A and B, so keep your records.

7   The group of four should discuss the coding and the transcriptions.

8   What patterns emerged in the interaction? Were there any utterances that could not be coded?

9   Reverse roles of picture sequencers and observers so that the former observers now become A and B picture sequencers. (If there are more than four in the group, it is better to have extra observers than extra picture sequencers.)

10 In the second round, picture sequencers are more likely to be self-conscious about the way their utterances will be coded. Did this happen? Did the patterns of the first interaction and the second interaction differ in any way?

In this section you have experienced two kinds of classroom interaction. You have created examples of different kinds of teacher error correction feedback and have worked to analyze data from a two-person cooperative picture-sequencing task. We will next turn to looking at how data from such observations can be compiled and analyzed.

Compiling classroom research data

We noted in both this chapter and in our previous discussion of introspective/retrospective studies that data are typically recorded on a tape (or video) recorder. The classroom interaction researcher will also have notes and/or have done partial transcriptions during data collection. Compiling the data for analysis will involve transcribing data from the tape recordings and interleaving notes and transcriptions made at the time of data collection.

We talked in the previous chapter about the critical task of *segmenting* the transcription so that each segment represents a unit of an apparent short thought or utterance. These segmented units become the core elements that you will code and analyze. In one sense, segmentation of classroom interaction data is easier than segmenting introspection data. The major segments in interaction data usually comprise each speaker's utterances. The beginning and end of segments are often signaled by change of speaker.

Teacher error-correction data

The word 'compile' comes from the Latin meaning 'Come, let us pile together' (well, almost). Certainly, one of the tasks of compiling is to get the data collected into piles of some sort for later analysis. For example, if you want to look at characteristics of certain kinds of teacher error correction, you will need to have all the error corrections of the same kind piled together. However, what seems obvious about sorting items into a pile for one researcher may not be so obvious to another researcher.

Exercise 4.5

In the previous section, you generated some learner errors and some examples of teacher correction types in response to those errors (Exercise 4.3). This is a good opportunity to check if the labels you gave your error correction examples would be the same labels as someone else would give to these examples. The following directions suggest how you may do this.

If you are working on your own, you will find samples of various kinds of teacher error corrections in Appendix 4.2 on pages 272–3. Your task is to classify your own earlier examples and the examples in Appendix 4.2 as to the type of teacher error correction you think each sample represents.

1   Retrieve your teacher error correction examples from Exercise 4.3. Since there were nine error correction types, there should be nine examples. Prepare nine slips of paper, each with a single example on it. Make sure that the error correction type label is not included on the slip.

2   If you are working in a class, form pairs and then join with another pair so that you have a group of four. Give the other pair your nine slips in random order.

3   Now with your partner, label the other pair's nine examples according to your judgement as to the error correction type. Write your error correction type label on the back of each slip.

4   Rejoin with the other pair and exchange your labels. Did you give the examples the same labels as the pair that created the examples did?

Discuss any differences and resolve them, by writing some new pairs, if necessary.

5   Now combine the piles of the two groups so that you have nine piles with two examples in each pile.

This is a good opportunity to combine all the piles from all class members. You would then have a comprehensive set of error correction examples as *produced and sorted by language teaching professionals*. While these are, perhaps, not quite the same as examples taken from actual classroom interaction, they are, in themselves, interesting data. They can, of course, now be used to compare with error correction examples taken directly from language classes. Combine the piles of slips for each of the nine error types so that the whole class can review all the error correction example types. You may want to glue or tape them to a single sheet of paper and post these on the wall of the class or produce photocopies for each member of the class. In this way, the whole class can review all the error correction example types.

Learner-to-learner interaction data

In the 'Experiencing classroom research' section of this chapter, you examined the interaction in a two-person, learner-to-learner cooperative picture-sequencing task. You now need to compile your data from this exercise.

Exercise 4.6

Draw or photocopy a data table like that shown in Table 4.4. (Sample entries for A and B are shown below.) If you feel there are other details you want to record, construct your own data table. Then follow these steps:

1   If you have tape recordings, you should transcribe these into the table now.

2   Get your coding notes and any notes made at the time of the observations.

3   Note any gaps in your notes and try to fill these.

4   Note any exchanges that were difficult or impossible to code.

5   Write down any particular problems in the sequencing—first picture, last picture, sequencing of similar pictures?

Table 4.4 Picture sequencing observation data table (www)

A/B	Said	Code	Pic no.	Comments
A	This looks like the start.	P-	D	Look at pics, don't say anything for a minute.
B	Mmmm	F	D	B looking at other pics

Photocopiable © Oxford University Press

Analyzing classroom interaction data

What are we looking for in the data from classroom interaction observation? Some early studies came up with the somewhat startling data that teacher talk took up 89% of classroom verbal interaction time, and that, 91% of the time, teachers already knew the answers to the questions they were asking (Nunan 1989: 26). These data were surprising but were they accurate, and did they indicate something good or bad? The initial thought of most teachers was, perhaps, 'MY classes aren't like that—at least, I don't think they are'. So some major questions of later research studies were:

1 How is class talk time divided between teachers and learners?
2 What are some of the different language patterns used in teacher–learner interaction?
3 How self-aware are teachers of how they use language in their interactions with their students?
4 What kinds of learning differences do different patterns of teacher talk make?
5 Can and will teachers re-create their teaching practices if it appears that better practices are available?

In this chapter, we are looking specifically to find answers to questions such as the following:

1   What kinds of learner errors are teachers most likely to correct?
2   What are some of the different ways in which teachers correct learners' errors in second language production?
3   Do teachers and learners have similar or different preferences in respect to error correction feedback?
4   What are some of the patterns of interaction in learner-to-learner communication in carrying out cooperative classroom tasks?
5   How do different interaction patterns facilitate or hinder learner-to-learner communication and the language learning of individual learners?

Teacher error-correction data

Sinclair and Coulthard (1975) claim that the most frequent kind of classroom interaction is conducted between teachers (T) and students (S) in the form of IRF exchanges, where I = Initiating move; R = Responding move; F = Follow-up move. For example:

I/T: What comes next?
R/S: Boy going.
F/T: Did you say that the boy is going somewhere?

As the IRF example suggests, I is frequently a question, R is a student response to the question and F is often some form of teacher identification or correction of student response errors.

In the previous section, we looked at a number of different types of learner errors and a number of different styles of teacher error correction. You found or made up examples of learner errors for the following seven error categories:

1   phonological   5   discourse
2   lexical   6   dialect
3   morphological   7   content
4   syntactic

You also composed some examples of nine common types of teacher error correction. The types of teacher error correction you examined were:

1   models correct form   6   (re)states teaching prompt
2   drills correct form   7   tells student what to say
3   repeats faulty form   8   reduces instructions
4   prompts correct form   9   expands directions
5   explains correct form

Exercise 4.7

Review all the error correction example types and their classification labels from the previous section (Exercise 4.5).

1   As a teacher, what would your preference be for these different types of error correction? Rank order the nine error type from your most favored (1) to least favored (9).

2   Consider the same error correction types from the your own perspective as a language learner. Rank the correction types from most favored (1) to least favored (9).

3   How similar are your two rankings, as teacher and as learner?

If you are using this text in a class group, each member of the class should now vote for which of the nine types of error correction strategies they, as teachers, personally prefer, using the same ranking system as above. The votes should then be tallied and added together to give a class ranking of favored error correction types. (In this election, the lowest number wins.) Your database of teacher error correction preferences is in this way enlarged.

It would also be interesting to see how much variation in individual class member rankings there is. (We will be returning in Chapter 6 to a consideration of how such ranking data can be handled more formally.)

We are now going to look at a longer piece of teacher–learner interaction (Appendix 4.2 on pages 272–3). In this interaction, there are several different kinds of teacher IRF sets. These are usually teacher questions → learner errors → teacher error corrections.

Exercise 4.8

Singly or in pairs follow these steps:

1   Consider the teacher questions. (The transcript has at least six clear questions.) Decide if the teacher knew or did not know the answer to each question before she asked it. If you think the teacher knew the answer to the question, label the question as D (standing for display question). If you think the teacher did not know the answer to the question, label the question R (standing for referential question). (This distinction as applied to teacher questions in second language classes is discussed in detail in Long and Sato 1983). Discuss why you gave the questions the label you did.

2   Consider the learner errors. Identify each of these and label it as to type using the error categories listed above (phonological, morphological,

etc.). Some errors may be ambiguous or of more than one type. Discuss why you gave the learner errors the labels you did.

3   Consider the teacher's error corrections. How many of the errors did she correct? What percentage of all errors was this? Identify each of the teacher's error corrections and label them using the error correction categories listed above.

4   Outline your conclusions based on this brief set of data.

5   Read and discuss the 'Author's Notes on Transcription' in the second section of Appendix 4.2 on page 273 (Allwright 1975).

Learner-to-learner interaction data

In the last section, you developed a data table for picture sequencing observation using a formatted coding system. Take a look back at that table now.

Exercise 4.9

Take notes as you answer the following questions:

1   What patterns are evident in the table? Who initiates most moves? Who talks most? Is there any evidence that one or both picture sequencers felt they did not get their fair say?

2   Rate how *interactive* or *individual* this activity was. Did partners work together or as two people each acting as if they were doing the task alone? What evidence would you offer for the *interacting* or *soloing* analysis?

3   Did cooperative interaction seem a good classroom activity for the pairs observed? Why or why not?

4   Any early suggestions as to how to revise the task to make it more balanced? More effective?

This is really the first look we have had at a formatted observation instrument constructed for the purpose of recording and analyzing some kinds of classroom interaction. One of the major sources of data has come from classroom observations using a variety of such observation instruments (also called schedules). With over 200 such observation instruments reported in the literature, 'It seems that every researcher who wants to investigate classroom interaction has felt bound to devise his/her own scheme' (Nunan 1989: 83).

Chaudron (1988) characterizes 26 of the instruments designed just for the analysis of interaction in second language classrooms. For each of these instruments, Chaudron indicates the following:

1 the recording procedure: is there a specific behavior noted on each appearance (a CATEGORY SYSTEM), or are all behaviors which occur within a specified time period noted (a SIGN SYSTEM)?
2 the degree of researcher intuition required: is it high or low ?
3 the number of categories in the system: in the instruments reviewed it varied between 7 and 73;
4 multiple coding: can behavior be considered in more than one category?
5 real-time coding: is coding done live during class observation or later using an audio or video recording of the class?
6 the unit of analysis: is the unit an arbitrary time interval or a specific analytical unit such as a move, a cycle, an episode, etc.?
7 the focus of observation: is it verbal, paralinguistic, nonlinguistic, cognitive, affective, pedagogical, content-related, discourse-related?

Exercise 4.10

Answer the following questions:

  1   If Chaudron were to characterize the coding system you used in coding the picture-sequencing task, how would he characterize this code with respect to the seven dimensions he proposes?

  2   If you were to look for a better coding system for this kind of observation of learner–learner interaction, what would you look for?

Designing your own classroom research

In this chapter we have so far looked at collecting, compiling, and analyzing some examples of classroom interaction data. We will now consider some of the issues involved in designing such a study.

In thinking about your own research design, you need to simultaneously consider your personal beliefs or *tenets*, your research *topic* and the research *technique* by which you might gather data on this topic.

Clarifying your beliefs, picking your tenets

Where are you coming from? What are your beliefs about what good teaching is? What are your beliefs about what effective learning looks like?

Most teachers and non-teachers alike have views about what constitutes good teaching. Often these views are widely shared and held to be axiomatic. Many of these axioms are built into teacher preparation programs and might be phrased as follows:

Axiom 1 Learners learn more effectively when given positive feedback (praise, approval) than negative feedback (criticism, disapproval).
Axiom 2 Learners learn from hearing, reading, and interacting with well-formed examples of how the L2 is used to communicate. Giving ungrammatical or *negative* examples is not helpful in second language acquisition.
Axiom 3 Giving learners time to think after a teacher's question (encouraging a longer 'teacher-wait time') is a good thing and will produce longer and more thoughtful learner responses.
Axiom 4 Real questions to learners will produce more interaction than phony questions to which the teacher already knows the answer.
Axiom 5 The more language interaction involving learner participation that goes on in class, the better the opportunities for language learning.

Exercise 4.11

Consider the five axioms presented above and answer the following questions:

Do you agree or disagree with these? How strongly?

   Assign to each axiom a rating using the following scale:
   0 = Strongly disagree
   1 = Disagree
   2 = No opinion
   3 = Agree
   4 = Strongly Agree

   1   Compare your ratings with other students if possible. Which items do most people concur on?

   2   On which items do people not concur?

To many these axioms seem reasonable, and classroom researchers have looked for classroom evidence that bear them out. Researchers positively inclined towards these principles often find evidence in their data to support them, while other researchers, perhaps a bit more skeptical, often suggest that the evidence is less convincing.

The literature is full of both positive research evidence to support these axioms and negative research evidence suggesting that there is no reported effect on learner achievement. As evidence for the evidence, so to speak, here is a list of some of the research reports for and against:

For axiom 1
positive evidence was found by Rosenshine and Furst (1973), and
negative evidence is cited by Long (1983).

For axiom 2
positive evidence is offered by Schwartz (1986), and
negative evidence is cited by White (1991).

For axiom 3
positive evidence is given by Holley and King (1971), and
negative evidence is cited by Long (1984).

For axiom 4
positive evidence is given by Brock (1986), and
negative evidence is cited by Long (1984).

For axiom 5
positive evidence is reported by Seliger (1977), and
negative evidence is reported by Day (1984).

This is not to say that these axioms are bad, or incorrect, or useless as
teaching principles. Nevertheless, it is true that such principles are often
hard to confirm consistently in studies of what actually takes place in the
classroom. As teachers know, there are complex interactions going on
simultaneously in any classroom; neat answers are hard to find. Recently
there has been growing reluctance among practitioners to prescribe and
proscribe teaching practices. Good practice is held to be an individual matter
directed by the specific content to be taught, by the beliefs, experience, and
preferences of the teacher, by the situational context in which teaching
occurs, and by the needs, interests, and personalities of the learners.

Johnson quotes Kent, a teacher-in-preparation who 'got the message' during
his practicum experience:

> This experience [the practicum placement] has opened my eyes to
> some very different ways of teaching. I used to think that there must be
> one right way to teach and all I had to do was figure out the right way
> and then do it. I now see that there are lots of right ways. What makes
> it right depends on what students want and need, and that is always
> different. (Johnson 1995: 33)

This kind of open-ended view of teaching makes classroom interaction
analysis somewhat problematical. What *is* good teaching and what kinds of
interactions are we looking for in second language classes? It is important for
researchers to be clear about their own tenets and candid in their reports
about how such tenets shaped their research.

Picking a topic

There is a host of potential topics on which to conduct your own classroom interaction research. We have mentioned a variety of teacher-focused topics: teacher questions, teacher error corrections, quantity of teacher speech, teacher explanations, teacher 'wait-time' for learner responses, etc. A similar range of topics on learner-focused themes could be considered.

While we know of no checklist of potential classroom interaction research topics, there have been several attempts to sketch out the factors affecting how teachers teach and how learners learn. You might find looking at one of these will stimulate your interest in looking more closely at how one of these factors is realized in the classroom. Shavelson and Stern (1981), for example, sketch the broad range of issues comprising the factors which impact on how teachers teach. Look at the adaptation of their view of this domain shown in Figure 4.1.

Exercise 4.12

Examine the array of factors in Figure 4.1 which are claimed to influence how teachers teach.

> 1   As you consider undertaking a classroom interaction research study, choose six of the factors that seem to be of most interest to you.
>
> 2   Which of the factors do you find confusing?

If possible, discuss with a partner why you chose those factors you did. Also discuss any factors you found confusing to see if you can come to a better understanding of them.

Figure 4.1 The domain of research on teachers' judgements, decisions and behavior

	Teacher characteristics	Teacher cognitive processes Information selection and integration
	Beliefs	Attributions
Antecedent conditions	Conceptions of subject	Heuristics
Information about students	Matter	Availability
Ability	Cognitive complexity	Representativeness
Participation		Anchoring
Behavior problems		Saliency
		Conflict/stress
Nature of instructional task		
Goals		**Inferences**
Subject matter		Judgements
Students		Expectations
Activities		Hypotheses
		Decisions

Classroom/school environment
Groupness
Evaluative climate
Extra-class pressures

**Consequences for teachers planning
Instruction**
Selection of content
Grouping of students
Selection of activities
Interaction with students
Teaching routines
Behavior problems
Tutoring

Teacher evaluation   **Consequences for students**
Of judgements
Of decisions
Of teaching routines

(Shavelson and Stern 1981)

Picking a technique

As we have indicated, classroom interaction research is an extremely active and important area of second language research. There is a wide range of books and journals focused in whole or in part on the subject. Doing such research requires spending a great deal of time in classrooms recording and taking notes.

We have seen that much classroom interaction research has been based on the use of classroom observation instruments; you used an example of one in your look at learner–learner interaction in a cooperative learning task. Otherwise, we have not done much with observation instruments in this chapter. This is so for several reasons:

1 There is a huge range of such classroom observation instruments available (200+) and exposure to one or two will not tell much about the range.
2 Most of the instruments take considerable training to use, and such training is not within the scope of this book.
3 Transcription and analysis of observational data is extremely time-consuming (15–20 hours per hour of observation) and usually complicated.
4 Classroom observations using these instruments represented the dominant method of research on classrooms in the 1960's and 70's. This practice declined considerably following sharp attacks on the use of such observation instruments (for example, Stubbs 1975).

5 The proliferation of observational instruments 'has resulted in many studies of similar phenomena that lack true comparability' (Chaudron 1988: 180) and this has led to the existence of many *stand-alone* studies which do little to advance understanding of classroom processes.

6 Observation is usually done over a period of time in live classes where the personalities in the class are unknown to the researcher. It is challenging to find such classes and the time to undertake such observations.

7 As we pointed out in the previous section, classroom observation instruments are inevitably biased towards some particular research perspective. Given some current lack of consensus on what constitutes good teaching and the general lack of success in finding consistent relationship between classroom behavior and learner achievement, it is hard to recommend any one observation instrument.

All of this is *not* to say that the practice of schedule-based classroom observation is dead, or that useful research reports based on the use of classroom observation instruments are not found in the literature, or that you should not consider undertaking a classroom interaction research study using a classroom observation instrument. (If this is the direction you wish to go in, you will find useful overviews of observation instrument types used in second language classroom research in Allwright 1988; Day 1990; and Nunan 1989.)

There are, however, a variety of alternative research techniques that have been and are being employed. These include:

1 diaries	8 simulated classroom data
2 journals	9 protocol analysis
3 ethnographic records	10 action research
4 field notes	11 stimulated recall
5 interviews	12 case studies
6 questionnaires	13 formal experiments
7 checklists	

In fact, all of the research methods discussed in this book (and a few more) have been employed in the study of what goes on in classrooms. Let us consider in slightly more detail three of these alternatives: (a) action research, (b) simulated classroom data, and (c) stimulated recall.

ACTION RESEARCH is 'a form of self-reflective enquiry undertaken by participants in social situations in order to improve the rationality and justice of their practices …' (Carr and Kemmis 1985: 220). It is a less stylized, more situational form of classroom research and thus avoids some of the criticisms leveled at other methods. Kemmis and McTaggart (1988) outline the steps to be taken in action research as follows:

Phase I: Develop a plan of action to improve what is already happening.
Phase II: Act to implement the plan.
Phase III: Observe the effects of action in context
Phase IV: Reflect on these effects

SIMULATED CLASSROOM DATA We have already looked at procedures for generating simulated classroom data when we asked you to generate and rank alternative techniques by which teachers correct learner errors. This is not as precise a method as classroom observation for examining how teachers actually correct student errors over a longish period of time, but it is considerably less taxing, and it does provide data that are interesting and useful for classroom practitioners.

STIMULATED RECALL is a technique in which the researcher records and transcribes parts of a lesson and then gets the teacher (and where possible, the learners) to comment on what was happening at the time that the teaching and learning took place. (Nunan 1989: 94)

Exercise 4.13

We are going to ask you to do a stimulated recall of a class period. You can use an upcoming class in which you are enrolled (maybe, a class in this course). If you are not enrolled in a class you may be able to use a movie or television class. The analysis will be similar. Using whatever data you can get, do the following:

I   Pick a period in the day when you have time and energy to do this, maybe with the foreknowledge of your teacher. It is useful to have a tape recorder running, to remind you later of what went on in class. In addition, set aside a piece of paper on which to make notes of what is going on in class. Try to note distinct sections of the class and some of the things you noticed that went on in each section. If a textbook was used, you can probably also use this as a guide to how the lesson was organized.

2   At the end of the day, replay the tape, go back over your notes, any text material used, and your own memory of the recently transpired events.

3   Describe briefly what went on in each segment of the lesson and your reaction to it. Your reactions might be to one of more of the following questions: Was the segment relevant? Did it relate to what went before and came after? Was the point of the segment made clear? Who participated in each segment and how? Was this segment of the lesson interesting, memorable?

Interpreting classroom research

In this chapter you have so far collected and analyzed several different kinds of classroom interaction data. Each of these lends itself to particular kinds of interpretation. We will now first examine some general views and reservations about the interpretation of such data. We will then consider how these might shape the interpretation of data collected and analyzed thus far.

Michael Stubbs cites with some concern the following procedures typical of classroom interaction research:

> Researchers return from the field with video recordings, audio recordings, notebooks, or other data. From these recordings or notes, they *select* for quotation and discussion, short *extracts* of, say, teacher–pupil dialogue. From these extracts, and probably more generally also within the corpus of the data, they *further select* particular *features* of language which they regard as *evidence* for educational statements. (Stubbs 1981: 63. Author's italics.)

Thus, what the reader sees is a very reduced and researcher-shaped version of the original data. Reductions from classroom situation to researcher interpretation run something like this:

1 The world of classroom interactions ⇩
2 Interactions the researcher observed ⇩
3 Interactions the researcher recorded as data ⇩
4 Interactions the researcher selected for analysis ⇩
5 Extracts from interactions selected for reporting ⇩
6 Features selected from extracts for focus ⇩
7 Features highlighted as evidence for interpretations

Interpretations, then, are very strongly influenced by the *selection* of data made at several points along the research trail. The implication is also that, having made a different selection of data, we might have been led to a different interpretation. Some have even questioned if it is possible for researchers to be altogether objective in selecting data for interpretation when they have already invested in a particular hypothesis in terms of what they expect to find. One way to check which factors may have influenced your interpretation is to look at how another researcher might interpret the same or similar data.

Researchers try to interpret their own research findings in relationship to what is already known, to the research that has preceded their own. We have already seen that the variety of different approaches to such research and the huge array of observational, coding, and reporting formats constitutes a particular problem in classroom interaction research. Indeed, the comparison and interpretation of a current research study with other studies using different observational or analytical models often provides a key challenge to the researcher.

You have already seen one system taken from Nystrom (1983) for classifying techniques which teachers use in correcting learner errors in speaking. Nystrom's table (Table 4.5) contains no examples though you have, we trust, assembled and classified a set of examples which you feel represent the error correction types identified there.

Another system for such classification is presented in Chaudron (1988). This system has been used by a variety of researchers working in this area. Yucel (2000) used an adaptation of Chaudron's typology to compare learner *preferences* with teacher *practices*. Yucel used Chaudron's classification system and examples to look at teacher error correction practices and learner error correction preferences. Tables 4.6 and 4.7 summarize Yucel's findings.

Table 4.5 Nystrom typology of teacher error correction strategies
Teacher response profiles (in percentages) (N = 4)

(For a characterization of the teachers in the study referred to here, see Appendix 4.1 on page 271.)

Teacher Corrections	A-1	A-2	B-1	B-2
Models correct form	10	20	–	17
Drills correct form	6	10	–	10
Repeats faulty form	10	16	–	12
Prompts correct form	13	13	–	13
Explains correct form	3	4	–	7
(Re)states question/prompt	3	12	–	8
Tells student what to say	14	10	–	5
Reduces directions	2	–	–	–
Expands directions	3	4	–	4

Nystrom's observational data on four teachers' error-correction behaviors, already discussed. (Context: primary school bilingual classes in U.S.)

(Adapted from Nystrom 1983: 175)

Table 4.6 Yucel's report of teacher error-correction behaviors

T 'What did you do at the weekend?'
S 'I go to the cinema.'
T ....

Corrective behaviors observed of teachers in class N = 10

Example of teacher error correction	Type of correction	In-class instances	%
1 *Don't say go; say went.*	1 Negation	–	–
2 *I went to the cinema.*	2 Repetition with change	13	26
3 *Yesterday, I ...*	3 Prompt	5	10
4 *Go is the present tense. You need the past tense here.*	4 Explanation	–	–
5 *What's the second word?*	5 Question	–	–
6 *Students?* (class gives answer)	6 Transfer	2	4
7 *Mmmmm* (disapproval)	7 Disapprove	–	–
8 *Please repeat the sentence.*	8 Repeat (explicit)	4	8
9 *What?*	9 Repeat (implicit)	–	–
10 *Again. Where did you go?*	10 Altered question	–	–
11 *Really? Which film did you see?*	11 Ignore	19	38
12 *When you went to the cinema, did you have a good time?*	12 Provide and expand	7	14

Yucel's observational data on 13 teachers' error-correction behaviors. (Context: university-level English preparatory classes in Turkey.)

(Adapted from Yucel 2000: 150–1)

Table 4.7 Yucel's report of learner error-correction preferences
Error correction preferences of 22–25-year-old students   N = 84

Example of teacher error correction	Type of correction	Number of Students
1 *Don't say go; say went.*	1 Negation	–
2 *I went to the cinema.*	2 Repetition with change	13
3 *Yesterday, I . . .*	3 Prompt	10
4 *Go is the present tense. You need the past tense here.*	4 Explanation	29
5 *What's the second word?*	5 Question	2
6 *Students?* (class gives answer)	6 Transfer	–
7 *Mmmmm* (disapproval)	7 Disapprove	–
8 *Please repeat the sentence.*	8 Repeat (explicit)	8
9 *What?*	9 Repeat (implicit)	–
10 *Again. Where did you go?*	10 Altered question	9
11 *Really? Which film did you see?*	11 Ignore	5
12 *When you went to the cinema, did you have a good time?*	12. Provide and expand	8

Yucel's questionnaire data on error-correction preferences of 22–25-year-old English language learners. (Context: same as Table 4.6.)

(Adapted from Yucel 2000: 150–1)

There are several interpretation issues that arise in trying to compare the data presented in Tables 4.5, 4.6, and 4.7. These issues involve comparing:

1 data from different learner/teacher populations
2 averaged and un-averaged teacher behavior counts
3 percentages and raw data
4 data using different systems of error correction classification
5 data from teacher behavior and learner-expressed preferences

Exercise 4.14

Examine the three tables and discuss the following:

1   Which error-correction types appear to be similar in Nystrom's and Yucel's classification systems? Which types are unique to each system? Are there any that you find questionable?

2   Why would there be significant differences in two systems meant to classify all teacher error-correction types?

3   What issues need to be considered in comparing teacher error correction behavior and learner error-correction preferences from the Yücel study?

4   Which error classification would you prefer to use if you were to conduct a study of teacher error correction? Why?

5   How might you *balance* these three sets of results in interpreting them?

You have compiled and analyzed some cooperative learning task data using a relatively simple nine-code observational system (Table 4.3). Another more elaborate interaction coding system was adapted by Lim (2000) in her study on cooperative task work. The task in Lim's case included having cooperating pairs reconstruct a dictated text from memory. Although codes in the two cooperative studies reflect task differences, there are several codes that appear to refer to similar kinds of cooperative or non-cooperative behavior between the partners. Our adaptation of Lim's system is shown in Table 4.8.

Exercise 4.15

Now, review your data table on cooperative interaction (Table 4.4), and answer the following questions:

1   Which of the Lim codes could be used in coding the picture sequencing data?

2   What codes might usefully be added to the picture sequencing code set?

3   Are there any codes in the original set that Lim's codes do not include?

Significance of classroom research

Mid-twentieth-century linguistic studies and the interpretation of these in guides intended for language teachers tended to focus somewhat independently

Table 4.8 Scaffolding functions in two-person student exchanges

<small>POSITIVE CODES</small>

Recruitment of Interest (RI):
Nominating or initiating topics and identifying of points for discussion.

Modelling (M):
Offering behaviour for imitation. It may involve completion or even explication of a solution already partially executed by the partner.

Feedback (F):
Providing partner with information on a performance as it compares to the required standard. Partner may also assist by highlighting the features of the task that are relevant.

Direction Maintenance (DM):
Keeping each other in pursuit of the task and working towards its completion. It involves deployment of questions and invitation to proceed to the next step.

Group Maintenance (GM)
Maintaining harmony in the group and lowering affective barriers through speech acts. Attempts to control frustration level in self and peer in order to complete the task

Questioning (Q1):
Requesting for verbal response that assists by producing a mental operation the partner cannot or would not produce alone. This interaction assists further by giving the assistor information about the partner's understanding.

Questioning (Q2):
Asking questions for the purpose of clarification as well as requests for help. Requests for help here refer to issues being discussed and not new problems.

Propositional Knowledge (PK):
Contributing new ideas, information or detail recalled that assists in the successful completion of the task.

Task Structuring (TS):
Helping partner and self to participate in the task by structuring. For example, sequencing, segregating or structuring a task into or from components to modify the task.

Negative Codes

Erroneous Feedback (EF):
Giving misleading feedback or inaccurate information offering garbled explanations. Includes pointing out problems and expressing doubt when the solution is already correct.

Assertions without Explanations (A):
Making assertions or categorically stating a point of view without offering any explanation or justification. Repeating a point of view without elaboration.

Lack of Frustration Control (FC):
Expressing overt exasperation with partner or task. This frustration can manifest itself in words or tone of voice.

Inauthentic Questions (NQ):
Posing questions that do not genuinely seek clarification or understanding, including questions asked with no particular purpose beside trying to confirm personal views.

(Adapted from Lim 2000: 66–74)

on learner language production (speaking and writing) and learner language reception (listening and reading). A similar tendency is found in some more current discussions on language learning which turn on the relative importance of language 'output' of the learner versus language 'input' to the learner.

An interactional view sees speaking and listening—language output and input—as inextricably linked and, of necessity, considered as an integrated system. An interactional view sees language

> as a vehicle for the realization of interpersonal relations and for the performance of social transactions between individuals … Language teaching content, according to this view, may be specified and organized by patterns of exchanges and interaction or may be left unspecified, to be shaped by the inclinations of learners in interactions. (Richards and Rodgers 2001: 21)

There are three areas in which classroom interaction studies have had major influence on discussions of language pedagogy. These areas involve

a) Teacher–student interaction
b) Student–student interaction
c) Student–text interaction, in which the student reader or writer is perceived as involved in an interactive dialog comprising author and reader.

Let us consider each of these briefly.

a) In a recent meta-analysis of studies looking at the role of interaction in second language acquisition, Ellis (1999:8) concludes that there is 'clear evidence that social and intermental interaction are major forces in the acquisition of an L2'. In classroom situations, Ellis notes the central role of the teacher in controlling discourse as a means of learners' obtaining the quality of interaction likely to foster L2 acquisition. A number of techniques such as the teacher's 'recasting' of student responses into more grammatically correct or more socially appropriate forms have been demonstrated to support L2 learning.

b) Student–student interaction patterns and their role in language acquisition have been examined in some detail by researchers studying the impact of cooperative learning routines on language learning. Students working in cooperative classroom groups need to make themselves understood, so they tend to adjust their input to make it *comprehensible*. The student speaker in a pair or small group has the luxury of adjusting speech to the level appropriate to the listener to negotiate meaning—a luxury not available to the teacher speaking to a whole class.

Because students are at a somewhat similar learning stage, their utterances to one another tend to fall within Vygotsky's 'zone of proximal development' (Vygotsky 1978). The developmental level of any student is what he or she can do alone; the proximal level is what he or she can do with supportive collaboration. The student–student interaction student interactions are said to have a higher probability of being 'developmentally appropriate' than teacher–student interactions may be.

Finally, language acquisition is underwritten by input received repeatedly from a variety of sources. 'Redundancy' is critical for language learning, and the cooperative learning group is a natural source of redundant communication. In small group discussions, students each use a variety of phrases providing the opportunity for the listeners to hone in on meaning as well as gain the repeated input necessary for learning to move from short-term comprehension to long-term acquisition. One summary of research in this area concludes that

> Language acquisition is determined by a complex interaction of a number of critical input, output, and context variables. An examination of these critical variables reveals cooperative learning has a dramatic positive impact on almost all of the variables critical to language acquisition. (Kagan 1995:1)

c) A number of those interested in first and second language reading (and writing) pedagogy have also adapted an interactional stance in regards to classroom instruction in literacy. Grabe (1988) posits a notion of inter-activity in second language reading and makes a distinction between reading as an interactive process (interaction between top-down and bottom-up processing) and interactive models of reading (interaction between reader and author *as if* reader and author were engaged in a text-based conversation). One exercise favored in this approach to pedagogy has writers first construct a piece of prose argumentation as a two-person dialog before trying to put their argument into expository prose. Similarly, readers in the interactive mode are encouraged to direct questions to an author before beginning their reading, and then to search the text to see if their questions have been answered.

Exercise 4.16

We have mentioned several senses in which reading and writing have been considered interactively. However, some texts appear to be more interactive than others.

Below are two excerpts from school texts on American history. One was written by a history professor and text writer, Fremont P. Wirth (Sample A) and one by a novelist, Stephen Vincent Binet, under temporary hire as a writer of school history texts (Sample B). Compare the two texts and do the following:

1   As a class, discuss the ways in which the Binet text might be considered more *interactive* than the Wirth text.

2   Consider the pros and cons of each kind of text from the perspective of a second language learner.

Sample A:

The first permanent settlement in New England was made by the Pilgrims, or Separatists, who established a colony on the coast of Massachusetts in 1620. This settlement, like Jamestown, was promoted by a commercial company. These early settlers were interested in improving their economic condition, but there was another factor which played a very important part, namely, religion.
(Fremont P. Wirth. (1936). *American History*. N.Y.: American Book Co.)

Sample B:

The Pilgrims landed on November 11, 1620, from a ship called the Mayflower. Who were the Pilgrims and why did they come to America? Were they adventurers, conquerors, gold seekers?

No, they were not. A few of those on the Mayflower came on the chance of getting land and farms of their own. But most came for another reason. They came because they wished to worship God in their own way – a simple and faithful way, but not the way of the Established Church of the England of their time.

They were family men, for the most part. They brought their wives and their children with them on a 64-day voyage, in a small tossing ship. One child was born on the voyage, two others just after the landfall. The whole company numbered a little over a hundred human beings. It was backed by an English company whose investors put money into the venture. But the backbone of the venture was this group of quiet, family men, bringing their wives and children to a coast at the world's end.

Why did they do such a crazy thing? Why on earth did they take such a chance? Nobody ordered them to do it, bribed them to do it. They went to great trouble and pain, uprooted their homes, left everything they had known behind, from the memories of childhood to the things in the house that one looks at and cannot take because there will be no room, and yet remembers.

They wanted to worship God in their own way. They were resolved and determined to worship God in their own way.
(Stephen Vincent Binet (1944). *America*. NY: Holt, Rinehart, and Winston.)

Linguistic studies of human interaction have been most insightful where the social relations between interactors are somewhat fixed and agreed upon by interactors. Key studies include the Sinclair and Coulthard (1975) analysis of teacher/student interaction, the study of therapist/client interaction in psychotherapy by Labov and Fanshel (1977), and the examination of doctor/patient interaction by Candlin, Leather, and Bruton (1978). Thus, the study of classroom interaction has been seminal in the attempts to understand more generally the patterns of human interaction. As we have noted previously, a number of classroom observational techniques continue to be proposed, the intent of which is to track interaction patterns more clearly and to link these to successful practice. Thus, classroom interaction studies continue to have a central place in current linguistic examination of human interaction.

Reflecting on classroom research

You have had a chance to look at several different uses of classroom interaction research, both with respect to teacher–learner interaction and learner–learner interaction. Classroom interaction research has addressed a variety of key issues in classroom instruction using a variety of observational and reporting techniques. We have seen that there is such a rich array of these techniques that it is often difficult to find common ground in comparing findings and in getting a sense of cumulative understanding. We have also seen that some teaching axioms that seem reasonably commonsensical and straightforward have been difficult to validate by means of classroom interaction studies. And yet, with these difficulties acknowledged, classroom interaction research is one of the most active areas in contemporary second language learning studies.

Consider some possible reasons that might justify current enthusiasm for classroom interaction research:

1 *Universal experience* Almost everyone is a veteran observer of classroom interaction, having spent many years of life as a classroom learner. It is interesting to know something deeper about a topic in which you are an expert and an insider.
2 *Importance of educational improvement* Education occupies the biggest budgets of most governmental agencies and almost no one, regardless of their schooling location or the subject of instruction, is fully satisfied with the ways that classes work. So there are almost always, almost everywhere, movements afoot to improve the delivery of education, to make classroom interaction more efficient, more effective, maybe more inspiring.
3 *Unsettling findings* Early classroom studies came up with some somewhat startling data. We previously referred to research that suggested that in many classrooms, teacher talk took up most of the interactional time and that most of that time, teachers asked questions to which they already knew the answers. Were the findings accurate and how should they be interpreted?
4 *Uniqueness of second language classes* Research in second language classrooms shares many of the same interests and techniques of inquiry

with research in other subject area classrooms. However, classroom inter-action research in second language classrooms is unique in that language is both the medium of instruction and the content of instruction. This overlay of medium and content of instruction provides both special challenges and the opportunity for special insights.

5 *Further professionalization of teaching* There has been a growing interest in the further professionalization of teaching, including involvement of classroom teachers in the process of research. This move ties in with other decentralizing trends in both general and second language education. These trends include school-based curriculum development, field-based teacher preparation, and professional self-evaluation projects. The classroom is the teacher's home territory, a place where teachers are experts in their field and masters of their environment. The classroom seems the ideal setting for more rigorous inquiry by teachers.

6 *Bridging the theory–practice gap* Some of the citations in our introductory chapter suggest the alienation that some practitioners feel towards 'research'. One of the goals of classroom interaction research is to narrow the gap between theory and practice, allowing teachers to become enthusiastic producers as well as consumers of educational research.

7 *The durability of classroom patterns* Classrooms have looked pretty much the same for the last 1,000 years. Despite changes in content, technologies, methods, educational priorities, and professionalization of teaching, school classrooms and the activities that go on within school classrooms have not changed much over the last millennium. The role and orientation of teachers and learners have been maintained although content has varied. So it appears that analyzing what happens in *regular* classrooms involving teachers and learners is likely to stay in fashion and relevant to improving education for the foreseeable future. (One thing that has changed is the importance placed in former times on corporal punishment.)

8 *Classrooms as ideal environments for the study of talk* The classroom has features that make it a particularly attractive environment for the study of talk in general. Ethnographers of communication examine how talk is systematically patterned in ways that reveal, or define, how the speakers perceive their relationships and situation. Classrooms represent a strongly marked *local social system* in which relationships and situations are somewhat fixed, allowing researchers intimate looks at the language which marks these relationships and situations.

9 *Homegrown nature of classroom research* Many of the techniques for conducting SLA research and even motivation for particular kinds of research typically come from outside the field of applied linguistics. However, with respect to studies of classroom talk, educational researchers acknowledge that the initial impetus behind the investigations of classroom talk came not from educational researchers but from applied

linguists, such as Hymes, Gumperz, Sinclair, and Coulthard. The widely influential model of *communicative competence* emerged from classroom interaction studies by socio-linguist Dell Hymes (1971), whose research concerns were largely directed towards the problems encountered by children from one cultural background who entered classrooms where communicative demands were defined primarily in terms of another. In a sense, then, critical aspects of the study of classroom interaction can be said to have been *home-grown*, to have been initiated and developed within the field of applied linguistics. Applied linguists writing on the subject of classroom interaction research continue to be widely read and cited by researchers from other traditions.

10 *Context for many current controversies* It may seem odd to cite 'controversy' as grounds for significance of an area of research. However, as Hammersley (1986: xii) notes, 'given its recent history, classroom research has been the site for some major theoretical and methodological debates'. These debates take place not only across disciplines, as might be expected, but also within disciplines where many key issues find focus in how classroom research is best done. Thus, educational psychologists, second language specialists, social anthropologists, linguists, sociologists, and ethnomethodologists all assert a multiplicity of views as to how classroom interaction research should be carried out both within their own areas of specialization as well as in the wider context of teaching and learning generally.

Exercise 4.17

Consider the above claims regarding the significance of classroom interaction research. Then do the following:

  1 Pick three of these that you find interesting and/or compelling.

  2 Jot down your reasons for selecting each of the three.

  3 What insights have you had about classroom interaction that may be useful in your own teaching?

Summary

In this chapter, you have traveled the path of classroom research from your own experience as the participants being studied to your reflections on designing classroom interaction research studies of your own. You looked closely at two key areas of classroom interaction—the interaction between teachers and learners (when teachers correct learner errors) and the interaction between learners (when learners work in pairs carrying out a cooperative task). Then you considered different ways of grouping and coding interaction data and saw that there were a rich array of alternative systems that researchers have proposed for carrying out this aspect of classroom interaction research. You also explored ways to code both linguistic and non-linguistic data, both of which play important roles in human interaction.

Researchers make choices about what classroom interactions they observe and report. Only a small portion of classroom interaction is actually isolated for recording, analysis, and interpretation, so both as researcher and reader you found that you need to be critical of drawing conclusions too facilely from tip-of-the-iceberg displays of data. You examined your own beliefs about what effective classrooms comprise and also reviewed candidate topics for research and techniques for examining those topics. Choices here critically shape the kind of classroom interaction study you might do and the results you might obtain.

You then looked at the diffuse range of ways in which *interaction* is used in contemporary second language discussions and noted a variety of the other factors that have contributed to the widespread interest in classroom interaction research. We invited you to consider not only the academic significance of interaction studies but also the very personal benefits that a more focused look at the classroom can bring in the way of insights and ideas to the practicing teacher.

PART THREE

Quantitative research

5 DESCRIPTIVE STATISTICS RESEARCH: SURVEY ANALYSIS

Introducing descriptive statistics research

Statistics have shown that mortality increases perceptibly in the military during wartime.
ALPHONSE ALLAIS, 1855–1905
French writer and humorist

Absurdity, n.: A statement or belief manifestly inconsistent with one's own opinion.
AMBROSE BIERCE, 1842–1914?
American journalist and writer
The Devil's Dictionary, 1911

Whether we like it or not, most of us are affected in one way or another by surveys. We get phone calls (invariably at dinner time) from people wanting to survey our opinions on commercial products, or political issues; we receive surveys in the mail or with products we buy and perhaps send them back to the big computer in the sky; we watch advertisements placed on television stations largely on the basis of ratings determined by yet another survey.

Surveys have also been used in the second language teaching and learning literature. There have been articles about individual learning differences like motivation, learning styles, personality, anxiety and language learning, attitudes toward language learning, and so on. (See, for example, Oxford 1990; Dörnyei and Schmidt 2001.) Other subjects covered have included needs analysis for language programs (for example, Johns 1981), evaluation of language programs (for example, Lynch 1992, 1997), usefulness of teacher training programs (for example, Ochsner 1980), and there have been many others. From time to time you may need to use a survey in order to understand better how things are really operating in your own, personal environment—in your classroom or other learning setting—or to describe the abilities, performances, and other characteristics of the learners, teachers, and administrators involved in your professional life.

Once you have the information from a survey, what can you do with it? In parts of Chapters 2 to 4, you experienced ways of describing such characteristics in various qualitative ways. In this chapter, you will experience doing DESCRIPTIVE STATISTICS RESEARCH, that is, any research that describes a setting or events in numerical terms. This experience will also initiate you into the strategies and uses of QUANTITATIVE RESEARCH METHODS, which are any investigative procedures used to describe in numerical terms a setting and the things going on in it.

Experiencing descriptive statistics research

We will focus on a widely-used questionnaire survey designed to measure the belief systems of language teachers. Every teacher, whether trained or untrained, has ideas about how language teaching should be done. Even teachers who are completely untrained will have beliefs, perhaps based on their experiences as language learners (Brown 1995b: 4–5). Horwitz put it more negatively: 'Prospective foreign language teachers enter the methods class with many preconceived ideas about how languages are learned and how they should be taught. These beliefs can directly interfere with their understanding of and receptivity to the information and techniques presented in the methods class' (Horwitz 1985: 333).

Trained teachers are more likely to be aware than untrained ones of their options in language teaching. They may favor more innovative or up-to-date teaching methods like communicative and task-based techniques. Alternatively they may choose to be *eclectic* and combine features of grammar-translation, audiolingual approaches, the Silent Way, Community Language Learning, Suggestopedia, and Total Physical Response, as well as communicative and task-based techniques. (See Table 7.7 on page 214 for a list of the distinctive features of some of these methods and for more complete overviews, see Brown 1995b; Larsen-Freeman 2000; Oller and Richard-Amato 1983; Richards and Rodgers 2001.)

Williams and Burden take a different perspective in their 1997 book *Psychology for Language Teachers*. They suggest that, for language teachers to come to grips with what it means to be a good teacher, it may be relatively unimportant for them to learn about particular methods. Instead, it may be crucial for them to understand what their own beliefs are 'about themselves, about learning and its educational relevance and about learners' (Williams and Burden 1997: 63). Let's explore some of your language teaching beliefs in a few warm-up exercises.

Exercise 5.1

(Warm-up)

For each of the following language teaching methods, indicate your impressions as follows: if you have a positive impression, put a plus (+); if you have a negative impression, use a minus (–); and if you don't know or don't have an impression one way or the other, put a zero (0).

Impression	Teaching Approach
_____	Audiolingual approach
_____	Cognitive approach
_____	Communicative language teaching
_____	Community Language Learning
_____	Content-based teaching
_____	Grammar-translation approach
_____	Natural approach
_____	Silent Way
_____	Situational language teaching
_____	Suggestopedia
_____	Task-based language teaching
_____	Total Physical Response
_____	Whole Language approach

Photocopiable © Oxford University Press

Let's suppose that the major linguistic elements to be taught to language students are pronunciation (P), vocabulary (V), grammar (G), and conversational strategies (C). The views of a teacher who feels all four deserve equal time could be represented by a PIE CHART equally divided into four sections like that shown in the example.

V	C
25%	25%

G	P
25%	25%

Exercise 5.2

Draw a pie diagram indicating approximately how much time you think should be accorded each of these elements in a *beginning* language course.

Now, with a partner, discuss your two diagrams, and in another circle, draw a *compromise* pie chart with which you can both agree.

Learner and teacher beliefs

The type of survey where respondents are asked to register their reactions on a 4 3 2 1 scale is commonly referred to as a LIKERT SCALE. For example, in a course evaluation, you might want learners to respond to the following item:

	Strongly agree	Agree	Disagree	Strongly disagree
My teacher is very well organized.	4	3	2	1

For other examples, see Horwitz 1985, 1988.

Likert scales can be on a 1 to 4 scale like the example above, or on a 1 to 5 scale, a 1 to 7 scale, etc., depending on how fine-tuned you want the respondents' answers to be. (See also Exercise 5.20 below.) Likert scales are generally useful for getting at respondents' views, judgments, or opinions about almost any aspect of language learning.

There is considerable evidence that teachers teach more effectively when their classroom methodology matches their belief system. The *Language Teaching/Learning Beliefs Questionnaire* (shown below) can help you bring your own beliefs about language teaching to a level of conscious awareness so you can compare them with the beliefs of other teachers and with your own classroom teaching practices. Note that the first part of the questionnaire asks for biodata information, that is, information about your background and individual characteristics. These biodata questions are OPEN-RESPONSE ITEMS because you respond to them in your own words in writing. The rest of the questionnaire is made up of SELECTED-RESPONSE ITEMS, that is, items you must answer by selecting from among alternatives by merely circling or checking their choices.

Language Teaching/Learning Beliefs Questionnaire

Name _____ Age _____ Gender (circle one): M F

Years of language teaching _____
Years of studying second languages _____
Number of languages you speak _____

Directions: Circle the number that corresponds to your degree of agreement with the statements listed on the left [strongly agree = 4; agree = 3; disagree = 2; strongly disagree = 1]:

	Strongly agree	Agree	Disagree	Strongly disagree
1 Some people have a special aptitude for learning foreign languages.	4	3	2	1
2 Teachers should be facilitators rather than directors of L2 classes.	4	3	2	1
3 Student writers should get their ideas on paper and not worry about correctness.	4	3	2	1
4 In learning a foreign language, it is important to repeat and practice a lot.	4	3	2	1
5 Striving for native-like pronunciation is not a useful goal in language teaching.	4	3	2	1
6 It is important that sentences be grammatically correct when spoken.	4	3	2	1
7 Vocabulary words are the most important part of learning a new language.	4	3	2	1
8 Students should be speaking from the first day of learning a new language.	4	3	2	1
9 If learners are allowed to make errors, these will be hard to correct later.	4	3	2	1
10 The most important part of a new language is learning its grammar.	4	3	2	1
11 Language teaching should rely on a strong base of linguistics.	4	3	2	1
12 In communication, meaning is all-important; form is of little importance.	4	3	2	1
13 A foreign language will improve only if it is used often for communication.	4	3	2	1
14 Listening is more important than speaking in the early stages.	4	3	2	1
15 Everybody can learn a foreign language following the same teaching techniques.	4	3	2	1
16 Listening, speaking, reading, and writing skills should first be taught separately.	4	3	2	1
17 In writing, the final product is critical, not the process by which it occurs.	4	3	2	1
18 Grammatical rules should be 'discovered' by students rather than explicitly taught.	4	3	2	1
19 In oral practice, the teacher should not correct student errors during practice.	4	3	2	1
20 First and second language learning follow the same basic processes.	4	3	2	1

Exercise 5.3

Now for a more detailed look at your teaching beliefs, fill in the biodata information and open-response items at the top of the *Language Teaching/Learning Beliefs Questionnaire* above, and then answer all 20 of the selected-response items.

Compiling descriptive data

Exercise 5.4

Now, as a class, using whatever strategy works best for you, compile the results for the *Language Teaching/Learning Beliefs Questionnaire* you did in Exercise 5.3. How you do this is up to you. You may wish to divide the task up among yourselves and do it at home, or work it out as a group on the board in class. Organize the data in a manner similar to that shown in Table 5.1. Table 5.2 shows some example data taken from one of our classes at the University of Hawaii. (Readers who are using this book on their own can enter their data at the bottom of Table 5.2 and use those data for the appropriate exercises.)

Much of the rest of the chapter will be dedicated to explaining how to describe the results of the survey once you have them.

Exercise 5.5

As a class, discuss the questionnaire results and try to decide which three items (in numbers 1 through 20) show the most agreement and which three show the least agreement.

Analyzing descriptive data

Now that you have compiled your numerical data in a clear table, the question now is how to make sense of all those numbers. You can describe your results in terms of frequencies or percentages, or you can show them in graphs or charts. Or you can sort through a set of numbers by calculating descriptive statistics. DESCRIPTIVE STATISTICS are used to characterize or describe a set of numbers in terms of central tendency and to show how the numbers disperse, or vary, around the center. Frequencies and percentages,

Table 5.1 Form for compiling data for classroom mini-study (www)

Student name	Age	Gender	Years teaching languages	Years studying languages	Number of foreign languages	1	2	3	4	5	6	7	8	9	10	11	12	13	14	15	16	17	18	19	20
Joe Example	29	m	8	4	2	1	2	1	4	1	2	3	2	3	4	3	3	3	2	3	1	2	2	3	2

Table 5.2 *Example data from the University of Hawaii group (www)*

Name	Age	Gender*	Yrs Lg Tch	Tch/No Tch**	Yrs Lg Std	#Lgs	1	2	3	4	5	6	7	8	9	10	11	12	13	14	15	16	17	18	19	20
C	24	1	2.5	2	18	2	3	3	2	3	3	2	2	2	2	2	2	2	3	3	2	2	2	2	2	2
E	25	1	0	1	12	2	4	3	2	4	3	3	4	1	2	2	2	2	2	4	3	4	1	3	3	2
F	26	1	1	1	20	2	3	3	3	4	2	2	3	3	3	3	2	3	3	2	1	2	1	3	3	2
A	28	1	2	2	8	2	4	3	3	4	3	2	2	2	4	2	2	2	3	3	2	1	1	3	2	2
J	28	1	0	1	13	2	3	3	2	4	3	3	2	3	2	2	2	2	3	3	2	2	2	3	3	2
D	29	1	0	1	18	2	3	2	3	3	3	2	2	1	1	2	2	2	3	3	2	2	2	2	2	1
I	29	1	4	2	17	2	4	4	4	3	2	2	1	3	2	2	2	2	2	2	1	1	1	2	4	2
G	30	1	0	1	28	4	3	4	2	2	2	3	2	2	2	2	2	3	2	2	2	3	2	2	2	3
H	30	2	3	2	12	2	4	4	3	3	3	2	1	1	2	3	1	2	2	2	1	2	2	3	3	2
B	36	1	10	2	10	2	4	3	2	3	3	3	3	3	3	2	2	2	2	3	2	1	2	2	2	2
Single reader																										

* 1 = female; 2 = male

** 1 = teaching experience; 2 = no experience

N = 10

graphical display of data, central tendency, and dispersion are the four topics we will cover in this section.

Frequencies and percentages

FREQUENCIES, also known as tallies, are used to count up the number of things or people in different categories. For instance, let's say the respondents to the *Language Teaching/Learning Beliefs Questionnaire* turned out to be seventeen people and you wanted to analyze their gender. You could count up the frequencies in two categories: male and female. If it turned out that there were six males and eleven females, six and eleven would be your frequencies for males and females. Such results can be expressed as RAW FREQUENCIES as in the previous sentence, or they can be converted to PERCENTAGES. This can often be a clearer way of expressing the information. As you know, percentages are calculated by dividing the total number in one category by the total number in all categories and multiplying the result by 100. For instance, using the example above, if you want to know what percentage of the total group is represented by the males, you would divide the number in the male category (6) by the number in all categories (males + females = 6 + 11 = 17), which would be calculated as follows: (6 / 17) x 100 = .353 x 100 = 35.3% or about 35%

Percentages are easier for many people to understand than raw frequencies. Telling people that your study included 35% males and 65% females may be clearer for them than saying that you studied six males and eleven females. Other people may find the actual raw frequencies clearer than the percentages, so you may find it best to report both the raw frequencies and percentages.

Such frequency and percentage analysis could equally well be applied to the answers that participants give to the various items. For instance, in analyzing the participants' answers to item number one in the survey, '1. Some people have a special aptitude for learning foreign languages', it might turn out that nine of the participants out of seventeen selected 'strongly agree', four selected 'agree', three selected 'disagree', and one selected 'strongly disagree'. Presenting those frequencies in prose, as we just did, or in a table would be helpful in analyzing the results. It might also be useful to calculate the percentage of participants who selected each (by dividing the number who selected each by the total of seventeen and moving the decimal point two places to the right). The result for the item one example above would be as follows: 52.9% of the participants selected 'strongly agree', 23.5% selected 'agree', 17.6% selected 'disagree', and 5.9% selected 'strongly disagree'. You might have noticed that these percentages add up to 99.9% rather than 100%, a difference that you would have to attribute to what is called ROUNDING ERROR.

Graphical display of data

Another way of showing frequency (or percentage data) is to graph them out in a HISTOGRAM. For example, you could represent the gender frequencies of six males and eleven females discussed in the previous section as follows:

```
Frequency
11      X
10      X
 9      X
 8      X
 7      X
 6      X       X
 5      X       X
 4      X       X
 3      X       X
 2      X       X
 1      X       X
       _____
        Females   Males
```

Graphing of frequencies is not only useful for data in categories like 'male' and 'female', but can also prove helpful for continuous scales like 'ages'.

For example, look at these ages for the same seventeen people:

21 22 24 24 25 26 26 26 27 27 27 27 28 28 29 30 31

They could be plotted as follows:

```
Frequency
4                           *
3                       *   *
2               *       *   *   *
1       *   *   *   *   *   *   *   *   *   *
       _____
Age   21  22  23  24  25  26  27  28  29  30  31
```

As you can see in the two example histograms shown here, you can use Xs, asterisks, or any other symbol that strikes your fancy. The point is to graphically display the frequency, or number, as shown along the frequency scale on the *left* of the histogram for each gender category or age bracket as shown along the *bottom* of the histogram.

Graphing data can take many forms. For example, the histogram given above for six males and eleven females could equally well be shown as a pie chart, with the percentages given rather than the raw frequencies, as follows:

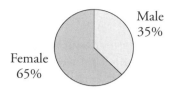

Histograms like the ones shown in this section are commonly used to show the frequency in each category for categorical variables, or at each value along continuous scales. Pie charts may prove clearer when the number of categories is small, while histograms may prove more useful when the number of categories is large or the scale is continuous (as in ages).

Exercise 5.6

Now look at the following ages for another, smaller group answering our questionnaire, and make a histogram:

Name	Age
Sonya	40
Maria	35
Hans	34
Hachiko	31
Juanita	31
Tatanya	30
George	29
Toshi	29
Greg	27
Celeste	27
James	25

Exercise 5.7

Now, look back at the survey results that you compiled in Exercise 5.4 and select the responses from any single item. How many participants selected each response (strongly agree (4), agree (3), disagree (2), or strongly disagree (1)) for that item? Now, make a histogram for those responses.

Central tendency

Another convenient way of summarizing data is to find a single statistic, called the central tendency, which represents an entire set of numbers. CENTRAL TENDENCY can be defined as the propensity of a set of numbers to cluster around a particular value. Three statistics are often used to find central tendency: the mean, the mode, and the median.

Mean The most widely used measure of central tendency is the MEAN, which is more commonly called the AVERAGE. The mean is the sum of all the values in a distribution divided by the number of values. The formula is written as follows:

$$M = \frac{\Sigma X}{N}$$

where: M = mean
Σ = sum of (or add up)
X = values
N = number of values

Look at these ages for yet another group of respondents to the questionnaire:

24 26 26 27 28 29 29 29 31 32

Using the formula $M = \Sigma X / N$, the mean for these ages is

$(24+26+26+27+28+29+29+29+31+32)/10 = 281/10 = 28.1$

Mode The MODE is that value in a set of numbers that occurs most frequently. In a way, the mode is the simplest of the three central tendency statistics discussed here because it requires no computation. You simply need to examine the number of occurrences of each value.

Look at the respondents' ages again: 24 26 26 27 28 29 29 29 31 32

In this case, the mode is 29 because it is the most frequent age.

Note that there can also be more than one mode in a distribution. For instance, in the set of ages that we have been working with, if we were to add one additional 26-year-old, there would be two modes (26 and 29) as follows:

24 26 26 26 27 28 29 29 29 31 32

When there are two modes, the distribution is referred to as BIMODAL. If there are three modes, it is TRIMODAL, and so on.

Median The MEDIAN is the point in the distribution below which 50% of the values lie and above which 50% lie. To find the median, you should first place the age values in order from low to high. Then, examine the age above and below which 50% of the ages lie.

Consider once again the ages of the respondents to the *Language Teaching/ Learning Beliefs Questionnaire* (still with that extra 26-year-old):

24 26 26 26 27 *28* 29 29 29 31 32

The median is 28 (in bold italics)—that is the age that has half of the other values (24, 26, 26, 26, and 27) below it and half the other values (29, 29, 29, 31, and 32) above it.

However, without that extra 26-year-old added, the ages would be as follows:

24 26 26 27 *28 29* 29 29 31 32

In this case, no single age has 50% of the other ages above and below it; the median involves splitting the difference between the two ages (the 28 and 29 in bold italics) that do divide the others 50/50. Thus, the median is 28.5, which is the difference between 28 and 29, the two ages that split all the ages into two halves: the lower half (24, 26, 26, 27, and 28) and the higher half (29, 29, 29, 31, and 32).

Exercise 5.8

Note: we will indicate exercises where you need a calculator in parentheses like this: (Calculator needed.)

Look at the following participants' ages (also used in Exercise 5.6) and calculate and record three descriptive statistics: the mean, the mode, and the median. You will find the answers in the Answer key on page 258.

Name	Age
Sonya	40
Maria	35
Hans	34
Hachiko	31
Juanita	31
Tatanya	30
George	29
Toshi	29
Greg	27
Celeste	27
James	25

Exercise 5.9

(Calculator needed.)

Now, look back at the survey responses for whatever single item you used in Exercise 5.7 and (using the response numbers 4, 3, 2, and 1 to represent the responses from strongly agree to strongly disagree) find and write down the mean, the mode, and the median.

Dispersion

Knowing about the central tendency of a set of numbers is very helpful way of characterizing the most typical behavior in a group. It doesn't, however, tell us anything about the way the numbers spread out around that central or typical behavior. Consider the following two sets of ages for groups answering the *Language Teaching/Learning Beliefs Questionnaire*:

Group A	Group B
65	54
61	53
60	51
54	50
50	50
50	50
47	49
41	47
22	46

Exercise 5.10

Work out the mean, the mode, and the median for Group A and Group B.

A quick look at all the ages in each group displayed as histograms will reveal that the way the ages vary away from the central tendency is quite different for the two groups:

Group A histogram

```
                            x
  x                 x    x  x  x      xx   x
  _____
  20  25  30  35  40  45  50  55  60  65
```

Group B histogram

```
                            x
                            x
                     xx xxx xx
  _____
  20  25  30  35  40  45  50  55  60  65
```

Notice that, even though the two groups have the same means, the ages for Group A are widely spread out from 22 to 65 years, while the ages for Group B are more narrowly spread out from 46 to 54. In descriptive statistics, this concept is referred to as DISPERSION, which can be defined as the degree to which the individual numbers vary away from the central tendency. There are three primary ways of examining dispersion: the low-high, the range, and the standard deviation.

Low-high The LOW-HIGH involves finding the lowest value and the highest value in a set of numbers. Look at these ages: 24 26 26 27 28 29 29 29 31 32

In this case, by putting the numbers in order from high to low, you can see immediately that the lowest age is 24 and the highest age is 32. Thus, the low-high is 24 to 32, or 24–32.

Range The RANGE is the highest value minus the lowest value plus one. You must add one because otherwise you will be excluding either the highest number or lowest number from the range. The formula is written as follows:

> *Range* = $H - L + 1$
> where: H = high number
> L = low number

Look at these ages: 24 26 26 27 28 29 29 29 31 32

> *Range* = $32 - 24 + 1 = 9$

Thus the range is nine including both the 24 and 32, as you can see by counting up the nine possible numbers in that range: 24 25 26 27 28 29 30 31 32

Standard deviation The best overall indicator of dispersion is the STANDARD DEVIATION. Brown (1988: 69) defined it as 'a sort of average of the differences of all scores from the mean'. The standard deviation is 'a sort of average' because you are averaging some values by adding them up and dividing by the number of values, just as you did in calculating the mean. So the equation for the standard deviation starts with adding *something* up and dividing by the number of *somethings*. In calculating the standard deviation, the *something* you are adding up is the 'differences of all scores from the mean,' or $\Sigma(X-M)$. So, the equation for the standard deviation includes $\Sigma(X-M)$ (for summing up the differences from the mean of each student divided by the number of students):

$$\frac{\Sigma(X-M)}{N}$$

Because half the students will be above the mean and half below the mean, the differences will tend to cancel each other out when you sum them up. Hence they will add up to something close to zero, which would tell you nothing. To get around this problem, statisticians eliminate the minus signs (for those students below the mean when you subtract the mean from each student's value) by *squaring the result for all students* before adding them up (rather than simply adding up the absolute numbers). So, the equation for the standard deviation includes (for summing up the distances from the mean *squared* for each student divided by the number of students):

$$\frac{\Sigma(X-M)^2}{N}$$

Because the distances of the values from the mean are squared, you need to take the square root of the result (when you are finished summing and dividing) in order to bring it back down to the original scale. This is for the sake of ease of interpretation. (Note that the squaring and square root part of the equation are why Brown (1988) began his definition with '*a sort of average*' (emphasis ours).) So, the full equation for calculating the standard deviation requires you to subtract the mean from each value and square that result for each student, then add those squared values up, divide the result by the number of students, and take the square root of the result of that division.

$$SD = \sqrt{\frac{\Sigma(X-M)^2}{N}}$$

Where: SD = standard deviation
X   = values
M   = mean of the values
N   = number values

Let's consider an example calculation of standard deviation. Look at these ages:

24 26 26 27 28 29 29 29 31 32

From calculations earlier, you already know that the mean of these ages is 28.1.

You should begin by lining the ages up vertically (as shown in column C1) with the mean next to each one (as in column C2). Next, calculate the difference between C1 and C2 for each student by subtracting C2 from C1 and put the result in column C3. Then square each of the values in C3 and put the result in column C4, and add up all the values in C4 at the bottom of that column.

C1		C2		C3	C4
ages	−	*mean*	=	*difference*	*squared difference*
24	−	28.1	=	−4.1	16.81
26	−	28.1	=	−2.1	4.41
26	−	28.1	=	−2.1	4.41
27	−	28.1	=	−1.1	1.21
28	−	28.1	=	−0.1	.01
29	−	28.1	=	0.9	.81
29	−	28.1	=	0.9	.81
29	−	28.1	=	0.9	.81
31	−	28.1	=	2.9	8.41
32	−	28.1	=	3.9	15.21

$52.90 = \Sigma\,(X - M)^2$, or the sum of squares
$10\ \ \ \ = N$, or the number of participant ages

You now have everything you need to calculate the standard deviation. So, plug the sum of squares and number of ages into the equation for the standard deviation, then divide, and take the square root, and you have the standard deviation: 2.3.

$$ SD = \sqrt{\frac{\Sigma(X - M)^2}{N}} = \sqrt{\frac{52.90}{10}} = \sqrt{5.29} = 2.3 $$

This value indicates critical information about the spread or dispersion of the data, which we describe in more detail in the next section.

Exercise 5.11

(Calculator needed.)

Look once again at the ages used to calculate the three central tendency statistics in Exercise 5.6 and Exercise 5.8 and calculate the standard deviation for those ages.

The ages were:

Name	C1 ages −	C2 mean =	C3 difference	C4 squared difference
Sonya	40			
Maria	35			
Hans	34			
Hachiko	31			
Juanita	31			
Tatanya	30			
George	29			
Toshi	29			
Greg	27			
Celeste	27			
James	25			

$\qquad\qquad = \Sigma(X - M)^2$, or the sum of squares

$= N$, or the number of ages

$$SD = \sqrt{\frac{\Sigma(X - M)^2}{N}}$$

Low-high = ＿＿＿＿   Range = ＿＿＿＿   Standard deviation = ＿＿＿＿

Exercise 5.12

(Calculator needed.)

Now do the same for the Group A data at the top of this section on Dispersion (page 130):

C1	C2	C3	C4
ages	− mean =	difference	squared difference
65			
61			
60			
54			
50			
50			
47			
41			
22			

$= \Sigma(X - M)^2$, or the sum of squares
$= N$, or the number of ages

$$SD = \sqrt{\frac{\Sigma(X - M)^2}{N}}$$

Low-high = _____ Range = _____ Standard deviation = _____

Exercise 5.13

(Calculator needed.)

Now do the same calculations for the Group B data at the top of this section on Dispersion (page 130).

Exercise 5.14

Now, look back at the three sets of dispersion statistics that you just calculated. Remember the three sets have nearly the same mean (52.9, 50, and 50, respectively). Yet they differ considerably in the dispersion, or spread, of scores. Now answer the following questions:

   1   Which of the three is the most widely dispersed?

   2   Which of the three has the narrowest dispersion?

Normal distribution

In any set of values that form a NORMAL DISTRIBUTION (commonly referred to as a BELL CURVE), the standard deviation can become a useful way of describing the dispersion of the scores. Let's say we have a large set of ages that range from 22 to 82. We calculate the mean and standard deviation, and they turn out to be 52 and 10, respectively, each ten-year period being one standard deviation. In the following graph, we have shown how the mean can be marked off in the middle of the distribution, and how the 10 years of the standard deviation can be used to mark off standard deviation units across the bottom:

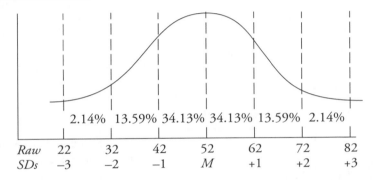

Notice that the mean of 52 is exactly in the middle. Notice also that one standard deviation above the mean is 62 (52 + 10 = 62); two above the mean is 72 (52 + 10 +10 = 72); and so forth. Next, notice that one standard deviation below the mean is 42 (52 −10 = 42); two standard deviations below the mean is 32 (52 − 10 − 10 = 32); and so forth. Thus we can refer to a student as being three standard deviations below the mean, or being two standard deviations above the mean, or being right in the middle (that is, exactly on the mean).

Based on experience with large groups of data, we can expect certain percentages of students to fall within one standard above the mean (34.13%), between one standard deviation and two above the mean (13.59%), and between two standard deviations and three above the mean (2.14%). Since the distribution is symmetrical, the same percentages also apply below the mean −1, −2, and −3 standard deviations. Thus the percentage of participants who will fall within the area between one SD above and one SD below the mean is 68.26% (34.13 + 34.13 = 68.26).

Exercise 5.15

(Calculator needed.)

As homework, divide up the teaching/learning beliefs items (numbers 1 to 20) so that each student can calculate the mean (M) and standard deviation (SD) for some of the items, and the percentage (based on frequency) of responses for each possible answer 4, 3, 2, and 1. For the sake of accuracy and for checking answers, make sure that the items are divided up such that at least two students do the calculations for each item. Create a table modeled on Table 5.3.

Look at the results shown in Table 5.4 for a group of 39 teachers in Turin, Italy, who answered the same questionnaire you did. Note that not all of the teachers in that group answered all of the items on the questionnaire. Thus the means, standard deviations, and other statistics are based solely on those teachers who did answer in each case.

The results in Table 5.4 are presented just as yours should have been in Table 5.3. Such similar displays of results make it possible to make comparisons.

Exercise 5.16

Form groups of three to four people. Each of the groups that you formed previously should now look at Tables 5.3 and 5.4 and compare the Turin group and your class by answering the following questions:

1 What differences and similarities do you see between the Turin group's biodata information and that for your class?

2 Which items does the Turin group agree with more strongly than your class?

3 Why do you think the Turin group agrees more strongly with certain items than your class?

4 Which items does the Turin group disagree with more strongly than your class?

5 Why do you think the Turin group disagrees more strongly with certain items than your class?

Table 5.3 Form for compiling results of the classroom mini-study (www)

Category	N	M	SD	Frequency strongly disagree 1	Frequency disagree 2	Frequency agree 3	Frequency strongly agree 4	Percent strongly disagree 1	Percent disagree 2	Percent agree 3	Percent strongly agree 4
Age				–	–	–	–	–	–	–	–
Sex M		–	–	–	–	–	–	–	–	–	–
F		–	–	–	–	–	–	–	–	–	–
Yrs teach				–	–	–	–	–	–	–	–
Yrs study				–	–	–	–	–	–	–	–
# Langs				–	–	–	–	–	–	–	–
–	–	–	–	–	–	–	–	–	–	–	–
Items	–	–	–	–	–	–	–	–	–	–	–
1											
2											
3											

4																	
5																	
6																	
7																	
8																	
9																	
10																	
11																	
12																	
13																	
14																	
15																	
16																	
17																	
18																	
19																	
20																	

Table 5.4 Results of the Turin group's classroom mini-study (www)

Category	N	M	SD	Frequency strongly disagree 1	Frequency disagree 2	Frequency agree 3	Frequency strongly agree 4	Percent strongly disagree 1	Percent disagree 2	Percent agree 3	Percent strongly agree 4
Age	39	25.71	2.56	--	--	--	--	--	--	--	--
Sex M	14	--	--	--	--	--	--	--	--	--	--
F	25	--	--	--	--	--	--	--	--	--	--
Yrs teach	39	8.47	2.97	--	--	--	--	--	--	--	--
Yrs study	39	5.60	.76	--	--	--	--	--	--	--	--
# Langs	39	3.21	.51	--	--	--	--	--	--	--	--
--	--	--	--	--	--	--	--	--	--	--	--
Items --	--	--	--	--	--	--	--	--	--	--	--
1	39	3.23	0.48	0	1	28	10	0.00	2.56	71.79	25.64
2	39	3.28	0.50	0	1	26	12	0.00	2.56	66.67	30.77
3	34	2.29	0.62	3	18	13	0	8.82	52.94	38.24	0.00

4	39	3.44	0.59	0	2	18	19	0.00	5.13	46.15	48.72
5	35	2.37	0.68	2	20	11	2	5.71	57.14	31.43	5.71
6	36	2.42	0.76	4	15	15	2	11.11	41.67	41.67	5.56
7	36	2.47	0.73	3	15	16	2	8.33	41.67	44.44	5.56
8	39	3.00	0.32	0	2	35	2	0.00	5.13	89.74	5.13
9	36	2.36	0.75	4	17	13	2	11.11	47.22	36.11	5.56
10	37	2.19	0.65	5	20	12	0	13.51	54.05	32.43	0.00
11	33	2.76	0.74	1	11	16	5	3.03	33.33	48.48	15.15
12	37	2.32	0.81	5	18	11	3	13.51	48.65	29.73	8.11
13	38	3.11	0.50	0	3	28	7	0.00	7.89	73.68	18.42
14	37	2.49	0.72	2	18	14	3	5.41	48.65	37.84	8.11
15	37	1.86	0.53	8	26	3	0	21.62	70.27	8.11	0.00
16	38	1.97	0.58	7	25	6	0	18.42	65.79	15.79	0.00
17	28	2.43	0.62	1	15	11	1	3.57	53.57	39.29	3.57
18	38	2.71	0.68	3	7	26	2	7.89	18.42	68.42	5.26
19	35	2.51	1.00	6	12	10	7	17.14	34.29	28.57	20.00
20	36	2.06	0.57	5	24	7	0	13.89	66.67	19.44	0.00

Designing your own descriptive research

Earlier in the chapter, you took part in a survey of teaching/learning beliefs. You may, however, still have questions about what surveys are and how you should go about writing good survey items. Those are the issues we will address in this section.

What are surveys?

SURVEYS are any procedures used to gather and describe the characteristics, attitudes, views, opinions, and so forth of students, teachers, administrators, or any other people who are important to a study. Surveys typically take the form of interviews or questionnaires or both. Naturally, the difference between interviews and questionnaires is that INTERVIEWS are done orally in a face-to-face format, on the telephone, or even in groups (as in an interview with a group of students who are not happy with a particular part of a language program), while QUESTIONNAIRES are administered in writing to individuals (as in a mailed questionnaire) or members of a group (as in a questionnaire passed out and completed in class).

Interviews are typically made up of fairly open-ended questions, but can be carefully planned in what is called an INTERVIEW SCHEDULE. This may involve a list of questions or prompts (sometimes with follow-up questions and prompts) for the interviewer to use when conducting the interview. Questionnaires may also include OPEN-RESPONSE ITEMS in the form of fill-in and short-answer questions, but generally speaking, questionnaires are predominantly made up of more CLOSED-RESPONSE ITEMS such as Likert scales, multiple-choice, yes-no, and ranking. (For more information on the variety of survey item types, see Brown 2001.)

Interviews are most useful for discovering what the issues are in a particular survey project or even for finding out which questions should be asked. They are, however, very time-consuming. If large-scale information is needed from a great many people, questionnaires are typically a more efficient way of gathering that information. It is not unusual for questionnaire designers to first conduct interviews to help them (a) understand the issues involved, (b) work out the questions to ask, and (c) formulate the items to be included on the questionnaire.

Writing good surveys

Writing good items is the first step in doing survey research. To do this, you need to be very clear about what you want to survey. You may first want to make a clear written statement of what it is you are setting out to accomplish in your survey and keep that in mind when you are actually writing items. Once you have written the survey, whether it be in the form of an interview schedule or questionnaire, you will also need to get feedback from colleagues on the quality of the items and/or to pilot the survey instrument with participants similar to the ones you will eventually be surveying. You may even want to interview those colleagues or participants after they have gone through the survey instrument to find out what was going on in their minds as they interacted with it.

During the item writing and item revision processes, you may find it useful for you (and your colleagues) to refer to Table 5.5, which gives some suggestions about how to write good survey items. Notice that Table 5.5 is presented in a negative way, that is, it gives a list of things that should be avoided in writing good survey items. The list starts with some self-explanatory things to avoid: (1) overly long items, (2) unclear or ambiguous items, (3) negative items, and (4) incomplete items.

Table 5.5 Things to avoid in writing good survey items

AVOID:
 1 Overly long items
 2 Unclear or ambiguous items
 3 Negative items
 4 Incomplete items
 5 Overlapping choices in items
 6 Items across two pages
 7 Double-barreled items
 8 Loaded word items
 9 Absolute word items
10 Leading items
11 Prestige items
12 Embarrassing items
13 Biased items
14 Items at the wrong level of language
15 Items that respondents are incompetent to answer
16 Assuming that everyone has an answer to all items
17 Making respondents answer items that don't apply
18 Irrelevant items
19 Writing superfluous information into items

(Adapted from Brown 1997b)

Other things to avoid may need a little explanation. Overlapping choices (5), for instance, are those which occur when the alternatives the respondents see are not independent of one other; that is, they are not mutually exclusive. For example:

The best location for the new foreign languages building would be:
1 In Los Angeles County
2 In the city of Burbank
3 In Burbank High School
4 Other: (specify) _____

In the example, the options are overlapping in the sense that Burbank High School is located in the city of Burbank and in Los Angeles County so the options are not independent. Thus answering such an item can be very confusing.

Items should also be presented so they appear on a single page (6) so respondents will not overlook any part of the item.

Double-barreled items (7) are items that simultaneously address more than one issue. For example:

The State of Hawaii should spend more on education (especially bilingual education) and less on prisons.

Agree _____   Disagree _____   Don't know _____

In this example, the question actually contains three questions that could be asked separately: questions about (a) spending on education, (b) money for prisons, and (c) funds for bilingual education.

Loaded words (8) are words or phrases that prompt the respondent to automatically answer in a positive or negative way, usually because they are weighted in an emotionally loaded way. For example:

Naturally, Hawaiian is the language to study if you live in Hawaii.

Agree _____   Disagree _____   Don't know _____

In the example, the word 'naturally' is emotionally loaded.

Words that express an absolute (9) can be particularly problematic—words such as 'all', 'every', 'always', 'never', etc. For example, the question 'All Americans are rich' provokes a negative response because most people recognize that absolute statements including words like 'all' are false.

Leading questions (10) are questions that openly push respondents to answer in a particular way. For example: 'You don't believe in the old-fashioned notion of grammar-translation, do you?'

Prestige questions (11) can also be problematic. For example, when asked point-blank, many respondents may maintain that their speaking ability in a language is better than it actually is or that they read more pages per day than they actually do because it is perceived that those are the prestigious ways to answer.

Embarrassing questions (12) are questions that some groups of respondent might find embarrassing. For example, some respondents might find questions containing sexually explicit words to be objectionable.

Biased questions (13) are questions that indicate bias or prejudice against a particular group of people. Such biases may be based on age, ethnic background, gender, national origin, race, religion, or any other characteristics about which people may be sensitive.

Other types of questions that should be avoided are questions at the wrong level of language (14) and questions that participants are incompetent to answer (15). In addition, it is best to avoid (16) assuming that everyone has an answer to all questions, (17) making participants answer questions that don't apply to them, (18) using irrelevant questions, and (19) giving superfluous information in questions.

Exercise 5.17

Have a look at the questions that follow in light of the guidelines provided in the previous section (including Table 5.5). List any problems that you see in questions 1 through 5.

Question	Strongly Agree	Agree	Disagree	Strongly Disagree
ex. *All teachers should use the same teaching method.*	4	3	2	1
1 Grammar is obviously a worthwhile component for any curriculum.	4	3	2	1
2 Pennsylvania Dutch teachers are often boring.	4	3	2	1
3 Funding for education (especially language teaching) is more important than funding for the military.	4	3	2	1
4 The one grammarian who has not influenced language teachers is not Chomsky.	4	3	2	1
5 The space race was clearly won by the Russians.	4	3	2	1

Exercise 5.18

Have another look at the *Language Teaching/Learning Beliefs Questionnaire* on page 121. Don't change your answers, but do look at the questionnaire in terms of the guidelines provided in Table 5.5. List any problems that you see in the *Questionnaire*. To start you off, we have noticed problems with questions 12, 15, 17, and 18. The problem with question 12 is that it is a double-barreled item that is asking two questions at the same time, one about meaning and the other about form. List the problems with the other three items as well as any other problems you notice elsewhere in that questionnaire.

Exercise 5.19

If you are working in a class situation, compare your answers to Exercise 5.18 with colleagues. Discuss your answers and decide how the problems you spotted in the questionnaire might affect the interpretation of the answers to those questions involved. Also decide how you would re-word the questions so the interpretation of the responses would be clearer.

Another issue we have not yet addressed is the number of options that you should use in Likert-scale items. Should an item contain 3, 4, 5, 6, or 7 points along the scale? That question can be answered in terms of how far you want answers spread out, or how fine you want the gradations to be along the scale. You will have to address those issues based on what you know about the context and your purposes for the Likert-scale items. Another issue is whether the number of points should be an even or an odd number.

Exercise 5.20

Consider the following two Likert scales and then answer the questions that follow:

A	Strongly Disagree	Disagree	Agree	Strongly Agree	
	1	2	3	4	

B	Strongly Disagree	Disagree	No Opinion	Agree	Strongly Agree
	1	2	3	4	5

1 What is the difference between the two scales?

2 What advantages might scale A have over B? And scale B have over A?

3   If you thought your respondents were likely to be overly timid in their responses (i.e. that many would stick to the middle road of 3: no opinion), which type of scale would you choose? Do you want to press respondents to state an opinion as in scale A? Or should you allow them to have no opinion, if that is their choice?

Interpreting descriptive research

According to Brown (1997b), surveys (including interviews and questionnaires) are most often used in language education for research and various kinds of curriculum development projects. For example, if the teachers and administrators in a language program are interested in what their students think about the curriculum, some form of curriculum analysis and research will probably prove interesting and useful to everybody involved. The two curriculum components that typically involve surveys are needs analysis and program evaluation. (For more on these curriculum components, see Brown 1989, 1995a, 1995b; and the final chapter of this book.)

Surveys can also be used for research not directly connected to curriculum. They can, for instance, be used to obtain information about language teachers' teaching/learning beliefs (such as the questionnaire you answered at the beginning of this chapter). Other surveys have been used to investigate topics such as the characteristics of graduate level language teacher-training programs (Ochsner 1980). One asked questions like 'How well did your MA program meet your professional goals?' Still other surveys may ask for opinions of members of a national professional organization (see Brown, Knowles, Murray, Neu, and Violand-Hainer 1992) with questions like 'What do you think is the biggest single problem facing ESL/EFL teachers today?' In fact, language surveys can be used to answer any research questions that require exploration, description, or explanation of peoples' characteristics, attitudes, views, and opinions.

In this section, we will focus on interpreting survey results as they are presented in tables. That does not mean that you should avoid examining the characteristics of the survey itself. However, because the focus of this chapter is on descriptive statistics, we will focus here on interpreting the numerical tables of frequencies, percentages, and descriptive statistics that are inevitably used to present survey results.

Consider the results shown in Table 5.6 (from the same TESOL survey project discussed in Chapter 1).

Table 5.6 Personal characteristics of groups sampled

Characteristic	All respondents
Gender (%):	
Female	71.0
Male	29.0
Nationality (%):	
U.S.	86.7
Other	13.3
First language (%):	
English	89.7
Latin language	5.0
Germanic	1.5
Sino-Tibetan	2.8
Other	1.0
Average age	44.2

(Adapted from Brown, Knowles, Murray, Neu, and Violand-Hainer 1992)

Notice in Table 5.6 that you can immediately tell that over two-thirds of the respondents were female, and the lion's share (or more appropriately, the lionesses' share) was made up of Americans and native speakers of English. In addition, their average age was 44.2 years old. Note also that using this table to present this numerical information about categories of people along only one dimension may not have been a very efficient use of space; it could have been more economically presented in prose. Tables of numbers become much more useful when multiple categories of numerical information are presented along two or more dimensions. For example, Table 5.7 shows a fuller version of Table 5.6 with categories of information listed down the left side and groups labeled across the top. In the survey involved, 1000 questionnaires were sent out to the general membership (GEN MEM) of TESOL, and 200 to members in each of four interest sections within the organization: Applied Linguistics (AL), Higher Education (HE), Research (RE), and Teacher Education (TE).

Notice in Table 5.7 that such a data display allows you to readily compare groups. For instance, you can immediately see that the Higher Education interest section has the highest percentage of females (with 82.3%) and that the Research and Teacher Education interest sections have the lowest (with 62.5% and 62.9%, respectively). You can also quickly spot the fact that the Higher Education interest section has the highest proportion of US citizens (98.4%) who are native speakers of English (96.8%), and so forth. To

Table 5.7* Personal characteristics of groups sampled

Characteristic	Interest sections					
	**GEN MEM	AL	HE	RE	TE	Total
Gender (%):						
Female	72.1	72.7	82.3	62.5	62.9	71.0
Male	27.9	27.3	17.7	37.5	37.1	29.0
Nationality (%):						
U.S.	89.6	72.7	98.4	79.0	84.1	86.7
Other	10.4	27.3	1.6	21.0	15.9	13.3
First language (%):						
English	89.7	83.3	96.8	90.1	88.9	89.7
Latin language	5.8	4.5	1.6	3.7	6.3	5.0
Germanic	0.9	4.5	1.6	2.5	0.0	1.5
Sino-Tibetan	2.7	6.1	0.0	2.5	3.2	2.8
Other	0.6	1.5	0.0	1.2	1.6	1.0
Average age	44.7	41.9	45.0	42.6	45.3	44.2

* Note that this is only one of the 10 tables presented in the original document.
** Abbreviations are as follows: GEN MEM = General Membership; AL = Applied Linguistics Interest Section (IS); HE = Higher Education IS; RE = Research IS; TE = Teacher Education IS

(Adapted from Brown, Knowles, Murray, Neu, and Violand-Hainer 1992)

provide the same information in prose would be very cumbersome indeed. Tables have a clear advantage when it comes to the presentation of multiple categories of numerical information along two or more dimensions.

Notice also that all of the information provided in Table 5.7 is in percentages, except for the last row, which shows ages on a different scale. In contrast, Table 5.8 (taken from Bailey and Brown 1996) shows several types of information including means, standard deviations, and frequencies. Bailey and Brown surveyed language-testing teachers from around the world with respect to the amount of coverage they give some main topics that are typical of such courses. Table 5.8 reports their responses to Likert scale questions (on a 0–5 scale with 0 being 'none). For example, on average, these language testers rated 'Item Writing' as a 3.24, which is fairly high compared to the other topics. However, the standard deviation of 1.46 also indicates that the responses to that item were a bit more varied, or spread out, than those for the other topics. The frequencies to the right also show you exactly what percentage of the language testing teachers selected each of the possible options. Thus 2.4% do not cover 'Item Writing' at all, while 14.3% give this topic some coverage, 26.2% give it extensive coverage, and so on. Clearly, the way information is presented in Table 5.8 is a good way to present Likert scale information because it provides a good estimate of central tendency (the mean) and dispersion (the standard deviation) as well as a clear picture of the actual percentages for each of the points along the Likert scale.

Table 5.8* General topics covered in language testing courses

| | Likert | | Percent negative responses | Percent positive responses | | | | |
| | | | | Some | | Moderate | | Extensive |
Topic	Mean	StdDev	0	1	2	3	4	5
Item Writing	3.24	1.46	2.4	14.3	13.1	29.8	20.2	26.2
Test Administration	2.06	1.34	15.7	20.5	22.9	26.5	12.0	2.4
Test Scoring	2.42	1.32	6.0	21.7	24.1	26.5	15.7	6.0
Test Score Interp.	3.10	1.26	1.2	10.7	21.4	23.8	29.8	13.1
Test Revision	2.45	1.42	8.5	20.7	22.0	22.0	19.5	7.3
Test Critiquing	3.38	1.35	4.8	4.8	11.9	28.6	26.2	23.8
Test Taking	1.89	1.28	9.8	36.6	25.6	14.6	9.8	3.7

* Note that this is only one of six tables in the original paper.

(Adapted from Bailey and Brown 1996)

Exercise 5.21

Look again at Table 5.8. Then answer the following questions:

1   Which topics get the lowest and highest average Likert scale ratings?

2   Which topic has the most agreement, that is, the least variation, in answers?

3   Which topic has the highest percentage of negative responses?

4   What percentage of the language testers give extensive coverage to Test Administration and Test Taking?

5   Which single topic seems to be the most popular among these language testers? How do you know that?

Significance of descriptive research on teacher beliefs

Ample evidence supports the notion that human beliefs are powerful. Beliefs cause couples to wed and soldiers to fight. Beliefs sicken and heal. Norman Cousins, in his book *Healing and Belief,* summarizes medical data showing that the efficacy of medicines and medical treatment generally is 25% due to the drug or treatment sourced and 75% the result of patient belief in the drug or treatment (Cousins 1989). His review of the literature and his own personal experience with healing led him on a 10-year quest to find evidence that positive beliefs are actually biochemical factors which combat disease. It is tempting to wonder if something like this isn't going on in teaching and learning, as well. Teaching, like medical practice, seems to have two components —a mechanical component and a mental component.

Richards identifies 'two different kinds of knowledge [that] influence teachers' understanding and practice of teaching. One relates to subject matter and curricular issues, and to how the content of a lesson can be presented in an effective and coherent way. This is the aspect of teaching that has to do with curricular goals, lesson plans, instructional activities, materials, tasks, and teaching techniques. The other kind of knowledge relates to teachers' implicit theories of teaching—that is, their personal and subjective philosophies and their understanding of what constitutes good teaching' (Richards 1998: 51).

Certainly, the notion of the power of belief in teaching and learning is itself not new. The prominent educational philosopher John Dewey noted that beliefs are the best indicators of the decisions that people make throughout their lives (Dewey 1933). While it has taken some time to formalize this assumption, a number of researchers are currently exploring the issue. These recent studies of teaching have taken more of an insider's view—a teacher's eye view—of teaching rather than (or in addition to) an outside observer's view of teaching. The insider's view includes the knowledge systems, beliefs, attitudes, values, and experiences of individual teachers, which shape teaching on a day-to-day and even moment-to-moment basis.

We have used the cover term 'beliefs' to refer to these various kinds of internal teacher perspectives. There are several assumptions implicit in this approach:

1 It is possible to get a sense of what terms like knowledge systems, beliefs, attitudes, values, and experience mean and how they are different or similar.
2 It is possible to assess these beliefs and belief systems in individual teachers.
3 Teaching behaviors can be observed (perhaps by the teachers themselves) and matches and mismatches between beliefs and behaviors can be noted.

4 Such noticing is likely to produce a change in teaching beliefs or behaviors, or both.

5 Teachers whose beliefs and teaching behaviors are in accord will be well-matched, will be more effective teachers, and will have more successful students than those teachers for whom beliefs and behaviors are in conflict.

It seems fair to say that the research is still at an early stage in evaluating these assumptions. As participants in this study of teacher beliefs, you have been part of this early stage.

The question of teacher beliefs is obviously a complex one. A recent overview acknowledges this complexity in its title: 'Teachers' beliefs and educational research: Cleaning up a messy construct' (Pajares 1992). Pajares notes that 'the difficulty in studying teachers' beliefs has been caused by definitional problems, poor conceptualizations, and differing understandings of beliefs and belief structures' (Pajares 1992: 307). In language teaching research, one approach to clearing up some of the 'messiness' has been to sub-classify different areas of language teachers' beliefs. Williams and Burden (1997) discuss language teacher beliefs about learning, about learners, and about themselves. Nespor (1987: 315) states that 'relatively little attention has been accorded to the structures and functions of teachers' beliefs about their roles, their students, the subject matter areas they teach, and the schools they work in'. And Richards notes that 'Teachers' belief systems are stable sources of reference, are built up gradually over time, and relate to such dimensions of teaching as the teachers' theory of language, the nature of language teaching, the role of the teacher, effective teaching practices, and teacher-student relations' (Richards 1998: 51–52).

Let us consider a few of these and involve you briefly in some of their methods of inquiry. We provide below an outline of some of the alternative conceptualizations of several areas of teacher belief systems as they have been reported in the applied linguistics and general education literature.

A Teacher Beliefs About Learning (Gow and Kember 1993)
   Learning can be alternatively conceptualized as:

1 a quantitative increase in knowledge
2 material committed to memory
3 the acquisition of material which can be retained and used in practice
4 the abstraction of meaning
5 a process aimed at understanding of reality
6 some form of personal change

B   Teacher Beliefs about Learners (Meighan and Meighan 1990)
     Learners may be alternatively thought of metaphorically as:

1   resisters
2   receptacles
3   raw material
4   clients
5   partners
6   individual explorers
7   democratic explorers

C   Teacher Beliefs about Teaching (Weinstein 1989)
     Good teachers are alternatively thought to have as key characteristics:

1   patience
2   high IQ
3   warmth
4   creativity
5   ability to be humorous
6   commitment to teaching
7   good grades in college
8   ability to relate to different kinds of people
9   organizational skills
10   outgoingness

Exercise 5.22

Now consider your own beliefs about these elements in the world of language teaching.

1   Pick one of these conceptualizations of key categories of teacher beliefs from the sets A–C above.

2   Rank-order (from most preferred to least preferred) the elements in the list you have chosen. List all elements. If an element is one you don't fully understand or are completely negative about, put that element at the end of your list.

3   Compare your listing with another participant who has chosen the same category as you did. Discuss why you think your ranks were similar or different.

If you are working on your own, you might rank order the elements in list C and compare this with the rating of how the participants in Weinstein's study (C. Teacher Beliefs about Teaching) rated importance of these elements. The Weinstein participants' rank of critical characteristics of good teachers was as follows (most important to least important): Commitment to teaching, Patience,

Creativity, Ability to relate to different kinds of people, Organizational skills, Warmth, Outgoingness, Ability to be humorous, Good grades in college, High IQ.

Exercise 5.23

Look at your answers to Exercise 5.22 and write answers to the following questions:

1   Why did you choose the category you chose?

2   What does your selection say (if anything) about which aspects of language teaching you believe are most central?

3   Which are most critical for you as a language teacher?

In sum, it appears that teaching is heavily influenced by the belief systems of its practitioners. But why are teachers so influenced by their belief systems rather than by training, texts, or methods? Nespor (1987) suggests that belief systems come into play in 'dealing with ill-structured and entangled domains'. He considers teaching to be such a domain. The personalities of individual classes, drawn from the same population, vary widely year-to-year and even day-to-day. National, community, and school demands on teaching time are unpredictable, frequently changing and often at odds with each other. Teachers themselves are influenced by mood, season, and their own sense of immediate priorities. For these and other reasons, teaching is often necessarily experienced as an 'ill-structured and entangled domain'. When invariant procedures meet with highly variable responses, beliefs kick in to explain the phenomenon or to re-structure the procedures. For language teachers especially, the current emphasis on task-based language teaching and second language acquisition research has a particular consequence with respect to belief systems. A number of authors have noted that 'beliefs perform the function of "framing" or defining the task at hand' (Nespor 1987: 322). That is, belief systems often determine how language-learning tasks are chosen, modified, sequenced, and contextualized by teachers and researchers alike.

Reflecting on descriptive research

In this chapter, you have experienced descriptive statistics research in terms of the following steps: (a) compiling data, (b) analyzing the results with descriptive statistics, (c) reporting the results, (d) designing your own descriptive research, and (e) interpreting a descriptive study.

Exercise 5.24

Look at the steps in the previous paragraph (and back through the chapter if necessary) and answer the following questions:

1 Which of those steps do you think is the most difficult part of doing such research in terms of the amount of work involved?

2 Which do you think is the most difficult in terms of intellectual challenge?

3 Which do you think is the most important in terms of understanding the results?

4 Which do you think taught you the most?

5 Which do you think was the most interesting?

The *Language Teaching/Learning Beliefs Questionnaire* contains a number of key belief systems mostly grounded on the following contrasts:

1 Skill learning for product or process?
2 L1 learning like L2 learning?
3 Vocabulary or structure primary?
4 Production or reception primary?
5 Correctness or communication primary?
6 Language theory or learning theory based?
7 Universal method or specific method?
8 Fluency or accuracy?
9 Relaxation or pressure best for language learning?
10 Grammar teaching: explicit or implicit?
11 Skills integrated or separated?
12 Errors useful or harmful?

Exercise 5.25

Read through the above list of contrasts and answer the following questions:

1 Can you match the contrasts with particular survey items?

2 Are there other issues that you feel are of equal importance but are not found in the survey?

3 Are there survey statements that do not appear to be reflected in the above contrasts?

4 Have your views on language teaching changed since you started this chapter? If so, how?

Summary

In this chapter, we introduced descriptive statistical research used in survey analysis and, with that introduction, we began our discussions of quantitative research methods. You experienced exercises that helped you think about various teaching methods and how you and your students relate to them, and then you became a participant in a questionnaire study by answering the *Language Teaching/Learning Beliefs Questionnaire*. After compiling the data for your whole class in a single table, you calculated frequencies and percentages, made graphical displays of data, and analyzed central tendency (including the mean, mode, and median) and dispersion (including low-high, range, and standard deviation statistics). You then reported descriptive research results by comparing the results of the responses of your class to the *Language Teaching/ Learning Beliefs Questionnaire* with those of a group of teachers in Turin, Italy. After considering what surveys are (including interviews and questionnaires) and how to write good survey items, you critically examined some sample tables taken from a survey of ESL/EFL teachers. You then examined the central role that beliefs play in how teachers teach and why they do it the way they do. Finally, you examined your own views of language teaching, reviewed the various descriptive statistics covered in the chapter, and thought about the key belief systems involved in the *Language Teaching/Learning Beliefs Questionnaire*.

6 CORRELATIONAL RESEARCH: LANGUAGE LEARNING/TEACHING ATTITUDES

Introducing correlational research

Native speakers of English who are learning Czech, Finnish, Spanish, or Polish are delighted to discover that the pronunciation of a word in these languages can be predicted with a high degree of accuracy by its spelling. Unfortunately, in English the correlation between spelling and pronunciation is not as close.
The American Heritage Book of English Usage: A practical and authoritative guide to contemporary English, 1996

The most merciful thing in the world ... is the inability of the human mind to correlate all its contents.
H. P. LOVECRAFT, 1890–1937
American author of horror stories

In our daily lives, all of us think about how things fit together, how things are related, or in more technical terms, how they are correlated. Questions like the following come up every day:

1 Are big kids really faster runners?
2 Do blondes really have more fun?
3 Do students who get to school first in the morning get higher grades?
4 Do young males really drive faster than older males?

In each case, we could gather information in the form of numbers and examine the degree to which those numbers correlate. In the case of the four questions above, we could:

1 Study the correlation of students' heights to their times in the 100-meter dash (perhaps for a group of fifth and sixth graders).
2 Examine the degree to which blondeness (as rated by a panel of experts) correlates with the amount of fun the participants report having in life , as measured by a self-report questionnaire in which the respondents rate in a

variety of ways the amount of fun they have on average. (We could also do a before-and-after survey of people who dye their hair blonde.)

3 Investigate the relationship between the average number of minutes a certain group of high school students arrive early (or late) to school and compare their averages over a semester to their grade point averages (on a scale of 0 to 4).

4 Explore the relationship between the number of speeding tickets received by males in a particular year and the age of the drivers who got them.

Similarly, in formal research, one purpose is often to explore the degree to which two sets of numbers are related to each other in one way or another. Let's say you have developed a test you call the *New English Placement Examination* (NEPE) with the purpose of assigning students into the different levels of study in your ESL program. One interesting research question about the NEPE might be whether students' scores on the test are related to their scores on the *Michigan Test of English Language Proficiency* (MTELP). To investigate that question you might use the NEPE for placing students, then administer the MTELP one week later. To find out how much relationship there is between these two sets of scores, you could just line up the students' scores on the NEPE next to their MTELP scores as shown in Table 6.1.

Table 6.1 Example data comparing two sets of scores for a group of ESL students (www)

Name	**NEPE**	**MTELP**
Fahtima	100	98
Jose	94	92
Maria	86	89
Jaime	89	86
Abdullah	78	75
Noriko	76	79
Hans	64	69
Tatania	61	54
Jürgen	55	51

Photocopiable © Oxford University Press

Clearly, just by examining the scores in Table 6.1, you can see that Fahtima and Jose have the highest scores on both tests and Tatania and Jürgen have the lowest. You can also see that the other students line up pretty much in the same order on both tests, but not in exactly the same order. In other words, you can see that the scores are related to some degree, but it is difficult to say exactly how much they are related. To get more precision, you will need to find out the CORRELATION, or degree of relationship, between the two sets of scores. This type of research is generally known as 'correlational research' (which we will define later).

Experiencing correlational research

In this chapter, we will focus on comparing the attitudes among different groups of people (for example, among students and teachers, different groups of students, etc.) toward various types of teaching/learning activities.

Exercise 6.1

(Warm-up)

Consider the following ten language classroom activities:

    A grammar lecture

    B group debates

    C group project work

    D minimal pair drills

    E pair work on tasks

    F peer feedback on an essay

    G student presentations

    H translation of a paragraph

    I   writing an in-class essay

    J   written grammar exercises

Now make a list of numbers from 1 to 10 in a column. Then, list the letters of the ten activities above in the spaces to the right of the numbers arranged from the one you consider the most useful for learning (1) to least useful (10). When you are finished with your list, form pairs with another student and copy their preferred activities in a column to the right of your own. If you are working alone, you might try first ranking the activities as you think students would view them, then rank them a second time in terms of your own personal preferences.

What percentage of your preferences had the same rank as your partner's? To calculate this percentage, you need to examine the number of activities you ranked the same (i.e. agreed on), then count up the number of such agreements, divide that number by the total number of activities, ten in this case, and move the decimal point two places to the right (for example, if you agreed on two of the ten activities, the percentage would be $2/10 = .20$, which would be 20%). In this exercise, you get a sense of the kind of questions that correlational analyses deal with: How much do two sets of data go together? However, as you will see in the next warm-up exercise, the types of data we are interested in are numbers, not just lists of preferences upon which we can agree or disagree.

Exercise 6.2

In this exercise, you and your partner should think about your two lists and, using your experience as language teachers, together come up with a third list of seven activities that you agree are useful. Write them down.

Now, without looking at each other's work, each of you should rank those preferences from one to seven, that is, from your favorite (1) to your least favorite (7), as in the previous exercise. When you are finished ranking the activities, copy your partner's rankings just to the right of your own. How much do the rankings go together? Eye-balling them, you might be able to say things like they go together *a little*, or *moderately*, or *a fair amount*, or *a lot*. Next, once again calculate the percentage of agreement between your two sets of ranks, and write the result down. Again this percentage of agreement gives you some idea of how much the two sets of ranks are similar.

There are more precise numerical ways to estimate how much two sets of rankings go together than the ones used in the previous exercise. For the moment, however, just put your rankings aside. Keep them handy, though, because we will come back to this exercise later in this chapter.

We will now look at another study, a questionnaire-based survey adapted from Willing's (1988) research into students' attitudes towards various learning styles. Our adaptation was designed to gather teachers' attitudes towards parallel teaching activities.

Exercise 6.3

Respond to the *Language Teaching Activity Preference Survey* opposite. Consider each statement carefully and circle the option on the right (*no, a little, good,* or *best*) that most accurately describes how much you like to use each activity in your language teaching.

Language Teaching Activity Preference Survey (based on Willing 1988: 106–107)

1	In the language class I teach, I like students to learn by reading.	*no*	*a little*	*good*	*best*
2	In class, I like to use cassettes for listening practice.	*no*	*a little*	*good*	*best*
3	In class, I like to use games.	*no*	*a little*	*good*	*best*
4	In class, I like to have students practice conversation.	*no*	*a little*	*good*	*best*
5	In class, I like to use pictures, films, video.	*no*	*a little*	*good*	*best*
6	I think students should write everything in their notebook.	*no*	*a little*	*good*	*best*
7	Students should each have their own textbook.	*no*	*a little*	*good*	*best*
8	As a teacher, I like to explain everything to the students.	*no*	*a little*	*good*	*best*
9	I like to give the students problems to work on.	*no*	*a little*	*good*	*best*
10	I like to help students talk about their interests.	*no*	*a little*	*good*	*best*
11	I like to correct all the students' errors.	*no*	*a little*	*good*	*best*
12	I like to let the students find their own mistakes.	*no*	*a little*	*good*	*best*
13	I like students to study English by themselves (alone).	*no*	*a little*	*good*	*best*
14	I like students to learn by talking in pairs.	*no*	*a little*	*good*	*best*
15	I like students to learn in small groups.	*no*	*a little*	*good*	*best*
16	I like students to learn with the whole class.	*no*	*a little*	*good*	*best*
17	I like to take the students out as a class to practice English.	*no*	*a little*	*good*	*best*
18	I like to teach grammar.	*no*	*a little*	*good*	*best*
19	I like to teach many new words.	*no*	*a little*	*good*	*best*
20	I like to teach the sounds and pronunciation of English.	*no*	*a little*	*good*	*best*
21	I like to teach English words through students seeing them.	*no*	*a little*	*good*	*best*
22	I like to teach English words through students hearing them.	*no*	*a little*	*good*	*best*
23	I like to teach English words through students doing something.	*no*	*a little*	*good*	*best*
24	At home, students should learn by reading newspapers, etc.	*no*	*a little*	*good*	*best*
25	At home, students should learn by watching TV in English.	*no*	*a little*	*good*	*best*
26	At home, students should learn by using cassettes.	*no*	*a little*	*good*	*best*
27	At home, students should learn by studying English books.	*no*	*a little*	*good*	*best*
28	I like students to learn by talking to friends in English.	*no*	*a little*	*good*	*best*
29	I like students to learn by watching and listening to native speakers.	*no*	*a little*	*good*	*best*
30	I like students to learn by using English in shops and daily life.	*no*	*a little*	*good*	*best*

Compiling correlational data

Exercise 6.4

Now as a class, compile the data for the *Language Teaching Activity Preference Survey* you did in Exercise 6.3 in whatever way works best for you. You might want to code the data in the format shown in Table 6.2 using the following values as shown in the example data in Table 6.3. Once again, if you are working alone, you may want to add your data to the example data provided in Table 6.3 and work with those data in doing the exercises that follow.

> Code *no*   as *0*
> Code *a little* as *1*
> Code *good*   as *2*
> Code *best*   as *3*

Exercise 6.5

(Calculator needed.)

Now that you have compiled your numerical data in clear columns and rows, the question is: How do we make sense of all those numbers? The first thing you will want to do for almost any statistical study is to calculate the basic descriptive statistics and look at the results. Do so following these steps:

1   Using the data that you compiled in Table 6.2, calculate the number (*N*) of people who responded to each item, the mean (*M*) for each item, the standard deviation (*SD*), the *number* who selected 1, 2, 3, or 4 and then the *percentage* who selected 1, 2, 3, or 4. (You will probably want to divide up the calculations among the members of the class. It is best to have two students calculate the statistics for each item in order to minimize mathematical errors.)

2   Put the results of these calculations into Table 6.4. You may notice that Table 6.4 is very similar to Table 5.3 on page 138 in the previous chapter. If you have any questions about how to calculate these statistics or where to put them in the table, please go back to the previous chapter and review the text dealing with Table 5.3.

Table 6.2 Form for compiling data for classroom mini-study (www)

Student Name	1	2	3	4	5	6	7	8	9	10	11	12	13	14	15	16	17	18	19	20	21	22	23	24	25	26	27	28	29	30
Jill Example	*1*	*2*	*3*	*0*	*1*	*2*	*3*	*0*	*1*	*2*	*3*	*0*	*1*	*2*	*3*	*0*	*1*	*2*	*3*	*0*	*1*	*2*	*3*	*0*	*1*	*2*	*3*	*0*	*1*	*2*

Table 6.3 *Example data from the University of Hawaii group (www)*

Student name	1	2	3	4	5	6	7	8	9	10	11	12	13	14	15	16	17	18	19	20	21	22	23	24	25	26	27	28	29	30
A	2	1	2	3	2	0	3	2	2	2	1	1	2	2	2	1	1	3	1	1	2	2	2	1	1	1	1	1	1	1
B	2	2	2	3	2	0	1	0	2	3	0	3	1	3	3	2	1	2	2	1	0	2	3	2	3	0	1	3	2	3
C	2	3	2	3	3	2	3	2	3	3	3	2	2	2	3	2	2	2	2	2	2	2	3	2	2	2	3	3	3	3
D	3	3	3	3	3	1	2	0	3	3	1	3	0	2	3	1	2	2	1	1	2	2	3	3	3	2	3	3	2	3
E	3	2	2	2	2	1	2	0	2	2	0	2	1	2	3	1	1	1	1	1	1	2	2	2	1	1	1	2	2	3
F	2	2	1	2	2	0	2	1	2	3	0	2	1	2	2	2	1	2	2	2	2	2	1	2	2	2	2	2	2	2
G	2	2	2	2	1	0	1	0	1	1	0	1	1	2	2	2	2	1	1	1	2	2	2	1	2	2	2	2	2	2
H	2	3	2	2	3	1	3	1	3	3	1	3	2	2	2	1	1	2	2	3	2	2	3	2	3	2	3	3	3	3
I	2	2	2	3	3	1	3	2	2	3	1	3	0	3	3	2	1	1	2	1	3	3	3	3	3	2	2	3	3	3
J	2	2	2	3	3	1	2	1	2	3	2	3	2	3	2	2	2	2	2	1	2	2	3	2	2	2	2	2	2	2
K	2	2	2	2	2	1	2	2	2	2	2	2	2	2	2	2	2	2	2	2	2	2	2	2	2	2	2	2	2	2

Photocopiable © Oxford University Press

Table 6.4 Form for compiling results of the classroom mini-study (www)

Question	N	M	SD	no 1	a little 2	good 3	best 4	Percent no 1	Percent a little 2	Percent good 3	Percent best 4
	1										
	2										
	3										
	4										
	5										
	6										
	7										
	8										
	9										
	10										
	11										
	12										
	13										
	14										
	15										
	16										
	17										
	18										
	19										
	20										
	21										
	22										
	23										
	24										
	25										
	26										
	27										
	28										
	29										
	30										

Exercise 6.6

Now that you have calculated descriptive statistics and put them in Table 6.4, discuss your results as a class by addressing the following questions:

1   Looking at the means, which of the activities did you (as a class) like best? Which did you like the least?

2   Looking at the standard deviations, which did you (as a class) agree on the most? Which did you disagree on the most?

All of the descriptive statistics that you have calculated and analyzed so far in this chapter have just been preliminary, but they were also necessary spadework for the correlational analyses that you will do later. Later in the chapter, we will be returning to these data to analyze the correlation between your class' results and those of the students in the Willing (1988) study.

Analyzing correlational data

How do we make sense of all those numbers? One way we can do so is to do CORRELATIONAL RESEARCH. This involves gathering and compiling data and then calculating a statistic called a CORRELATION COEFFICIENT. Correlation coefficients indicate the degree of relationship between two sets of numbers represented as the ratio of go-togetherness to total score variation. Thus correlation coefficients can range from 0.00 (if the ratio is zero, indicating absolutely no relationship) to 1.00 (if the ratio is perfect, indicating that there is a 100% relationship and that both sets of numbers are going in the same direction). For instance, the following numbers, representing, say the number of words spelled correctly in a spelling test of ten items, are perfectly correlated at 1.00 (because they are in a perfect relationship and going in the same direction):

Student	Set A	Set B
Marie	9	8
José	8	7
Jeanne	7	6
Hachiko	6	5
Raphael	5	4
Yuka	4	3
Hossein	3	2
Tamara	2	1
Hans	1	0

Naturally, all the numbers between 0.00 and 1.00 are also possible and, as they vary, they indicate differing degrees of relationship. So a correlation of .97 would be considered very high, and one of .09 would be very low, and others of .15, .27, .51, .67, .72, and .83 would be at different points in between.

Correlation coefficients can also range from 0.00 (again, for no relationship at all) to −1.00 (for a perfect relationship with the two sets of numbers changing together but in opposite directions). For instance, the following numbers, from, say, a different spelling test, would be perfectly correlated at −1.00:

Student	Set A	Set B
Marie	9	1
José	8	2
Jeanne	7	3
Hachiko	6	4
Raphael	5	5
Yuka	4	6
Hossein	3	7
Tamara	2	8
Hans	1	9

Naturally, all the coefficients between 0.00 and −1.00 are also possible and, as they vary, they indicate differing degrees of relationship. So a correlation of −.97 would be considered very high in a negative direction, and one of −.08 would be very low in a negative direction, and others of −.17, −.25, −.57, −.63, −.75, and −.84 would be at different points in between.

At this point, the important things to remember about correlation coefficients are that (a) the size of the number indicates the degree of relationship relative to a low of 0.00 and a high of 1.00 and (b) the sign (+ or −) indicates the direction of the relationship in a positive (i.e. same) direction or negative (i.e. opposite) direction.

Now that you understand how correlation coefficients work in general, let's look at how correlational research is done. Typically, three basic steps are followed in doing a correlational analysis:

(a) figure out what kind of scales you are dealing with,
(b) decide what kind of correlation coefficient to calculate, and
(c) calculate the appropriate correlation coefficient.

We will now consider each of these steps in more detail.

Step 1: Figuring out the type of scale

The first step in correlational analysis is to figure out what kinds of scale you are dealing with. Three kinds of scale will concern us in language studies: rank-ordered, categorical, and continuous scales. We will briefly define each of these three scales and give an example or two for each.

RANK-ORDERED SCALES are any scales that arrange or sort the values according to order. If the scale can be expressed as ordinal numbers (1st, 2nd, 3rd, etc.) it is a rank-ordered scale. Rank-ordered scales are also called ORDINAL SCALES because they order things. The word 'order' is a key word that may help you remember the meaning of 'rank-ordered scales'. In the real world, ordering a group of people from best to worst (1st, 2nd, 3rd, etc.) by height, age, or speed in the 100-meter dash, creates an ordinal scale. In language teaching, when a teacher orders the test scores of fifteen students from the highest score (or 1st) to the lowest (15th) with everyone else ordered in between, this is a rank-ordered scale. Or, when researchers talk about the order of morpheme acquisition with one morpheme being learned first, another learned second, etc., those morphemes are also on a rank-ordered scale. (We looked at this in Chapter 2, and for more examples, see Anderson 1976, Brown 1983, Krashen 1977, Pienemann 1985.) The key to understanding rank-ordered scales is that only the order of the points in the scale is important, not the distance between those points. If you are second in line at the movies, standing close behind the person who is first does not make you any closer to the front of the line. You are still second no matter how close or far you stand from that first person.

If we use *number values* instead of *order* to organize data, the scale can be called a CONTINUOUS SCALE. Continuous scales are any scales that show the order of the values, but also show the distances between the values. If five students have continuous scale test scores of 100, 99, 81, 50, and 11, they are obviously in a particular order, but you can also readily see the distances between them: the distance between the 100 and 99 is a very small one point, the distance between 99 and 81 is a much bigger 18 points, the distance between 81 and 50 is an even bigger 31 points, etc. Ages, weights, language test scores, and years of language study are other examples of continuous scales.

CATEGORICAL SCALES are any scales that organize the data into categories or groups. Categorical scales are also referred to as NOMINAL SCALES because they 'name' categories, which is what this type of scale does. Your name is either Jezabel or it is not. Your name cannot be *sort of* Jezabel. In other words, in a categorical scale, each data point will clearly belong in or not belong in each category. Gender (as in male/female) is a binary, or two-category, categorical variable.

Examples of categorical variables with more than two groups would be nationality (as in German, Japanese, Indonesian, and Egyptian), language background (Chinese, Spanish, Arabic, Japanese, and French), or age expressed as categories (child 0–12, adolescent 13–19, young adult 20–25, adult 26–39, middle aged 40–55, senior citizen 56 or above.)

Table 6.5 shows an example of a continuous scale that has been turned into a rank-ordered scale, which in turn has been turned into a categorical scale. Notice that we used the continuous scale from Table 6.1 and put it in the second column labeled *NEPE*. We turned those continuous scale scores into ranks in the third column labeled *Ranks*. Then, we turned the ranks into a categorical variable that we labeled *Groups* in the fourth column (including High, Middle, and Low Groups).

Table 6.5 Examples of continuous, rank-ordered, and categorical scales (www)

Name	NEPE	Ranks	Groups
Fahtima	100	1	High
Jose	94	2	High
Maria	89	3	High
Jaime	86	4	Middle
Abdullah	78	5	Middle
Noriko	76	6	Middle
Hans	64	7	Low
Tatania	61	8	Low
Jürgen	55	9	Low

Photocopiable © Oxford University Press

As you saw in Table 6.5, the three types of scale discussed here are somewhat interchangeable. However, they are only interchangeable in one direction, from continuous to rank-ordered or categorical and from rank-ordered to categorical. In other words, a categorical scale cannot be turned into a rank-ordered or continuous scale, and a rank-ordered scale cannot be turned into a continuous scale. The message is that, if you want continuous data, you had better gather them that way to start with. Whereas you can always create rank-ordered or categorical scales at a later date if you have continuous scales to start with.

Step 2: Deciding on the appropriate correlation coefficient to calculate

The second step in correlational analysis is to figure out what type of correlation coefficient will be appropriate for the types of scales involved. We will discuss three different types of correlation coefficient. They differ primarily in terms of the types of scale they can analyze.

The Spearman (rho, or ρ) correlation coefficient can, for example, be used to analyze two sets of numbers if they are both rank-ordered scales, whereas the Pearson product-moment correlation coefficient (r) is appropriate if the two sets of numbers are continuous scales. The Phi (Φ) coefficient is appropriate if the two sets of numbers are categorical scales. Table 6.6 summarizes this information.

Table 6.6 Three types of correlation coefficients and the scales they can analyze

Type of correlation coefficient	What scales can it analyze?
Spearman (rho, or ρ)	Two sets of rank-ordered data
Pearson product-moment (r)	Two sets of continuous data
Phi (Φ)	Two sets of categorical data

Step 3: Calculating the correlation coefficient

The Spearman rank-order correlation coefficient The third step in correlational analysis is to calculate a correlation coefficient. Let's begin with the Spearman coefficient because it is conceptually the easiest to understand. The SPEARMAN RANK-ORDER CORRELATION COEFFICIENT is designed to estimate the degree of relationship between two sets of rank-ordered data. Since the 'Spearman rank-order correlation coefficient' is such a mouthful, it is often simply called SPEARMAN RHO, or symbolized by the Greek letter ρ. The equation for Spearman rho is as follows:

$$\rho = 1 - \frac{6\Sigma D^2}{N(N^2 - 1)}$$

where: ρ = Spearman rho correlation coefficient
D = the differences between the ranks
N = the number of cases

Note that, as in the previous chapter, the 'sum of' function is symbolized by the upper case Greek letter Σ. Here, too, you must square some of the values. The six in the equation is a constant that is needed to adjust the result to facilitate comparison with results attained by the Pearson r. (The Pearson r is an earlier—and therefore more prestigious—correlation coefficient. Spearman therefore has to adjust to Pearson, rather than the other way round.)

Let's look at an example: say some teenagers and their parents had seen the same ten movies. Would they like them equally well, or would the teenagers rank the movies differently from their parents? You could use a Spearman rank-order correlation coefficient to determine the degree to which the average rankings for teenagers and their parents were related.

Turning to a language teaching example, let's say two teachers had the same group of 11 students, and they wanted to know the degree to which they ranked the students in the same order in terms of overall performance in their courses as shown in Table 6.7.

Table 6.7 Two teachers' rankings of overall course performance for one group of 11 students (www)

Student	First teacher's rank	Second teacher's rank	Difference	D^2
Maria	1	4	-3	9
Juanita	2	3	-1	1
Toshi	3	1	2	4
Raul	4	2	2	4
Anna	5	5	0	0
Jaime	6	6	0	0
Hans	7	8	-1	1
Hachiko	8	9	-1	1
Tanya	9	7	2	4
Jacques	10	11	-1	1
Serge	11	10	1	1
			Total = 0	Total = 26

Photocopiable © Oxford University Press

To help them find the answer to their question, you would begin by lining up the students' names and each teacher's ranks as shown in the first three columns of Table 6.7. Then you would find the difference in ranks for each student by taking the first teacher's rank and subtracting the second teacher's rank, and putting that result in a column of its own (as shown in column 4 of Table 6.7). (Note that you could crosscheck your figures at this point by adding up the differences in the fourth column. That sum should turn out to be zero.) Next you would square each of the differences (D^2) and put the result in the fifth column. And then add up those squared values and put it at the bottom of the fifth column. (When + or − values are squared, all signs disappear.)

If you count up the number of students ($N = 11$ in this case) and check the total at the bottom right of Table 6.7 (in this case, $\sum D^2 = 26$), you will have all the information you need to calculate Spearman rho using the formula from above as follows:

$$\rho = 1 - \frac{6\Sigma D^2}{N(N^2-1)} = 1 - \frac{6 \times 26}{11(121-1)} = 1 - \frac{156}{1320} = 1 - .1181818 = .8818182 \approx .88$$

Given that the correlation coefficient can range up to 1.00, the result based on the ranks in Table 6.7 is high at about (notice that *about* is symbolized above as ≈) .88. In other words, the rankings of the first and second teachers are highly related.

Exercise 6.7

(Calculator needed.)

Now go back and look at the ranks you and your partner assigned to the various activities you listed in Exercise 6.2. Put those ranks in the spaces provided in Table 6.8. Then, using Table 6.8 and the explanation above, calculate Spearman rho for the ranks that you and your partner produced. (Note, N = 7.)

When you are finished calculating your Spearman rho, discuss what rho tells you about the degree to which you and your partner in Exercise 6.2 thought the activities were important (at least in terms of how you two ranked them).

Table 6.8 Activity preference ratings (you and your partner from Exercise 6.2) (www)

Activity preferences	Your ranking	Partner's ranking	Difference	D2
1				
2				
3				
4				
5				
6				
7				
			Total =	Total =

The Pearson product-moment correlation coefficient The PEARSON PRODUCT-MOMENT CORRELATION COEFFICIENT is the most commonly reported correlation coefficient. Often simply called the PEARSON *r*, or just *r*, it is designed to estimate the degree of relationship between two sets of continuous scale data. The *r* stands for regression coefficient, which is another name for the same statistic.

The equation for the Pearson *r* is as follows:

$$r = \frac{\sum(X - M_x)(Y - M_y)}{N S_x S_y}$$

where: X = the values for the X variable
Y = the values for the Y variable
M_X = the mean for the X variable
M_Y = the mean for the Y variable
S_X = the standard deviation for the X variable
S_Y = the standard deviation for the Y variable
N = the number of paired values for the X and Y variables (often the number of participants)

Note that, once again, the 'sum of' function is symbolized by the upper case Greek letter $\sum$.

As an example, Willing (1988: 116) presented one set of questionnaire results in two different ways: he gave the mean answers on each four-point Likert scale item as well as the 'percentage who marked this as "best"for each item'. You might legitimately ask how much these two different ways of presenting his questionnaire results might be related. To answer that question, you could investigate the degree of statistical correlation between the two sets of numbers. Since both sets can be considered continuous scales, the Pearson *r* would be the appropriate form of analysis. Notice that we present those data in Table 6.9 with the mean answers on each four-point Likert scale item given in the third column and the 'percentage who marked this as "best"' for each item given in column 6.

The steps involved in calculating the Pearson coefficient are as follows:

1 Subtract the mean (M_x) from each of the X scores and put the result of each calculation in the fourth column with the heading $X–M_X$.
2 Subtract the mean (M_y) from each of the Y scores and put the result of each calculation in the seventh column with the heading $Y–M_Y$.
3 Multiply each of the results in the fourth column of numbers ($X–M_x$) times the corresponding result in the seventh column ($Y–M_y$) for the same item and put the result in the eighth column with the heading $(X–M_X)(Y–M_Y)$.

Table 6.9 Example data for calculating the Pearson Product-Moment Correlation Coefficient (www)

1	2	3	4	5	6	7	8
Question	Likert scale means (X)	$-\ M_x$	$=\ X–M_x$	% who marked this *best* (Y)	$-\ M_y$	$=\ Y–M_y$	$(X–M_x)(Y–M_y)$
20	3.54	$-$ 2.96	= 0.58	62	$-$ 31.53	= 30.47	17.65
11	3.51	$-$ 2.96	= 0.55	61	$-$ 31.53	= 29.47	16.19
4	3.42	$-$ 2.96	= 0.46	55	$-$ 31.53	= 23.47	10.78
8	3.40	$-$ 2.96	= 0.44	54	$-$ 31.53	= 22.47	9.87
19	3.38	$-$ 2.96	= 0.42	47	$-$ 31.53	= 15.47	6.49
28	3.31	$-$ 2.96	= 0.35	48	$-$ 31.53	= 16.47	5.75
29	3.19	$-$ 2.96	= 0.23	39	$-$ 31.53	= 7.47	1.71
22	3.16	$-$ 2.96	= 0.20	37	$-$ 31.53	= 5.47	1.09
10	3.15	$-$ 2.96	= 0.19	35	$-$ 31.53	= 3.47	0.66
21	3.16	$-$ 2.96	= 0.20	38	$-$ 31.53	= 6.47	1.29
15	3.14	$-$ 2.96	= 0.18	35	$-$ 31.53	= 3.47	0.62
23	3.12	$-$ 2.96	= 0.16	36	$-$ 31.53	= 4.47	0.71
18	3.10	$-$ 2.96	= 0.14	39	$-$ 31.53	= 7.47	1.04
25	3.01	$-$ 2.96	= 0.05	26	$-$ 31.53	= $-$5.53	$-$0.27
7	3.00	$-$ 2.96	= 0.04	34	$-$ 31.53	= 2.47	0.10
30	2.96	$-$ 2.96	= 0.00	30	$-$ 31.53	= $-$1.53	0.00
9	2.92	$-$ 2.96	= $-$0.04	24	$-$ 31.53	= $-$7.53	0.31
17	2.91	$-$ 2.96	= $-$0.05	30	$-$ 31.53	= $-$1.53	0.08
27	2.87	$-$ 2.96	= $-$0.09	21	$-$ 31.53	= $-$10.53	0.96
1	2.84	$-$ 2.96	= $-$0.12	21	$-$ 31.53	= $-$10.53	1.27
2	2.77	$-$ 2.96	= $-$0.19	22	$-$ 31.53	= $-$9.53	1.82
6	2.77	$-$ 2.96	= $-$0.19	21	$-$ 31.53	= $-$10.53	2.01
12	2.76	$-$ 2.96	= $-$0.20	27	$-$ 31.53	= $-$4.53	0.91
24	2.73	$-$ 2.96	= $-$0.23	21	$-$ 31.53	= $-$10.53	2.43
5	2.72	$-$ 2.96	= $-$0.24	19	$-$ 31.53	= $-$12.53	3.02
16	2.68	$-$ 2.96	= $-$0.28	21	$-$ 31.53	= $-$10.53	2.96
26	2.63	$-$ 2.96	= $-$0.33	15	$-$ 31.53	= $-$16.53	5.47
14	2.63	$-$ 2.96	= $-$0.33	15	$-$ 31.53	= $-$16.53	5.47
3	2.35	$-$ 2.96	= $-$0.61	10	$-$ 31.53	= $-$21.53	13.15
13	1.69	$-$ 2.96	= $-$1.27	3	$-$ 31.53	= $-$28.53	36.26
Mean	2.96			31.53			
SD	0.37			14.53			Sum = 149.76

4 Add up all the results in the eighth column and put the result at the bottom of column eight next to the Sum =
5 Put that result into the numerator (above the line) of the equation in the spaces that follow and put the number of students and the standard deviations for each test in the denominator (below the line).
6 And finally, solve the equation to calculate the Pearson *r*.

$$r = \frac{\Sigma (X - M_x)(Y - M_y)}{N S_x S_y}$$

$$= \frac{149.76}{30(.37)(14.53)}$$

$$= \frac{149.76}{161.283} = .9285541 \approx .93$$

So the degree of correlation (as indicated by the Pearson *r*) between Willing's two different ways of presenting questionnaire results was .93 indicating that they are very similar (on this scale from .00 to 1.00) in the ways they order and represent the results on each item. Thus Willing was justified in using *% Who Marked This Best* as an important variable of focus in his study instead of the more general *Likert-Scale Means*, which might be considered more representative of the entire group, because the two ways of presenting the data are highly related and more-or-less equivalent.

For more on the interpretation of correlation coefficients, see the section below on **Interpreting correlational research** (pages 184–191).

Exercise 6.8

(Calculator needed.)

To calculate the Pearson *r*, let's use the example data from Table 6.1 again as they are shown in Table 6.10. Notice that the data in Table 6.10 are laid out with the means and standard deviations below each set of scores and the appropriate means next to each score for both the *NEPE* and the *MTELP*. Given this layout, you can easily follow the steps in the previous section and calculate all the information you need in order to apply the formula for the Pearson *r*. Using the formula given above, calculate the Pearson *r*. After you have finished, check your answer against the work shown in the Answer key (page 258).

Table 6.10 Data for Exercise 6.5 (taken from Table 6.1) (www)

Name	NEPE $(X) - M_X$	$= X-M_X$	MTELP $(Y) - M_Y$	$= Y-M_Y$	$(X-M_X)(Y-M_Y)$
Fahtima	100 – 78.11 =		98 – 77.00 =		
Jose	94 – 78.11 =		92 – 77.00 =		
Maria	86 – 78.11 =		89 – 77.00 =		
Jaime	89 – 78.11 =		86 – 77.00 =		
Abdullah	78 – 78.11 =		75 – 77.00 =		
Noriko	76 – 78.11 =		79 – 77.00 =		
Hans	64 – 78.11 =		69 – 77.00 =		
Tatania	61 – 78.11 =		54 – 77.00 =		
Jürgen	55 – 78.11 =		51 – 77.00 =		
Mean	78.11		77.00		$=\Sigma(X-M_X)(Y-M_y)$
SD	14.69		15.52		

Photocopiable © Oxford University Press

In previous exercises, you calculated the descriptive statistics for your class responses to each item on Willing's *Language Teaching Activity Preference Survey*. In the process, you calculated the percentage of your class members who selected each option (1, 2, 3, or 4) for each item. In Table 6.11, you will find the question number, Likert scale means, overall mean, and overall standard deviation already written in for all the students in Willing's study.

Exercise 6.9

(Calculator needed.)

Begin by filling in your class' means for each item in the column labeled *Likert Scale Means (Y) in Your Data*, then continue to calculate and fill in the necessary information for calculating the Pearson *r* for your data. (See Table 6.9 and the accompanying text for an example laid out in exactly the same way.)

Once you have calculated the Pearson *r* between your results and those reported for Willing's students, answer each of the following questions:

1   Did your class agree or disagree with Willing's students about the importance of the various language teaching activities?

2   How much did your ratings agree or disagree with the students' ratings?

3   How does the result you found in this exercise match your experience and how may it affect the language teaching activities you will select in the future?

Table 6.11 Example data for calculating the Pearson Product-Moment Correlation Coefficient (www)

Question	Likert Scale Means (X) in Willing Study	$- M_X$	$= X–M_X$	Likert Scale Means (Y) in Your Data	$-$	$M_y = Y–M_y$	$(X–M_X)(Y–M_y)$
1	2.84	$- 2.96$	$= -0.12$		$-$	$=$	
2	2.77	$- 2.96$	$= -0.19$		$-$	$=$	
3	2.35	$- 2.96$	$= -0.61$		$-$	$=$	
4	3.42	$- 2.96$	$= 0.46$		$-$	$=$	
5	2.72	$- 2.96$	$= -0.24$		$-$	$=$	
6	2.77	$- 2.96$	$= -0.19$		$-$	$=$	
7	3.00	$- 2.96$	$= 0.04$		$-$	$=$	
8	3.40	$- 2.96$	$= 0.44$		$-$	$=$	
9	2.92	$- 2.96$	$= -0.04$		$-$	$=$	
10	3.15	$- 2.96$	$= 0.19$		$-$	$=$	
11	3.51	$- 2.96$	$= 0.55$		$-$	$=$	
12	2.76	$- 2.96$	$= -0.20$		$-$	$=$	
13	1.69	$- 2.96$	$= -1.27$		$-$	$=$	
14	2.63	$- 2.96$	$= -0.33$		$-$	$=$	
15	3.14	$- 2.96$	$= 0.18$		$-$	$=$	
16	2.68	$- 2.96$	$= -0.28$		$-$	$=$	
17	2.91	$- 2.96$	$= -0.05$		$-$	$=$	
18	3.10	$- 2.96$	$= 0.14$		$-$	$=$	
19	3.38	$- 2.96$	$= 0.42$		$-$	$=$	
20	3.54	$- 2.96$	$= 0.58$		$-$	$=$	
21	3.16	$- 2.96$	$= 0.20$		$-$	$=$	
22	3.16	$- 2.96$	$= 0.20$		$-$	$=$	
23	3.12	$- 2.96$	$= 0.16$		$-$	$=$	
24	2.73	$- 2.96$	$= -0.23$		$-$	$=$	
25	3.01	$- 2.96$	$= 0.05$		$-$	$=$	
26	2.63	$- 2.96$	$= -0.33$		$-$	$=$	
27	2.87	$- 2.96$	$= -0.09$		$-$	$=$	
28	3.31	$- 2.96$	$= 0.35$		$-$	$=$	
29	3.19	$- 2.96$	$= 0.23$		$-$	$=$	
30	2.96	$- 2.96$	$= 0.00$		$-$	$=$	
Mean of $X =$	2.96			Mean of $Y =$			
SD of $X =$	0.37			SD of $Y =$		Sum $=$	

Calculating the phi coefficient

The PHI COEFFICIENT (Φ) is designed to estimate the degree of relationship between two categorical variables with two possibilities each. For example, let's say you want to know if there is a relationship between gender (female and male) and yes/no responses to the following statement:

I like to share things with other people. Y/N

The first step in calculating a phi coefficient is to arrange your data in a two-by-two table like this:

A	B
C	D

The equation for phi using the numbers in cells A, B, C, and D is as follows:

$$\Phi = \frac{BC - AD}{\sqrt{(A + B)(C + D)(A + C)(B + D)}}$$

We asked students in several classes of MA level ESL teachers in training at the University of Hawaii to respond to the item *I like to share things with other people. Y/N* and got the following results:

	Male	Female	
	A 2	B 14	Yes
	C 11	D 1	No

Putting those values in the equation for phi, you will get the following results:

$$\Phi = \frac{BC - AD}{\sqrt{(A+B)(C+D)(A+C)(B+D)}} = \frac{(14 \times 11) - (2 \times 1)}{\sqrt{(2+14)(11+1)(2+11)(14+1)}} = \frac{154 - 2}{\sqrt{(16)(12)(13)(15)}}$$

$$= \frac{152}{3\sqrt{7440}} \quad \frac{152}{= 193.49} = .7855703 \approx .79$$

This .79 shows a substantial, though not perfect, relationship in this group of graduate students between being male or female and answering yes or no to the question about sharing. This result appears to support the popular stereotypes that males do not like to share and females do, but it also shows that the relationship is not a perfect one, i.e. there are exceptions to the stereotype.

Exercise 6.10

(Calculator needed.)

Now let's say a group of Japanese teachers of English (in a small town in the north of Honshu) were asked to respond to the following two items:

1 I prefer to teach English using the grammar-translation method. Yes/No
2 I did my teacher training in _____. Japan/Other country

And, the results turned out as follows:

Training country

Other	Japan	
A 5	B 12	Yes
C 16	D 6	No

By looking at the contingency table above, you can see that there is some degree of relationship between country of training and whether or not the teacher prefers to use the grammar-translation method. Put those values into the following equation for phi and calculate the result:

$$\Phi = \frac{BC - AD}{\sqrt{(A+B)(C+D)(A+C)(B+D)}}$$

After you have done your calculations, you can check your answers in the Answer key (page 259).

Exercise 6.11

(Calculator needed.)

Next, divide your class roughly in half on the basis of years of teaching experience (or some other binary categorical variable like males/females if that works better). Put the following question to each group: should you teach speaking on the first day of students' language learning experience or should there be a period of listening only at the beginning? Use the cells in the diagram below to record the numbers of most-experienced and least-experienced teachers who think you should begin right away with speaking and those who think you should begin with a listening period:

	Begin class with	
Experience	Speaking	Listening
Teaching Most	A	B
Least	C	D

Now calculate phi for your data to find out the degree of relationship between teaching experience (most or least) and whether they think you should begin language teaching right away with speaking or with a listening period.

Designing your own correlational research

Earlier in this chapter, we defined 'correlation' as the degree of relationship between the two sets of scores. We also showed that such correlation coefficients can be either positive (if the numbers are related in the same direction) or negative (if they are related in opposite directions). In designing studies that use correlation coefficients, you must recognize two things: (a) the sign (i.e. positive or negative) and magnitude of a correlation coefficient are two different things, and (b) correlation coefficients only make sense if the assumptions underlying them are met.

Magnitude and sign of correlation coefficients

Positive correlation coefficients will sometimes make sense and at other times negative ones will. For example, even without calculating a correlation coefficient, you would expect some degree of correlation in any group of people between height and weight (i.e. the taller people are, the more they will probably weigh, and conversely, the shorter they are the less they are likely to weigh). Other similar examples might include relationships that you would expect between waist measurements and weight or between age and weight. In the realm of language teaching, you would probably expect some degree of relationship among your students between length of language study and proficiency in that language or between whether or not students have lived in the country where a language is spoken and proficiency in that language.

Negative correlations also occur in logical ways. For instance, because of various cultural factors, the number of children per family tends to be negatively related to the family income, i.e. as family incomes goes up, the number of children per family goes down and vice versa. Similarly, it would be reasonable to expect a negative relationship between worker efficiency ratings and number of hours worked, efficiency going down as workers spend more hours working and getting increasingly tired. (A personally more discouraging example was provided by some of our younger students who, observing us as older professors, suggested that there might be some negative correlation between age and ability to remember things.) In the realm of language teaching, you might expect a negative correlation between pronunciation test scores and the age at which students began studying the language (especially if some started as very young children). You might be surprised to find a negative correlation between the scores on a very detailed English grammar test and the number of years students have spent in the country where the language is spoken. Nevertheless one of the authors of this book found just such a correlation in Japan. His interpretation was that students still in Japan pay a great deal of attention to grammar and thus score well on a picky grammar test, while students who have actually acquired English in an English-speaking country haven't studied detailed grammar rules for years and so have trouble with them. Thus, in some cases, negative correlations are a natural consequence of the way some variables are counted and how they are related with other variables, while in other cases, negative correlations may present a surprise that you will have to try to interpret.

It is important to recognize that negative correlation coefficients are not lower than positive ones. The magnitude of the correlation, whether positive or negative, tells you the degree of relationship between the two sets of numbers, and the sign tells you the direction of the relationship. If you plan and understand your study properly, you should know well before you gather data which of your correlations are likely to be positive and which negative.

Assumptions underlying correlation coefficients

As Brown put it, '*Assumptions* are preconditions that are necessary for accurate application of a particular statistical test' (Brown 1992a: 639). Furthermore, as a researcher, you are responsible for planning and actually checking these assumptions before reporting the results of your statistical analyses. Thus ASSUMPTIONS are preconditions that must be checked in advance so you can accurately and responsibly apply a particular statistic.

Assumptions underlying the Pearson r

The assumptions underlying the Pearson *r* are as follows:

1 SCALES ASSUMPTION: both sets of numbers must be continuous scales.
2 INDEPENDENCE ASSUMPTION: the pairs of numbers within a data set must be independent of one another, i.e. each number in each pair must have been generated in ways which could not have influenced the generation of the other. (See below for examples.)
3 NORMALITY ASSUMPTION: both distributions must be normal, as defined in Chapter 5 (page 136).
4 LINEARITY ASSUMPTION: The two sets of numbers, if plotted on a SCATTERPLOT or graph, should be more or less in a line.

If you find all four assumptions are met, you can reasonably interpret the resulting correlation coefficient as the degree to which the two sets of numbers are associated. If you find that your data violate one or more of the assumptions, the resulting correlation coefficient may be an overestimate or underestimate of the true state of affairs in the group you are studying.

Check Assumption 1   (scales assumption) by examining each scale and confirming that each is continuous (according to the definition given earlier in this chapter).

Check Assumption 2   (independence assumption) (a) by making sure the students do not cheat or otherwise collaborate while you are testing or otherwise measuring them and (b) by examining the sets of numbers to make sure the same student does not appear twice in the data (i.e. did not generate two pairs of scores).

Check Assumption 3   (normality assumption) (a) by examining the descriptive statistics for normality, or normal distribution, (by examining them to see if you can fit at least two standard deviations on each side of the mean within the range of scores and/or (b) by creating a histogram or bar graph of the scores and deciding if it looks approximately normal.

Check Assumption 4   (linearity assumption) by plotting the two sets of numbers in a scatterplot and looking at them. For instance, if we plot the two sets of numbers that served as the basis of the demonstration calculations for the Pearson *r* (the *r* that turned out to be .93), we would get the SCATTERPLOT shown in Figure 6.1. Recall that we are examining the correlation between the Likert scale means for each item on Willing's questionnaire and the percentage who selected each item as 'best'. In the scatterplot the percentages are on the vertical axis and the Likert scale means are on the horizontal axis. Each item's pair of data points (percentage 'best' and Likert mean) in Table 6.9 is represented by a single diamond in Figure 6.1: from item 20 with 3.54 and 62, and item 11 with 3.51 and 61 all the way down to item 3 with 2.35 and 10 and item 13 with 1.69 and 3. Since the diamonds are more or less in a straight line (with the exception of that single student to the lower left, who makes the data look slightly curved), we can say that the two sets of numbers are approximately linear in relationship. If there were a marked curve in the data or if there was no clear pattern, this assumption would not be met. In such cases, correlations become very difficult to interpret.

Figure 6.1 Scatterplot to check linearity

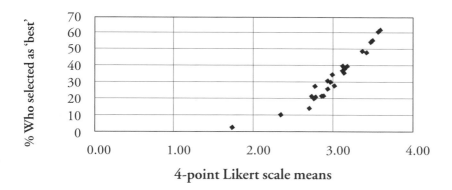

Assumptions underlying the Spearman rho, and phi coefficients

The other correlation coefficients covered in this chapter require fewer assumptions than the Pearson *r*. Spearman *ρ* assumes that the scales are rank-orders (for example, parent and child movie preferences) and requires independence and linearity. The phi coefficient (*Φ*) assumes that both scales are nominal (i.e. are named categories, with two possibilities each, like male and female), are independent of one another (for example, are not the same people repeated), and are in a linear relationship.

Interpreting correlational research

In earlier sections of this chapter, we showed how three types of correlation coefficient can be calculated: the Pearson *r*, Spearman *ρ*, and the phi coefficient (*Φ*). In all three cases, those coefficients are useful for understanding the degree of relationship between the numbers involved. However, certain cautions must be observed in interpreting such coefficients: even random numbers can show some degree of correlation; statistical significance does not imply meaningfulness; and correlation coefficients do not indicate causality.

Even random numbers can show some degree of correlation

One problem that was noticed early in the development of correlation coefficients was that they seldom turned out to be exactly zero. In fact, even when calculating a correlation coefficient based on randomly generated numbers (where absolutely no systematic relationship should exist), a correlation of .00 is very seldom found. Consider Table 6.12, where we repeatedly calculated correlation coefficients based on random number sets of varying sizes. The first column of numbers shows ten correlation coefficients based on 100 pairs of random numbers. Notice that these correlation coefficients range as high as 0.13 in the positive direction and –0.08 in the negative direction. The second column of numbers shows ten correlation coefficients based on 50 pairs of random numbers; these correlation coefficients range a bit more: from as high as 0.22 in the positive direction to –0.26 in the negative direction. The third column of numbers shows ten correlation coefficients based on 30 pairs of random numbers; these correlation coefficients range even more, from as high as 0.34 in the positive direction to –0.38 in the negative direction. The fourth column of numbers shows ten correlation coefficients based on ten pairs of random numbers; these correlation coefficients range still more, from as high as 0.48 in the positive direction to –0.49 in the negative direction. Finally, the last column shows ten correlation coefficients based on five pairs of random numbers; these correlation coefficients range the most: from a staggering 0.92 in the positive direction to an even larger –0.93 in the negative direction.

Table 6.12 Correlation coefficients calculated from random number sets of varying sizes

Trial	Number of random numbers				
	5	100	50	30	10
A	−0.04	−0.18	−0.12	−0.31	−0.23
B	0.01	−0.04	0.13	−0.05	−0.19
C	−0.08	0.22	−0.24	0.24	0.64
D	0.05	0.05	0.34	−0.49	0.92
E	0.04	−0.26	−0.04	0.48	−0.05
F	−0.02	−0.03	−0.37	0.02	0.40
G	0.13	0.02	−0.38	0.06	−0.93
H	0.06	0.08	−0.14	−0.17	−0.23
I	0.07	0.11	−0.06	0.35	−0.46
J	−0.07	0.01	0.29	0.18	0.65

Photocopiable © Oxford University Press

Exercise 6.12

(Calculator needed.)

Using numbers from a hat, or some similar technique, create two sets of random numbers and put them side by side. Then calculate the Pearson r correlation coefficient based on those ten numbers.

Is your result similar to the ones shown in Table 6.12 for ten pairs of random numbers? In other words, is your result between .48 and −.49 like those shown in Table 6.12 for ten pairs of random numbers?

What does all this mean? Two lessons emerge from Table 6.12: (a) correlation coefficients are very seldom zero even when the numbers are randomly generated and (b) the smaller the number of numbers (that is the smaller the *N*-size) involved in calculating a correlation coefficient, the more widely they are likely to range away from zero by chance alone.

In order to determine whether a particular correlation coefficient that you observe in your data is just a random result or probably a real relationship, you will need to determine the probability that your observed correlation is other than a chance finding. To do this, you need to consult tables that have been worked out in advance by statisticians. For instance, for the Pearson *r*, you could use Table 6.13, which shows the critical values, or values beyond which your observed value must be to have a certain probability of having

SIGNIFICANCE (that is, being other than a chance, or random, finding). To use Table 6.13, you will need to do the following:

1 Decide whether your decision is *directional* (i.e. you can reasonably expect the correlation to be either positive or negative) or *non-directional* (i.e. you have no idea what to expect in terms of the sign of the correlation).
2 Decide whether you want to be 99% sure, and set the acceptable level of probability at $p < .01$, or you can accept being 95% sure of your result, and set the acceptable level of probability at $p < .05$.
3 Make sure you know how many pairs of numbers were involved in calculating your correlation coefficient.

Once you have all of the above information, you can enter the correct column by finding the two that are directional or non-directional and then the one column that is $p < .05$ or $.01$. You will then need to move down to the row that corresponds to the number of pairs of numbers you used in calculating the correlation coefficient. For example, let's say you observe a correlation of .55 in your data, you know what direction to expect so it is a directional decision, and you are willing to be 95% sure of your result at $p < .05$. You also know that you used 12 pairs of numbers in calculating the correlation coefficient. Looking in the two columns for directional decisions, you find the one column labeled $p < .05$ and go down to the row where $N = 12$. The result? Your critical value is .4973. Since your observed correlation of .55 is greater than your critical value, you can say that the correlation of .55 is significant at $p < .05$, or that there is only a 5 percent chance that your correlation coefficient is due to chance alone. (For more on this concept, see Brown 1988 or Hatch and Lazaraton 1991.)

Exercise 6.13

1 A study had 102 students and therefore 102 pairs of scores, the observed *r* is .31 (the correlation between the number of hours students spend in the language lab and their grades in language courses), the decision is non-directional, and you want to be 99% sure (at $p < .01$) of the relationship. Using Table 6.13, what would the Pearson *r* critical value be for the study?
2 Would the observed *r* of .31 be significant?

(See the Answer key on page 259 for the answer.)

Table 6.13 Critical values for the Pearson Product-moment Correlation Coefficient (r)

N	Directional decision		Non-directional decision	
	$p < .05$	$p < .01$	$p < .05$	$p < .01$
3	.9877	.9995	.9969	1.0000
4	.9000	.9800	.9500	.9900
5	.8054	.9343	.8783	.9587
6	.7293	.8822	.8114	.9172
7	.6694	.8329	.7545	.8745
8	.6215	.7887	.7067	.8343
9	.5822	.7498	.6664	.7977
10	.5494	.7155	.6319	.7646
11	.5214	.6851	.6021	.7348
12	.4973	.6581	.5760	.7079
13	.4762	.6339	.5529	.6835
14	.4575	.6120	.5324	.6614
15	.4409	.5923	.5139	.6411
16	.4259	.5742	.4973	.6226
17	.4124	.5577	.4821	.6055
18	.3598	.4921	.4227	.5368
27	.3233	.4451	.3809	.4869
32	.2960	.4093	.3494	.4487
37	.2746	.3810	.3246	.4182
42	.2573	.3578	.3044	.3932
47	.2428	.3384	.2875	.3721
52	.2306	.3218	.2732	.3541
62	.2108	.2948	.2500	.3248
72	.1954	.2737	.2319	.3017
82	.1829	.2565	.2172	.2830
92	.1726	.2422	.2050	.2673
102	.1638	.2301	.1946	.2540

(Adapted from Fisher and Yates 1963)

Exercise 6.14

Another study had 27 students and therefore 27 pairs of scores, the observed *r* is .31 (the correlation between the hours per week students claim to study outside of class and their grades in language courses), the decision is directional, and you are willing to be 95% sure (at $p < .05$) of the relationship.

   1 Again using Table 6.13, what would the Pearson *r* critical value be for the study?

   2 Would the observed *r* of .31 be significant?

(See the Answer key on page 259 for the answer.)

In a similar way, you can find the critical values for any directional decision for Spearman ρ by referring to Table 6.14.

Table 6.14 Critical values for directional decisions when using Spearman rho

(N)	p < .05	p < .01
5	.900	1.000
6	.829	.943
7	.714	.893
8	.643	.833
9	.600	.783
10	.564	.746
12	.506	.712
14	.456	.645
16	.425	.601
18	.399	.564
20	.377	.534
22	.359	.508
24	.343	.485
26	.329	.465
28	.317	.448
30	.306	.432

(Adapted from Dixon and Massey 1951)

For the phi (Φ) coefficient, you can actually calculate (after Guilford and Fruchter 1973) the critical values for .05 and .01 as follows (where N is the total number of cases in the contingency table):

$$\Phi_{\text{critical (.05)}} = \frac{1.960}{\sqrt{N}}$$

$$\Phi_{\text{critical (.01)}} = \frac{2.576}{\sqrt{N}}$$

For example, in the section above on calculating phi for the relationship between gender (female and male) and yes/no responses to the statement 'I like to share things with other people', the ϕ observed turned out to be .79. To determine if that value is significant at .01, you would need to look back at the example and find out that the total number of cases in the contingency table was 28 (A + B + C + D = 2 + 14 + 11 + 1 = 28), and then you could use the second equation above to calculate the critical value as follows:

$$\Phi_{\text{critical (.01)}} = \frac{2.576}{\sqrt{N}} = \frac{2.576}{\sqrt{28}} = \frac{2.576}{5.2915} = .4868 \approx .49$$

Since the observed value of .79 is greater than the critical value at .01 of .49, you can say that $p < .01$, or put another way: there is only a 1% probability that this phi correlation occurred by chance alone.

Exercise 6.15

Consider a study in which you have seven pairs of ranks (ranking the relative importance of seven classroom activities to the students in a class, on average, and their teacher), you calculate an observed Spearman ρ of .65, you are making a directional decision, and you want to be sure at $p < .05$.

1   Using Table 6.14, what would the Spearman ρ critical value be for this study?

2   Would the observed ρ of .65 be significant?

(See the Answer key on page 259 for the answer.)

Exercise 6.16

In yet another study, you have a total of 57 observations in a contingency table, you calculated an observed ϕ of .30 (for the relationship between gender and whether or not homework was turned in today), and you want to be sure at $p < .05$.

1   Using the appropriate formula, what would the ϕ critical value be for the following study?

2   Would the observed ϕ of .30 be significant?

(See the Answer key on page 259 for the answer.)

Statistical significance does not imply meaningfulness

Statistical significance and the attendant p values of .01 or .05 help us to deal with the problem of random numbers being correlated by indicating that there is only a one percent or five percent probability that an observed correlation coefficient is a chance finding. However, we would like to stress here that nothing else should be inferred directly or indirectly from this notion of STATISTICAL SIGNIFICANCE. A *significant* statistical finding in this instance does not imply that it is *interesting* or *meaningful* as in the lay use of the word *significant*. So if a researcher interprets one coefficient as *more significant* than another in this lay sense of the word, you should be very wary. Any such phrasing you come across in the language teaching literature should be treated with the utmost suspicion.

How, then, can meaningfulness be inferred from a correlation coefficient? First, a coefficient must be statistically significant (at .05 or .01) to even have a chance of being meaningful; a correlation that is not statistically significant is perhaps a chance finding and therefore meaningless. However, once statistical significance has been established as a sort of minimal criterion, the meaningfulness of the correlation coefficient is dependent on its magnitude. Interpreting the magnitude of a correlation coefficient can be as simple as saying that a correlation of .81 is higher than one of .61.

Alternatively, you may prefer to square the correlation coefficient (if it is a Pearson *r*) and thereby calculate a statistic called the COEFFICIENT OF DETERMINATION, which is the proportion of shared variance between the two sets of numbers used to calculate the correlation coefficient. For example, a correlation coefficient of .80 squared would be .64, which indicates that the proportion of shared variance is .64. By moving the decimal point two places to the right, you can make the same interpretation, but in percentage terms. Thus, .64 would become 64%, which indicates that the correlation coefficient of .80 shows 64% overlapping or shared variance between the two sets of numbers involved. For some people, the coefficient of determination interpreted as a percentage is easier to understand than the associated correlation coefficient. What do you think? In the example, is it easier to understand that there is a correlation coefficient of .80, or that there is 64% overlap between the two sets of numbers involved?

Whether or not you decide to square the correlation coefficient, you should remember that a statistically significant correlation coefficient is simply one that probably did not occur by chance; the degree to which it is interesting or meaningful is an entirely different matter best determined by examining the magnitude of the coefficient within the particular context and research purposes involved.

Correlation coefficients do not indicate causality

Another issue in interpreting any of the correlation coefficients discussed in this chapter is that correlation coefficients do *not* indicate causality. As the late Stephen J. Gould put it, 'The fact of correlation implies nothing about cause. It is not even true that intense correlations are more likely to represent cause than weak ones' (Gould 1981: 242).

Correlation coefficients are no more than estimates of the degree to which two sets of numbers are related. The fact that a moderate or strong relationship exists between one set of numbers and another does not mean that the first set caused the second set, or vice versa. Even a correlation of .99 between, say, the number of days of language lab attendance and proficiency test scores would not indicate that increasing language lab attendance will cause proficiency to go up. Another equally plausible explanation could be that high proficiency students are just naturally interested in attending language lab more often than low proficiency students; another might be that students who are motivated tend to be proficient and tend to attend language lab more often, and vice versa. In short, many alternative explanations can be imagined for almost any relationship that is found, and great care must be taken in interpreting correlational results. In fact, the only statement you can safely make about any correlation coefficient is that it shows X degree of relationship between the two sets of numbers involved (either positive or negative).

Significance of correlational research comparing students' and teachers' attitudes

We looked in the previous chapter on survey research at the significance of human beliefs on behavior and, indeed, on physical health. Where teaching methods correlate with teacher beliefs, it appears that teachers do a more convincing and more effective job of teaching. Likewise, where students see their needs, interests, and preferences being well served, they are likely to be more motivated to study, more diligent in their work, and more convinced of the positive output of their efforts. Where there is a correlation between classroom pedagogy and student learning preferences, more effective instruction should result. In contrast, where there is a mismatch between what teachers do and what students perceive to be useful, there is a spinning of wheels and instructional discordance.

Nunan (1991: 91–3) presents a study that examines the relationship between the attitudes of students and teachers to the following ten activities:

1 Conversation practice
2 Error correction
3 Explanations to class
4 Language games
5 Listening to/using cassettes
6 Pair work
7 Pronunciation practice
8 Student self-discovery of errors
9 Using pictures/films/videos
10 Vocabulary development

As shown in Figure 6.2, the data he reports show 'clear mismatches between learners' and teachers' views of language learning' with 'mismatches in all but one activity investigated' (Nunan 1991b: 93).

Similarly, Brindley (1984) reports on the results of interviews that he conducted with students and teachers in an adult migrant education setting in Australia. He found that the beliefs of students and teachers about what constitutes good language teaching and learning were quite the opposite, i.e. they were not correlated.

Figure 6.2 Learning activity ratings (1 to 7 from very low to very high) of teachers and students

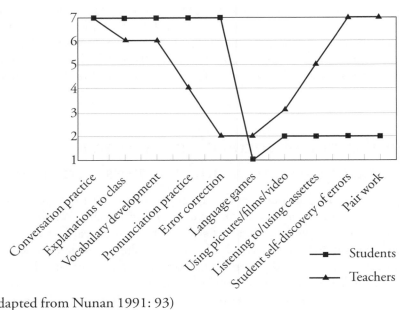

(Adapted from Nunan 1991: 93)

What the teacher *does* with such information is another issue. Some teachers might choose to modify their teaching to match the preferences of their students. Others might offer a *student choice day* during which learners get to set the learning agenda and pedagogical mode. Still others might spend time explaining to students why they have chosen the particular pedagogical path along which they are leading the learners. Regardless of which choice of action teachers might take, they cannot make the decision without information about the relationship between their own activity preferences and those of their students.

Reflecting on correlational research

In this chapter, you experienced correlational research in terms of compiling data and analyzing the results with descriptive and correlational statistics. You also learned how to calculate three different kinds of correlation coefficients and how people's views of language-teaching activities may vary.

Exercise 6.17

Answer the following questions about

The steps in correlational research

   I   Which of those steps do you think is the most difficult part in terms of the amount of work involved?

2   Which do you think is the most difficult in terms of intellectual challenge?

3   Which do you think is the most important in terms of understanding the results?

4   Which do you think taught you the most?

5   Which do you think was the most interesting?

Calculating correlation coefficients

6   Which is the most difficult to calculate?

7   Which is the easiest?

8   Did your confidence and efficiency in calculation improve with practice?

People's views on teaching activities

9   Have your views on the usefulness of various language-teaching activities changed since you started this chapter? How?

10   Do you think that your views on the relative merits of the various teaching activities will coincide with those of your students? Do they have to coincide?

11   Do you need to know what they are thinking in terms of which activities they like best and which they find most useful?

12   What would you do with information that your students' views disagree with yours?

Summary

In this chapter, we introduced correlational research, thereby continuing our discussions of quantitative research methods. You began by experiencing exercises that helped you think about various teaching activities and how much you and your colleagues agreed on their usefulness. You also responded to a language teaching preferences questionnaire. After compiling the data, you determined the means and standard deviations for all participants, as well as the number and percentage who selected each option. You also learned about three types of scales (rank-ordered, continuous, and categorical) and about three different types of correlation coefficients (Spearman rho, the Pearson *r*, and phi) and how they are related to different combinations of scales. After reviewing how the sign of a correlation coefficient and its magnitude are two entirely different things, you examined the assumptions underlying correlation coefficients, how to determine if a correlation coefficient is a chance finding, and why correlation coefficients do *not* indicate causality. Finally, you found that you are not the only language-teaching professional concerned about the differing attitudes of teachers and students toward various classroom activities.

7 QUASI-EXPERIMENTAL RESEARCH: VOCABULARY LEARNING TECHNIQUES

Introducing experimental research

Don't be too timid and squeamish about your actions. All life is an experiment. The more experiments you make the better.
RALPH WALDO EMERSON, 1802–1882
American essayist and poet

Nature is trying very hard to make us succeed, but nature does not depend on us. We are not the only experiment.
R. BUCKMINSTER FULLER, 1895–1983
American engineer, designer and architect

Many people assume that the most appropriate way to resolve a question about language learning or teaching is to conduct an experiment. Experiments are found in fields like chemistry and physics and so appear to have scientific rigor, which human studies sometimes seem to lack. Indeed, some have suggested that those of us in the humanities and social sciences who crave scientific rigor in our work suffer from physics envy.

The experience in this chapter involves an experiment comparing two ways that have been proposed to help learners study and remember second language vocabulary. After having taken part in the experimental situation, you will compile, analyze, and interpret your own results somewhat as you have done (and will do) in other chapters. In EXPERIMENTAL RESEARCH, there are particular techniques associated with these steps, which you will become familiar with during the process.

Experiencing experimental research

Vocabulary learning techniques have been the focus of some six hundred experimental reports published over the last twenty-five years. In part, this plethora of studies has come about because of a re-focusing of interest on the subject of second language vocabulary learning after a period of fairly prolonged neglect.

Current questions include the following: (a) what are the appropriate lexical units by which to define vocabulary, (b) how can vocabulary best be made available for use in conversation or in writing, and (c) why do some vocabulary items seem harder to retain and access than others? Interest in this topic of vocabulary learning also arises because of everyday curiosity about how we remember anything (names, numbers, facts, and so forth) and what we can do to increase our ability to recall things when we want to.

Exercise 7.1

(Warm-up)

The following is a vocabulary recall experiment. There are two lists of 25 words each—Lists A and B. The task is to study each list for two minutes and then to write down all the words you can remember from the list. You will need a timer or watch, or better, a partner to time you in this activity. If you are working on your own, try to find some friends or colleagues to do this with you.

1   Begin your study of List A. When the two minutes are up, set the list aside so you cannot see it and write down all the words you can remember.

 List A:
 bath, write, bed, crisp, dream, fresh, glass, shiny, jar, lie, cup, listen, window, new, pail, read, bright, think, rest, bucket, room, sleep, speak, relax, table

2   Now, begin your study of List B. When the two minutes are up, set the list aside so you cannot see it and write down all the words you can remember.

 List B:
 light, lamp, candle, bulb, lantern
 sit, stand, kneel, bend, jump
 old, ancient, tired, weak, bent
 tire, wheel, engine, gear, door
 student, desk, teacher, pencil, eraser

3   Look back at the original lists and count up the number of words you were able to correctly write down after studying List A for two minutes and the number you were able to write down after studying List B.

4   Compare your own scores for recall of words in Lists A and B. Is there a difference? With which list did you have greater recall? Why do think you got this result?

5   Collect recall data for both lists for all the students in your class (participants). Compute the average recall for each list for the whole class, as well as for males and females separately. Is there a difference between Lists A and B recall? Between males and females? Are the differences large? Small? In favor of which lists?

6   As a whole class, discuss what you think the differences were between List A and List B.

7   Organize the words in List A into five groups of five words each. What characteristics do these lists have? Are they similar to the ways in which the words in List B are organized? In what ways?

Comparing methods for learning L2 vocabulary

Now you are ready to try the central experimental experience of this chapter, which will be presented in two parts: one in Exercise 7.2 and the other in Exercise 7.3.

For readers who already know these Spanish words, we provide an alternative list of Russian vocabulary items on the book's Internet site www.oup.com/elt/teacher/L2research. (You will need to log in.)

Exercise 7.2

Instructions to be read by experimenter to class acting as participants:

This experiment deals with learning vocabulary pairs in two languages. The two languages are Spanish and English. In List E in Appendix 7.1 on page 278, you will find a list showing four practice items and 20 learning trial items, each consisting of a Spanish word and its English translation. I will state a number and then say the Spanish word that goes with that number. You will have ten seconds to practice saying the Spanish word and its English translation to yourself as many times as you can. After ten seconds, I will go on to the next numbered Spanish word. Again, practice saying the Spanish word and its English translation as many times as you can.

Experimenter reads each of the numbers and Spanish words in List E followed by a ten-second pause.

Now, turn to Test E (on the next page). Do not look back at List E. During the test, I will say a number and a Spanish word. Try to remember and write down what you think is the English translation of the Spanish word. I will do the same thing for all twenty Spanish words.

If you are working through the text alone, you can simulate the two vocabulary learning experimental trials, Test E and Test F. With a few exceptions, Spanish words are pronounced as a speaker of English or a European language would expect them to be pronounced. Using a sheet of paper across the List E and List F pages (Appendixes 7.1 and 7.2 on pages 278 and 279) so as to expose one pair of words at a time, repeat to yourself the Practice examples and the Learning Trial words following the text instructions and timing. At the finish of the exercise, check your recall of Test words as noted in the text.

Test E   Score _____

No.	Spanish word	Translation
1	Caracol	
2	Barro	
3	Toalla	
4	Vientre	
5	Carpa	
6	Comedor	
7	Tallarín	
8	Corazón	
9	Prado	
10	Parabrisas	
11	Sabor	
12	Pollo	
13	Sabio	
14	Herida	
15	Lata	
16	Jefe	
17	Polvo	
18	Espaldas	
19	Helado	
20	Viajero	

Photocopiable © Oxford University Press

Instructions for scoring to be read by the experimenter to class acting as participants:

Now compare your answers on Test E to the answers in the Answer Key for Experiment E (page 260). Count up the total of correct answers that you wrote on Test E and put that number in the space provided for a score in the upper-right part of the test.

Exercise 7.3

Follow a similar procedure for the Test F vocabulary learning Practice and
Learning Trial list as you did for Test E. Observe the new repetition instructions
for Test F. The 'keywords' are meant to sound very much like all or part of the
Spanish stimulus words, so you might modify your 'Spanish' pronunciations to
reflect the 'echo' relationship of the English keywords to the Spanish stimulus
words. Again, check your recall of Text F words as instructed in the text.
Remember to total your recall of correct responses for both trials on List E and
List F.

Instructions to be read to class by the experimenter acting as participants:

This experiment deals with learning vocabulary pairs in two languages. The two
languages are Spanish and English. In List F in Appendix 7.2 on page 279, you will
find four practice items and 20 learning trial items. For each number, there is first
a Spanish word; second, a keyword (that is, an English word or phrase that sounds
like part of the Spanish word); and, third, an English translation of the Spanish
word. I will state a number and then say the Spanish word that goes with that
number.

Listen to the Spanish word.

As I say the Spanish word, look at and learn the keyword in brackets that sounds
like the Spanish word. Next, try to make a picture in your mind that links the
keyword to the English translation. For example, if I say, 'number one—*pato*,' you
should look at and remember the sound-alike English keyword *pot*.

Now make a mental picture that connects *pot* and *duck*. Maybe, you see a duck
soldier with a pot on his head. Or a duck being cooked in a pot and crying.

So now when you hear the Spanish word *pato*, you think of the English keyword
pot. You might picture a duck cooking in a pot and crying. You then remember that
the Spanish word *pato* means *duck* in English.

Let's try one more example. If I say, 'number two—*butaca*,' the English keyword
sound-alike is *boot*: *butaca* – *boot*. The English translation is *armchair*. Make a mental
picture that connects *boot* and *armchair*: maybe, somebody sitting on the floor with
his dirty boots propped up on a nice armchair.

Now when you hear *butaca*, you think of the keyword *boot* and picture somebody sitting on the floor with his dirty boots on an armchair. So you remember the Spanish word *butaca* means *armchair* in English.

Experimenter reads each of the numbers and Spanish words in List F followed by a ten-second pause.

Now, look at Test F below. Do not look back at the Experimental List F. In the test, I will say a number and a Spanish word. Try to remember the key word, then the picture in your mind, and then the English translation of the Spanish word. Write the English word down. I will do the same thing for all twenty Spanish words.

Test F   Score _____

No.	Spanish word	Translation
1	Tarde	
2	Cama	
3	Fondo	
4	Ciudad	
5	Payaso	
6	Postre	
7	Muñeca	
8	Huevo	
9	Bombero	
10	Piso	
11	Saltamontes	
12	Ayuda	
13	Pulgado	
14	Bolsillo	
15	Arroz	
16	Arena	
17	Sábana	
18	Guerra	
19	Mujer	
20	Gusano	

Instructions for scoring to be read by experimenter to class acting as participants:

Now compare your answers on Test F to the answers in the Answer Key for Experiment F (page 261). Count up the total of correct answers that you wrote in Test F and put that number in the space provided for a score in the upper-right part of the test.

Compiling experimental data

Exercise 7.4

(Calculator needed.)

As a class, compile the results for the *Vocabulary Learning Experiments* that you did in Exercises 7.2 and 7.3. Compile the data in any way that makes sense to you as a group, in a format similar to that shown in Table 7.1. An example of how your compilation might look is shown in Table 7.2.

If you are working alone, you can add your own scores to the example data shown in Table 7.2 and use them for the ensuing exercises.

1   What is the class average (you will need to calculate means) for correct answers, first for Exercise 7.2, then for Exercise 7.3? Which class mean was higher? How much higher?

2   What were the highest and lowest scores for each exercise?

3   Which set of items was easier to remember? Why do you think those items were easier? Did most participants agree on which set of items was easier?

4   What were your impressions and strategies in participating in Exercises 7.2 and 7.3?

Analyzing experimental data

Let's look at some typical experimental data. A class group like yours did the warm-up experiment we called Exercise 7.1 in this chapter. The class consisted of 34 students, 17 men and 17 women. One of the women wondered if the women would remember more words from list learning than men because she felt women had to make more lists and remember things in lists more often than men. Some of the men objected, claiming they were dedicated list makers and users. So the class decided to compare the scores of the women and men, as well as the averages or means of recall of items on the lists A and B. Table 7.3 shows their recall data in table form.

Table 7.1   Table for compiling the data from the vocabulary learning experiments (www)

Student Number	Gender	Score on Exercise 3	Score on Exercise 4
1			
2			
3			
4			
5			
6			
7			
8			
9			
10			
11			
12			
13			
14			
15			
16			
17			
18			
19			
20			
21			
22			
23			
24			
25			
26			
27			
28			
29			
30			

Table 7.2 Example data for the vocabulary learning experiments (Exercise 7.1) (www)

Student Number	Gender	Score on List A	Score on List B
1	M	15	17
2	M	0	10
3	M	3	7
4	M	5	5
5	M	7	6
6	M	14	17
7	M	10	16
8	M	8	8
9	M	2	8
10	F	6	8
11	F	8	7
12	F	3	5
13	F	4	3
14	F	10	9
15	F	7	12
16	F	5	14
17	F	10	12
18	F	8	9
19	F	7	10
20	F	12	14

Photocopiable © Oxford University Press

Table 7.3 Example recall data (www)

	List A $M(SD)$	List B $M(SD)$
Women $N = 17$	18.5(2.5)	22.5(2.0)
Men $N = 17$	14.5(3.5)	21.5(2.5)

For List A in Table 7.3, the 17 women had a mean (*M*) recall of 18.5 items, while the 17 men averaged 14.5 word items. For List B, the women had a mean of 22.5 items, and the men recalled an average of 21.5 items. The standard deviations (measuring the spread of individual recall scores) were as shown in parentheses in the table. For example the standard deviation in recall for women for List A words was $SD = 2.5$.

Let us look more closely at the differences between men and women on List A word recall:

Women ($N = 17$)	Men ($N = 17$)
Mean $M_w = 18.5$	Mean $M_m = 14.5$
Standard Deviation $SD_w = 2.5$	Standard Deviation $SD_m = 3.5$

The first question is: Is there a difference between the two means? The answer: Yes. (Actually, it would be pretty strange if the means of the two groups were *exactly* the same.) So, yes, there is a difference. The second question is: What does the difference between means say about the memory of words for men and women? The answer: It looks like the women were better at remembering lists of words than the men, particularly if the words were randomly presented (as in List A) rather than organized in meaningful sets (as in List B).

The third question is: Is the difference between the means a big difference or a small difference? The answer: Well, for List A, it looks sort of biggish. But compared to what? What if the means were Women = 18.5; Men = 17? Is that difference biggish or smallish?

What if there were only two women and two men taking the test. We could still figure the means for the two groups. Let's suppose the means are still the same: Women's mean = 18.5; Men's mean = 14.5. Does it make any difference that now there are only four people involved instead of 27 as in the original example? Descriptions of data like 'biggish' and 'smallish' don't help much in answering questions like these. To give better answers, experimenters have invented some more formal ways of describing the differences between bits of analyzed data.

Formal experiments are almost always analyzed using inferential statistics. That is, they are analyzed using statistical computations that allow the experimenters to make *inferences* about what is going on—particularly what is going on with respect to their original research questions. As in analyzing descriptive research data (see Chapter 5), you can compute frequencies and percentages, display the scores on a histogram, determine measures of central tendency (mean, mode, and median), and calculate estimates of dispersion (low–high, range, and standard deviation). Once you have computed these, you will want to know if the difference between the two means is *significant* or not. SIGNIFICANCE is a statistical way of talking about whether the difference between two groups' means is *biggish* or *smallish*. When comparing pairs of means (say, the difference between two means related to two different methods of vocabulary presentation) the statistical measure typically used is the *t*-test.

Computing the t-*test in data analysis*

The *t*-TEST is the most frequently used measure in second language research when comparing mean scores for two groups. Suppose you want to know whether older students versus younger students or males versus females or those with pets versus those without pets performed better when taking the same test. A *t*-test would be the measure you would use to compare the mean scores of the two groups. The *t*-test, with a bit of adjustment, can also be used to compare mean scores of just one group, say between a pre-test and a post-test, when checking to see if some skill had been acquired by the group during training.

The *t*-test is represented (hold on to your hats) with the symbol *t*. It is a very useful measure because it can be used with very large or very small groups. The adjustment for group size is made by using a table that shows different values for various group sizes. Group size is (roughly) adjusted for by *degrees of freedom*. DEGREES OF FREEDOM (*df*) for *t*-tests can be determined by subtracting one from the number of participants in each group and then adding the two resulting numbers together.

Adjustments for differences in types of decisions is made by considering one-tailed and two-tailed decisions separately. These two concepts work very much like directional and non-directional decisions for correlational analyses (see page 186). *One-tailed* decisions for *t*-tests are like directional decisions in correlational analysis in the sense that you should use them when you can reasonably expect one mean to be higher than the other; *two-tailed* decisions for *t*-tests are like non-directional decisions in correlational analysis in the sense that you should use them when you have no reason to expect one or the other of the means to be higher.

For example, let's say we are comparing the mean *remembering* scores of men versus women on word List A. In our sample class, there were 17 women and 17 men, so we would subtract 17 minus 1 (17 − 1 = 16) and 17 minus 1 (17 − 1 = 16) and add these two results together (16 + 16 = 32) to determine that we have 32 degrees of freedom. When we check our *t*-value in the appropriate table, we would check in the row which has 32 degrees of freedom to decide if the difference between the means is significant or not.

So, let's compute a *t*-value for our sample class of word list learners. Table 7.4 once again shows a set of word recall means and standard deviations for Lists A and B for both women and men.

Table 7.4 Recall means and standard deviations in Exercise 7.5 (www)

	List A $M(SD)$	List B $M(SD)$
Women N = 17	18.5(2.5)	22.5(2.0)
Men N = 17	14.5(3.5)	21.5(2.5)

The difference in recall for List A between women and men looks interesting, so we'll consider that first.

Women (N_w = 17)   Men (N_m = 17)

Mean M_w = 18.5   Mean M_m = 14.5

Standard Deviation S_w = 2.5   Standard Deviation S_m = 3.5

In this case, because the group sizes are the same, the formula for computing the *t*-value would look like this:

$$t = \frac{M_w - M_m}{\sqrt{\dfrac{S_w^2}{N_w} + \dfrac{S_m^2}{N_m}}}$$

This equation is read as *t* equals the mean for women minus the mean for men divided by the square root of the standard deviation squared for the women divided by the number of women plus the standard deviation squared for the men divided by the number of men.

Let's take this equation a bit at a time. The top half of this equation is easy. So, $M_w - M_m = 18.5 - 14.5 = 4$. The bottom half of this equation is determined by squaring the women's standard deviation ($S_w^2 = 2.5^2 = 6.25$) and dividing the result by the number of women (N_w = 17) and adding to that the squared value of the men's standard deviation ($S_m^2 = 3.5^2 = 12.25$) divided by the number of men (N_m = 17) then taking the square root of the result. Computing this out step by step:

$$t = \frac{M_w - M_m}{\sqrt{\dfrac{S_w^2}{N_w} + \dfrac{S_m^2}{N_m}}}$$

$$t = \frac{18.5 - 14.5}{\sqrt{\dfrac{6.25}{17} + \dfrac{12.25}{17}}}$$

Table 7.5 Critical values for the t-*test statistic*

One-tailed	0.05	0.025	0.01	0.005
Two-tailed	0.10	0.05	0.02	0.01
df				
1	6.314	12.706	31.821	63.657
2	2.920	4.303	6.965	9.925
3	2.353	3.182	4.541	5.841
4	2.132	2.776	3.747	4.604
5	2.015	2.571	3.365	4.032
6	1.943	2.447	3.143	3.707
7	1.895	2.365	2.998	3.499
8	1.860	2.306	2.896	3.355
9	1.833	2.262	2.821	3.250
10	1.812	2.228	2.764	3.169
11	1.796	2.201	2.718	3.106
12	1.782	2.179	2.681	3.055
13	1.771	2.160	2.650	3.012
14	1.761	2.145	2.624	2.977
15	1.753	2.131	2.602	2.947
16	1.746	2.120	2.583	2.921
17	1.740	2.110	2.567	2.898
18	1.734	2.101	2.552	2.878
19	1.729	2.093	2.539	2.861
20	1.725	2.086	2.528	2.845
21	1.721	2.080	2.518	2.831
22	1.717	2.074	2.508	2.819
23	1.714	2.069	2.500	2.807
24	1.711	2.064	2.492	2.797
25	1.708	2.060	2.485	2.787
26	1.706	2.056	2.479	2.779
27	1.703	2.052	2.473	2.771
28	1.701	2.048	2.467	2.763
29	1.699	2.045	2.462	2.756
30	1.697	2.042	2.457	2.750
40	1.684	2.021	2.423	2.704
60	1.671	2.000	2.390	2.660
120	1.658	1.980	2.358	2.617
∞	1.645	1.960	2.326	2.576

(Adapted from Fisher and Yates 1963)

$$t = \frac{4.0}{\sqrt{.3676 + .7206}}$$

$$t = \frac{4.0}{\sqrt{1.0882}} = \frac{4.0}{1.0432} = 3.8344 \approx 3.83$$

Thus, the *t*-value in this case is about 3.83.

Next, we look in the *t*-test table (see Table 7.5) remembering that there are 32 degrees of freedom (*df*). If the exact *df* is not shown in the table, we take the closest value below it in order to be conservative. There is no row for 32 degrees of freedom in the table, so we take the closest value below 32, which is 30. In that row, the critical value for *t* at the .01 level of significance (two-tailed) is 2.750 (or 2.042 at the .05 level of significance). Since the *t*-value we calculated for the difference between women and men was 3.83 and that value is greater than the critical value found in the table at .01 or .05, we take the more conservative of those two values, which means that we have found a significant difference between women and men at *p* < .01. This indicates that the difference between women's mean and men's mean probably did not happen accidentally. There is only 1 chance in 100 (.01) that the difference in mean scores between women and men occurred by chance. Put another way, this result means that the women's mean is *significantly higher* than the men's mean score for List A recall.

An article describing this experiment might have this partial summary of findings:

ABSTRACT (partial)

An inquiry was conducted into gender differences on list recall of 25 common English words, listed randomly or in semantic categories. For the random list condition, women participants had a mean word recall of 18.5 (*SD* = 2.5) while men participants had a mean word recall of 14.5 (*SD* = 3.5). A *t*-test analysis of the differences between means yielded a *t* of 3.83. This was significant at the *p* < .01 level (with *df* = 32). It was concluded that, in this experiment, women participants were significantly better than men at remembering random lists of words.

In the above experiment, the number of men and the number of women were equal. Note that another equation should be used if the sample sizes are different for the two groups:

$$t = \frac{M_w - M_m}{\sqrt{\left[\frac{(N_w - 1)S_w^2 + (N_m - 1)S_m^2}{N_w + N_m - 2}\right]\left[\frac{1}{N_w} + \frac{1}{N_m}\right]}}$$

For instance, let's say the number of men in the example above had been nine instead of 17 and the number of women was still 17. The mean recall of words and standard deviations remain as given in the abstract. In that case, the t-value would have been calculated as follows:

$$t = \cfrac{M_w - M_m}{\sqrt{\left[\cfrac{(N_w - 1)S_w^2 + (N_m - 1)S_m^2}{N_w + N_m - 2}\right]\left[\cfrac{1}{N_w} + \cfrac{1}{N_m}\right]}}$$

$$t = \cfrac{18.5 - 14.5}{\sqrt{\left[\cfrac{(17-1)2.5^2 + (9-1)3.5^2}{17 + 9 - 2}\right]\left[\cfrac{1}{17} + \cfrac{1}{9}\right]}}$$

$$t = \cfrac{4.0}{\sqrt{\left[\cfrac{(16)6.25 + (8)12.25}{24}\right](.0588 + .1111)}}$$

$$t = \cfrac{4.0}{\sqrt{\left[\cfrac{100 + 98}{24}\right](.1699)}}$$

$$t = \cfrac{4.0}{\sqrt{\left[\cfrac{198}{24}\right](.1699)}} = \cfrac{4.0}{\sqrt{[8.25](.1699)}} = \cfrac{4.0}{\sqrt{1.4017}} = \cfrac{4.0}{1.1839} = 3.3787$$

This equation could also be used in situations where the group sizes are the same. For instance, in the original example above with 17 in each group, we found a t-value of 3.83 using the original formula and applying the formula for here, we get 3.84, which is within one one-hundredth of the same result.

$$t = \cfrac{M_w - M_m}{\sqrt{\left[\cfrac{(N_w - 1)S_w^2 + (N_m - 1)S_m^2}{N_w + N_m - 2}\right]\left[\cfrac{1}{N_w} + \cfrac{1}{N_m}\right]}}$$

$$t = \cfrac{18.5 - 14.5}{\sqrt{\left[\cfrac{(17-1)2.5^2 + (17-1)3.5^2}{17 + 17 - 2}\right]\left[\cfrac{1}{17} + \cfrac{1}{17}\right]}}$$

$$t = \cfrac{4.0}{\sqrt{\left[\cfrac{(16)6.25 + (16)12.25}{32}\right](.0588 + .0588)}}$$

$$t = \frac{4.0}{\sqrt{\left[\dfrac{100 + 196}{32}\right](.1176)}}$$

$$t = \frac{4.0}{\sqrt{\left[\dfrac{296}{32}\right](.1176)}} = \frac{4.0}{\sqrt{[9.25](.1176)}} = \frac{4.0}{\sqrt{1.0878}} = \frac{4.0}{1.0430} = 3.8351 \approx 3.84$$

Note that yet another equation must be used if the means being compared are for the same group of participants on two occasions as in a comparison of pre-test and post-test means. (For a full explanation and example, see Hatch and Lazaraton 1991). Notice also that there are now only 26 participants instead of 34, so a *t*-value of 3.84 may no longer be significant. You might check Table 7.5 to find out.

Exercise 7.5

(Calculator needed)

Now it's your turn. Using the equations and examples above, compute the *t*-test value for the difference between the scores of women versus men for List B in Exercise 7.1.

Exercise 7.6

(Calculator needed.)

Now it's time to compute *t*-test values for your own class vocabulary learning experimental data. To do this, you will need to assemble the means and standard deviations for the women and men in your class (or any other two groups, like native-speakers versus non-native speakers of English, or those with, say, five or more years of teaching experience versus those with less, etc.). If you are doing this exercise alone, you can use the data in Table 7.2 or add your own results to that table and then use the data to calculate the *t*-test for the difference between males and females.

Then, write answers to the following questions:

1   What is the *t*-test value for the comparison between those two groups' means? (Be sure to use the correct formula.)

2   Does the *t*-test value indicate a significant difference between the means?

3   Significant at what level?

Designing your own experimental studies

In this section, we will focus on (a) experimental approaches to language teaching research, (b) the big method-comparison studies, (c) creating research questions and the accompanying hypotheses, and (d) designing experiments to test hypotheses.

Experimental approaches to language teaching research

An experiment is defined as 'a situation in which one observes the relationship between two variables by deliberately producing a change in one and looking to see whether this alteration produces a change in the other' (Anderson 1969). This definition is a broad one covering experiments in physics, medicine, and psychology—in fact, in any discipline which considers itself a science.

The most formal kind of applied linguistics experiment might involve research that tests whether Method A or Method B is more effective in teaching, say, academic writing to first-year university students. Such a TRUE EXPERIMENTAL STUDY would have the following characteristics:

a students are randomly selected and assigned to two groups;
b two experimental conditions or treatments in the teaching of academic writing are provided; and
c for both groups, a pre-test and post-test are given, each involving some kind of academic writing.

The two groups of participants are assumed to be equivalent because they were assigned to the groups randomly. Both groups will be pre-tested on some measure of academic writing ability (helping to determine if the two groups are, indeed, equivalent). One group, usually called the control group, will receive a *control treatment* in the form of so-called *standard* first-year instruction in writing; the second group, often called the treatment group, will receive the *experimental treatment* in the form of some new approach to teaching academic writing (say, by using diagrams to suggest the nature of the parts and interaction of parts in an academic paper). Finally, both groups will receive a post-test, which will indicate what changes in academic writing ability have occurred in either (or both) groups. This is a typical *true* experimental design.

However, there are many studies reported in the literature which lack one or more of the defining characteristics of a true experimental study. At the lower end of the scale are studies which some commentators have called XO studies, where X is some kind of educational treatment and O is an observation following the treatment. As Campbell and Stanley note:

> Much educational research today conforms to a design in which a single group is studied only once, subsequent to some agent or treatment presumed to cause change. Such studies might be diagrammed as follows:

$$X\ O$$

> Such studies have such a total absence of control as to be of almost no scientific value ... It seems well-nigh unethical ... to allow, as theses or dissertations in education, case studies of this nature (Campbell and Stanley 1963: 176–177).

More adequate experimental designs are generally of one of four types. These four types (A, B, C, & D) are shown in Table 7.6. It would seem to follow from the above that an *ideal* experimental study would be of Type D, that is, like the writing example outlined above. Often, however, second language researchers are unable to obtain randomly selected groups of participants and have to deal in their experiments with already existing INTACT GROUPS. Thus, although the classes might be assumed to be at the same educational or language learning level and thus equivalent, they have not been pre-tested or randomly assigned to groups. Such variation from the formal requirements for a *true* experiment causes such a study to be called QUASI-EXPERIMENTAL. It is often difficult to conduct educational studies with human participants (i.e. real students and real teachers) that are pure experimental studies. Thus, most studies in our field tend to be quasi-experimental rather than truly experimental.

Table 7.6 Experimental approaches to language teaching research

	One treatment	Two treatments
One group	A Pre-test/Post-test. Single group followed throughout treatment.	B Treatments may be simultaneous or sequential. For example, one might involve two L2s taught with two different methods.
Two groups	C Groups vary on some assumed critical dimension such as age, sex, intelligence, motivation, etc.	D Classic method studies involving a control group and an experimental group, each taught by a different method.

In your reading of experimental studies you first might want to note which type of experimental study is being reported. If the design was not of the Type D shown in Table 7.6, what reasons did the researcher give for the alternative chosen? Did the reasoning seem valid?

Exercise 7.7

The following questions will help you understand how and why control groups are used:

1   Review the experiments you have participated in during your study of this chapter. Which type of study were these? Did any of the studies in other chapters involve separate control and experimental groups? Do you think they could or should have?

2   The experiments of this chapter are of the type often called *own control* studies. Explain what you think this means.

3   List the advantages and disadvantages you can think of for *own control* versus *separate control/experimental* group studies. Keep in mind
    a) the size of your class,
    b) the sequence of control and experimental treatments and their possible effect on results,
    c) the influence of the *teacher* or *experimenter*, and
    d) other variables you think might influence your decision.

4   You could group your class vocabulary experimental results by sub-groups. That is, you could separate and compare the data for males and females, or native and non-native speakers, or for those holding graduate degrees and those not holding graduate degrees, or for those having straight hair and those not having straight hair, or by any number of other differences. If you compared any pair of such differences, what experimental type on the diagram would your study resemble?

5   For the vocabulary experiment, between which two types of student would you expect there to be differences? Why?

The big method-comparison studies

The second half of the 20th century has been sometimes labeled 'The Age of Methods' in second language instruction. This came about because of the proliferation of methods proposed and marketed for teaching second and foreign languages during this period. In their analysis of language teaching methods, Richards and Rodgers (2001) list eighteen major methods and discuss their salient distinctions. These methods and their distinctive features are shown in Table 7.7.

Table 7.7 Some methods and their distinctive features

AUDIOLINGUAL METHOD: Importance of students having repeated and systematic productive practice.

COMMUNICATIVE LANGUAGE TEACHING: Role of meaningful communication is the focus of LT.

COMMUNITY LANGUAGE LEARNING: Focuses on the classroom as community with learners' larger lives involved in learning.

COMPETENCY-BASED LANGUAGE TEACHING: Specifies learning outcomes rather than learning processes.

CONTENT-BASED INSTRUCTION: Teaching organized around subject-matter structure rather than linguistic structure.

COOPERATIVE LANGUAGE LEARNING: Focuses on small-group interaction and on the learning contribution that learners make to fellow-learners.

GRAMMAR TRANSLATION: Detailed analysis of grammar rules leading to a translation of texts into and out of the target language.

LEXICAL APPROACH: Focuses on words and lexical chunks as critical learning and use elements of the language.

MULTIPLE INTELLIGENCES: Emphasis on accommodating different learner styles, preferences and capabilities.

NATURAL APPROACH: The importance of the teacher in helping make new language interesting and comprehensible.

NEUROLINGUISTIC PROGRAMMING: Set of general communication techniques based on modeling behaviors of successful language learners and users.

SILENT WAY: Focus on learning rather than teaching, with student problem-solving central to learning.

SITUATIONAL LANGUAGE TEACHING: Role of meaningful context in the situations in which language will be used.

STRUCTURAL METHOD: Focus of LT is on the phonological and syntactic structures of the language.

SUGGESTOPEDIA: Focus on the importance of relaxation and rhythm in learning.

TASK-BASED APPROACHES: Engaging and relevant tasks as LT focus.

TOTAL PHYSICAL RESPONSE: The tie between body and brain in LL.

WHOLE LANGUAGE: Perspective involving learner participation in authentic, interesting situations and the language which naturally emerges in such situations.

Not surprisingly, learners, teachers, and administrators sought to determine which of these methods was best for the typical language-teaching situation. In an attempt to respond to this issue, numerous large-scale experimental METHOD-COMPARISON STUDIES were undertaken with designs hoping to approximate *pure* experimental studies as far as possible. (See Brown 1995a for a comprehensive list of such studies up to that date.) The research was carried out 'on the assumption that it made sense to ask, "Which is the best method for modern language teaching?" and that presumably on the additional assumption that once the answer was determined it would then make sense to simply prescribe the "winning" method for general adoption' (Allwright 1988: 10).

Despite both the extent and expense of these studies, results have generally been inconclusive, and the research methodology of the studies was very heavily criticized. This was so much the case that 'method-comparison studies' became a phrase to be avoided and even smaller-scale, more carefully-designed comparative studies were for some time discouraged. One benefit of the failure of these research studies was the focusing of greater *qualitative* attention on what actually happened in classrooms rather than on what was claimed to transpire with respect to a particular teaching method. Now, both small-scale experimental comparison studies (like our writing example above) and qualitative studies based on classroom observations seem to co-exist harmoniously.

Creating research questions and hypotheses

In experimental research, you can use research questions and/or research hypotheses. In other words, the central issues of your research can be posited as RESEARCH QUESTIONS, which are questions that you will try to answer in the study, or the issues can be posited as RESEARCH HYPOTHESES, which are *claims* that you believe the experimental study might support (or perhaps disprove).

Look back at Exercise 7.1, the vocabulary list recall experiment. In one condition (List A), you were asked to briefly study and then recall a list of 25 randomly organized common English words. In the second condition (List B), you were asked to study for a similar period 25 common English words organized into sets of five words. Each set of five contained words that were a) the same part of speech—were syntactically similar (nouns, verbs, etc.) and b) came from a similar meaning set—were semantically similar (parts of a car, body action verbs, etc.). The researcher might have posed a research question and hypothesis for this experiment which looked like the following:

Research question 1 In recalling long lists of words (say 25 words), will words pre-organized into syntactically/semantically similar five-word clusters be easier to recall than like words presented in a randomly ordered list?

The researcher apparently feels that clustering words by parts of speech (syntactically) and by meaning (semantically) will support better recall than random, unclustered lists. A more direct way to phrase this assumption is in terms of a hypothesis that clearly states how the experimenter thinks the experimental results will turn out.

Hypothesis 1a In memorizing a long list of common English words, participants will better recall words pre-ordered in like syntactic/semantic clusters of five words than they will recall a similar list of words randomly ordered.

When experimenters phrase the subject of their research as hypotheses rather than as questions, they must also anticipate competing hypotheses to their principle hypotheses. Competing hypotheses are often called alternative hypotheses. For the vocabulary recall data, an ALTERNATIVE HYPOTHESIS might be that subjects will choose their own best strategy for recalling long lists of words and that *forcing* them to study words in fixed clusters of five will be less efficient than whatever strategy subjects might create on their own. This hypothesis might be stated as follows:

Hypothesis 1b (Alternative Hypothesis to 1a) In learning a long word list (say 25 words), pre-ordering of words into syntactic/semantic clusters of five will promote *less* successful recall than allowing subjects to apply their own strategies (whatever these may be) for word recall.

Another form of competing hypothesis is called the NULL HYPOTHESIS. In the word recall case the null hypothesis might be that neither the *random order* nor the *clustered condition* will prove superior to the other. They will prove to be equally effective (or ineffective) as measured by number of words correctly recalled. The null hypothesis might be stated as follows:

Hypothesis 1c (Null hypothesis to 1a) In memorizing a list of 25 common English words, participants will recall words pre-ordered in like syntactic/semantic clusters of five words no better than they will recall a similar list of words randomly ordered.

In all aspects of experimental research reporting—particularly in the hypothesis and literature review sections—views contrasting with the experimenter's must be fully and fairly stated. That is, if, in review of the literature, you find three previous experimental studies indicating that clustering *does not* help subjects in stimulus recall, you need to state this evidence in the literature review as completely and fairly as you might present evidence from six studies you found showing that clustering *does* help subjects in stimulus recall. You might want to explain why you think the three negative studies on clustering came out as they did, but you cannot ignore or downplay the findings of such studies that compete with your own hypothesis without good (stated) reasons.

Exercise 7. 8

Using the above examples of hypotheses as models, state a hypothesis, an alternative hypothesis, and a null hypothesis for the *keyword link* experiment featured in Exercises 7.2 and 7.3.

If your results are typical of other experiments based on the keyword technique, most of your class participants will have recalled more vocabulary items in List F using the experimental, keyword condition than they did in List E using the control, rote memorization condition. In one of the early tests of the keyword method, Atkinson reports as typical the finding that the control (rote) group 'recalled only 28% of the words. The keyword group recalled 88%' (Atkinson 1975: 824). However, there are several questions—objections even—that could and have been raised with respect to the use of the keyword method in learning L2 vocabulary. Maybe the several-step process (of associating an L2 word to an acoustic link, then to a visual link, and then to specific recall of the English meaning) interferes with speed or facility in using an L2 conversationally. Maybe you can remember vocabulary in the direction L2→L1 but not in the direction L1→L2. And so on.

Setting up experiments to test hypotheses

Below are listed a number of proverbs about human behavior in everyday life. Think of them as providing hypotheses of recognized *truths* about everyday human actions. For example, 'Two heads are better than one' could be quoted by proponents of cooperative learning to support the notion that everybody recognizes cooperation as being of high value in accomplishing a task. However, we could think of this as a hypothesis about human operations.

Hypothesis 1 Two heads are better than one.

Is there a competing hypothesis to Hypothesis 1? As it happens, there is also a proverb to provide the competing hypothesis:

Hypothesis 2 If you want something done right, do it yourself.

Many familiar proverbs could be said to represent competing hypotheses. Consider as hypotheses, the following pairs of proverbs:

Hypothesis 3 Look before you leap.
Hypothesis 4 He who hesitates is lost.

Hypothesis 5 Absence makes the heart grow fonder.
Hypothesis 6 Out of sight, out of mind.

Hypothesis 7 Better safe than sorry.
Hypothesis 8 Nothing ventured, nothing gained.

Hypothesis 9 You can't tell a book by its cover.
Hypothesis 10 Clothes make the man.

Hypothesis 11 You can't teach an old dog new tricks.
Hypothesis 12 It's never too late too learn.

Hypothesis 13 Never sweat the small stuff.
Hypothesis 14 God is in the details.

Hypothesis 15 Many hands make light work.
Hypothesis 16 Too many cooks spoil the broth.

Exercise 7.9

Write a paragraph describing an experiment (feel free to make these a bit humorous, if you wish) to test one of these hypotheses, using the other hypothesis as the alternative hypothesis. An example is provided to start you off:

Example:
Hypothesis: It's never too late too learn.
Alternative Hypothesis: You can't teach an old dog new tricks.

The participants are twenty doting grandparents—half male, half female—all of whom claim to be completely mystified by the video cassette recorders (VCRs) that their children gave them for Christmas and are unable to operate them at all. Ten of the grandparents (five males and five females) will constitute the control group, while the other 10 (five males and five females) will be the experimental group. The members of the control group are told that they will be given a demonstration (one more time) of how to operate the VCR and a simplified instruction manual with key operational sections noted with pink underliner. They are told further that if they are still unable to operate the VCR after two weeks, the givers will remove the VCRs and take them to a Salvation Army shelter for street people. The test of operational competence is defined as the ability to program the VCR to record the soap opera, 'The Days of Our Lives,' on weekdays. The members of the experimental group are also told that they will be given a demonstration (one more time) of how to operate the VCR and a simplified instruction manual with key operational sections noted with pink underliner. They are told further that they will prohibited from seeing their grandchildren for two months or until they are able to program the VCR to record 'The Days of Our Lives' on weekdays. Prediction is that a significantly greater number of the experimental group grandparents will learn to operate the VCR than control group grandparents supporting the hypothesis that 'It's never too late too learn' and providing counter-evidence to the hypothesis that 'You can't teach an old dog new tricks'.

New experimental research areas in vocabulary learning

We have looked in some detail at one aspect of vocabulary learning and its relationship to some other issues of language learning. But there are certainly a number of other researchable questions about vocabulary learning and its role in overall language learning. What are some of these issues?

Exercise 7.10

Think of five questions you might have about vocabulary learning and its role in language learning, generally. We have listed some of our own interests in a set of questions, which we have included in Table 7.8 (out of sight on the next page). Put together your own list before you look at ours.

Interpreting experimental studies

There have been a number of experimental studies conducted on the learning of second language vocabulary. Some are conducted orally; some in written form. Some test learning in the L1 to L2 direction; some in the L2 to L1 direction. There are a variety of questions you might ask of these studies: a) in order to assure you fully understand them, b) to see if the experimental work has been carried out and reported carefully, and c) to determine if the results of the studies are applicable to your own instructional or research questions.

Many of the experiments involving the keyword vocabulary learning technique report positive results in favor of the keyword experimental technique over the control vocabulary study technique. We mentioned one such study (Atkinson 1975) in the previous section.

Exercise 7.11

Reviewing your own experience and some of the issues raised above, list five questions in regard to keyword-based vocabulary experiments that would help you interpret these studies.

Table 7.8 Second language vocabulary: some possible research areas

1   Are there harder/easier L2 words to learn, remember and recall? If so, why?

2   What is the most effective way to group ways of L2 vocabulary for teaching?
    (frequency, pedagogical usefulness, memorability, conversational usefulness,
    familiarity, potency, personal preference, semantic categories, concreteness,
    etc.)

3   What methods do students favor in learning L2 vocabulary? Why?

4   What methods do teachers favor in teaching L2 vocabulary? Why?

5   What differences are there between a learner's active and passive vocabulary?
    How can these be measured?

6   Is vocabulary of some languages harder to learn than that of others (for
    example, German compared with Japanese)?

7   If lexical phrases are to be counted as vocabulary items, how can these be
    inventoried? How can they be taught?

8   How does vocabulary learning *fit* with other L2 skills—grammar,
    pronunciation, etc?

9   Is memory for L2 vocabulary related to other kinds of memory (of faces,
    figures, names, etc.)?

10 What is the role of context in vocabulary learning? How do students use
    context?

Photocopiable © Oxford University Press

Exercise 7.12

Following are some of the questions that have been raised in the scholarly
literature about various aspects of keyword experiments and about interpretation
of keyword techniques in practical situations. Now that you have had some
practice in hypothesis-making, state your hunch about the answer to each of these
questions in the form of a hypothesis statement. A hypothesis in response to the
first question is given as an example. You can use the sentence form of the
example as a model for your hypotheses in response to the questions raised.

Example Question 1: Does pre-training of subjects in use of the keyword technique
increase their scores on recall of vocabulary words using the keyword technique?

Your hypothesis?

> *Pre-training of subjects in use of the keyword vocabulary learning technique will
> significantly increase the scores of these subjects in keyword-based vocabulary
> learning and recall over those subjects who have a similar experimental condition but
> no pre-training.*

Question 2: Is it better if the experimenter invents the keyword and gives it to subjects or is it better if subjects invent their own keywords?

Your hypothesis?

Question 3: Is it better if the experimenter provides the image link (say, in the form of a cartoon) to subjects or is it better if subjects invent their own imagery links?

Your hypothesis?

Question 4: Is providing a sentence link as effective as providing an imagery link? For example, instead of imagining a picture of a duck with a pot on its head to help in the association of *pato* (Spanish) = *duck* (English), the subject creates/hears a sentence such as 'When the farmer put a pot on its head, the *pato* quacked.'

Your hypothesis?

Question 5: The keyword technique may facilitate the learning of vocabulary items in the direction of Given L2 word → Recall L1 word, but does it help in the learning of vocabulary in the direction Given L1 word → Recall L2 word?

Your hypothesis?

Question 6: Are some keywords better than other keywords?

Your hypothesis?

Question 7: The keyword technique may prove useful in laboratory learning, but is it of any use in real, regular classroom situations?

Your hypothesis?

Question 8: Does use of the keyword technique, because of its several steps, slow the speed of recall or impede the fluency of use of L2 in conversation?

Your hypothesis?

You will find the answers to the questions posed above in the Answer key for Exercise 7.12 on pages 262–3. The answers we provide are derived from research findings on use of the keyword technique. How do your hypotheses fit with the research findings? You should remember that the research findings are all reported by Raugh and Atkinson (1975), who cannot be considered entirely unbiased on the topic of keyword vocabulary techniques. Other researchers may be a bit skeptical of at least some of these findings. (See, for example, Levin and Pessley 1985.) Compare your hypotheses with these experimental results and see if your hypotheses were confirmed or disconfirmed by the experiments summarized in Raugh and Atkinson (1975). Indicate after each of the hypotheses you wrote above a C for a confirmed hypothesis or D for a disconfirmed hypothesis.

Significance of experimental research in teaching vocabulary

In educational history, vocabulary learning has at various periods been treated as both central and peripheral in learning a second language. After a considerable period of both research and pedagogical neglect during the 1950s and 1960s, renewed attention was given to vocabulary by the new methodologies that came into fashion in the 1970s (Communicative Language Learning, Silent Way, Suggestopedia, Natural Approach, etc.). Advocates of these new methodologies exhorted language educators to re-consider the role of vocabulary in second language learning as well as to promote successful strategies to help students learn and retain second language vocabulary for communicative use.

Learners may have always been more aware of the importance of vocabulary learning than have teachers or researchers. Krashen (1977) typifies one apparently commonsensical view when he notes that students traveling in a foreign country don't take a grammar book, they take a dictionary. (This assurance, however, does not appear to be based on interviews conducted by Krashen of student travelers.) In the commonsensical view, the logic might be put like this: there are two main elements of language—sound and meaning—and what holds these two together are words—vocabulary. You don't combine sounds to make sentences; you combine sounds to make words. When you teach how sentences convey meaning, you teach how words go together. So words are the central items that bring sound and meaning together.

In counterpoint to 'commonsensical' appeals is a variety of relatively recent theoretical overviews and research summaries which examine the role of vocabulary learning in mastering a new language. Such a formal/theoretical view is presented by Laufer and Hulstijn in a recent article intended to 'stimulate theoretical thinking and empirical research in the domain of L2 vocabulary learning' (Laufer and Hulstijn 2001). The authors note that 'Virtually all second language learners and their teachers are well aware of the fact that learning a second language (L2) involves the learning of large numbers of words.' They further observe that student apprehension of 'such an enormous task' has had the result that 'learners have always shown a keen interest in finding out how words can best be learned'. These authors observe that learning psychologists (as perhaps contrasted with language educators) have consistently followed William James's dictum that 'all improvement of the memory lies in the line of elaborating the associates', which they interpret to mean that 'the richer the associations that are made with existing knowledge, the higher are the chances that the new information will be retained' (Laufer and Hulstijn 2001:1). The vocabulary experiments in which you have participated in this chapter represent some of the techniques that have been proposed to enrich the association of new vocabulary words with existing knowledge.

In a recent research review (Gersten and Baker 2000) the authors summarize a variety of studies of effective practices for English-language learners, observing that the number one instructional variable identified was 'Building and Using Vocabulary as a Curricular Anchor'. They state that one clear point of agreement among the professional work groups interviewed as part of their research review was that 'vocabulary learning plays a major role in successful programs for English-language learners', and that successful instruction involved 'several approaches … to help students develop a deep understanding' of new vocabulary words (Gersten and Baker 2000: 462).

In another recent summary review, Schmidt identifies 'several fairly general principles that fall within the category of "generally accepted findings"' in relation to 'best practices in foreign language teaching' (Schmidt 2002). Among these principles are the following:

1 People are motivated to do things that are interesting, relevant to their goals, and enjoyable.
2 Different learners use different learning strategies. More successful learners use a broader range of strategies more flexibly.
3 Language aptitude includes (at least) the sub-components of sound discrimination (oral mimicry ability) and verbal memory ability.

We interpret that these 'generally accepted findings' support a view which encourages learners (and their teachers, perhaps) to experiment with different strategies for increasing verbal memory ability (for example, vocabulary learning) and to use more than one of these verbal memory strategies in language study, to the extent that they prove interesting, relevant to learning goals, and enjoyable.

Reflecting on experimental research

You have had an inside look at how experimental research is done and what some of its results are. In particular you have had a chance to focus on alternative approaches to learning second language vocabulary.

Exercise 7.13

Here are some questions for you to ponder, perhaps with a partner.

I   As a teacher, do you/would you provide time and guidance to help students become more effective vocabulary learners? Would you consider using either of the techniques for structuring vocabulary which you experienced in Exercise 7.1 (semantic clustering) and Exercise 7.2 (keyword technique) in your classes? Why or why not?

2   If you were to undertake study of a new second language would you use any of the vocabulary learning techniques that we looked at in this chapter? What would be your own preferred way of learning new vocabulary items?

3   Do you think it is possible or desirable to use the language class to conduct small experimental studies of your own interest? What kind of topic would most interest you in carrying out such a study in a class of your own?

4   Do you believe experimental results can be of any value to the classroom teacher or are they too laboratory-like to have a practical application in real language classrooms?

5   What is the most interesting thing you found out in studying this chapter? What would you like to know more about?

Summary

This chapter introduced you to a classic mode of educational research, the controlled experiment. You participated in a *vocabulary remembering* experiment in which you acted both the part of an experimental subject and a control subject. You analyzed the results of your experiment by comparing the means of item recall in the experimental condition versus the means of item recall in the control condition. The t-test was used to see if there were significant differences between the mean of correct recalls in the two conditions. You also saw that t-tests could be used to compare differences in means between men and women, between learners with greater and lesser years of language training, between those with pets and those without pets, or between pre-test and post-test means for the same individuals. You found that experiments are based on research questions or hypotheses that the researcher has about the expected results of the experiments, and you had some practice in analyzing and writing research questions and hypotheses of your own. Vocabulary/lexical learning is a key theme in current second language research, and you had a chance to examine why this is so. Finally, you considered how experimental designs and results might be of use to you in your own classroom situations.

PART FOUR

Conclusion

Completion

8 COURSE EVALUATION: COMBINING RESEARCH TYPES

Introducing evaluation research

Measure your mind's height by the shade it casts.
ROBERT BROWNING, 1812–1889
English poet

I have never let my schooling interfere with my education.
MARK TWAIN, 1835–1910
American writer

He gave man speech, and speech created thought, which is the measure of the universe.
PERCY BYSSHE SHELLEY, 1792–1822
English poet

The Olympic Games could be said to meet in full the three conditions of the definition of 'evaluation' proposed by Scriven: 'The discipline of evaluation is devoted to the systematic determination of merit, worth, or significance' (Scriven 1999: 1). In this chapter, we are looking at language program evaluation, a somewhat narrower focus than the Olympic Games.

We will explore ways to do language course or program evaluation by combining the various research techniques covered in earlier chapters, and we will apply these in an evaluation of this book.

When we use the term EVALUATION we are *not* referring exclusively to TESTING. Alderson (1986: 5) put it this way: 'Evaluation is the process of seeking to establish the value of something for some purpose, a test is an instrument for gauging learning outcomes.' Evaluation includes all the practices and instruments involved in gathering and compiling the data necessary to make judgments about the value of a language course or program; this may or may not include students' test results. More specifically, in using the phrase LANGUAGE PROGRAM EVALUATION, we mean 'the systematic collection and analysis of all relevant information necessary to promote the improvement of a curriculum and assess its effectiveness and efficiency as well as the participants' attitudes within the context of the particular institutions involved' (Brown1989: 223).

Teachers and administrators do course or program evaluations for many different reasons. Teachers may, for example, do evaluation in order to improve the effectiveness of their

1 course materials
2 classroom activities
3 teaching
4 students' learning processes
5 students' learning

and there will be many other reasons.

Exercise 8.1

(Warm-up)

All of the reasons for doing evaluation in the list above are from a teacher's point of view. Discuss in pairs the importance of evaluation from your points of view as students. List at least five good reasons . If you are working in a class, you may want to discuss the lists of five reasons created by all the pairs to see if any general trends arise across all the pairs.

Exercise 8.2

(Warm-up)

As homework, write a short retrospective essay about what you liked and disliked about this book and about how your views of the book have changed as you have worked your way through it. You might want to review Chapter 3 on Introspection. You might also find it useful to take another look at the Preface and Table of Contents and impressionistically react to how accurately these predicted what you have actually experienced.

Experiencing evaluation research

In order to set up exercises that realistically allow you to experience evaluation research, we have chosen to focus the exercises in this chapter on course book evaluation. The course in question is the research methods course in which you are using this book. However, the same evaluation techniques could equally well be applied to other aspects of the course or to a total program evaluation; the difference is simply one of scale.

The first step in any evaluation is to figure out the purpose of the evaluation and the issues involved in achieving that purpose. In this case, we will define it fairly narrowly:

> The purpose of this evaluation is to determine the effectiveness and efficiency of the course book as well as the attitudes of various interested parties toward the course book.

Naturally, the purpose of the evaluation could be expanded to include evaluation of the teacher's performance, classroom dynamics, students' performances, available resources, etc. but we choose to limit it in this way to make it relatively clear and easy.

Determining the issues involved in achieving the purpose of our evaluation is the second step in the process. One way of figuring out what the issues are is to interview the interested parties. But what questions should you ask as the interviewer? One useful framework for figuring out the questions to ask is provided by Rossett's (1982) five types of questions that cover the important issues in a survey study: (a) problems, (b) priorities, (c) abilities, (d) attitudes, and (e) solutions.

Applying Rossett's framework, we developed a set of interview questions for ourselves as the authors of this book (i.e. Ted and JD). We then used the interview questions to interview each of us separately by e-mail (try not to get too twisted up in the pronouns here). In developing this open-ended questionnaire for ourselves, we used the framework of problems, priorities, abilities, attitudes, and solutions and asked each other two open-ended questions for each category:

1 What problems do you think students might have with the content of this book?
2 What problems do you think teachers might have with presenting the content of this book?
3 Which chapter or chapters do you think are most important?
4 Which of the sections (experiencing, compiling, analyzing, designing, interpreting, significance, and reflecting) that are found across all the chapters do you think are the most important?
5 What abilities does the book assume on the part of the students?
6 What abilities does the book assume on the part of the teacher?
7 What are your attitudes toward the qualitative research types presented in Chapters 2, 3, and 4 in this book?
8 What are your attitudes toward the quantitative research types presented in Chapters 5, 6, and 7 of this book?

9 Give one solution to a problem or issue you raised in the first eight questions above.

10 Give a solution to at least one other problem or issue you raised in the first eight questions above.

The results of the interviews with authors are shown in Appendixes 8.1 and 8.2 on pages 280–6.

Table 8.1 Table for summarizing the results of author e-mail interviews (www)

Issue	Ted Rodgers	JD Brown
Problems (Qs 1 & 2)		
Priorities (Qs 3 & 4)		
Abilities (Qs 5 & 6)		
Attitudes (Qs 7 & 8)		
Solutions (Qs 9 & 10)		

Photocopiable © Oxford University Press

Exercise 8.3

As individuals, go through the answers given by the authors and try to summarize them very briefly in an expanded version of Table 8.1 (i.e. compile them in brief in categories of problems, priorities, abilities, attitudes, and solutions in two columns, one for Ted and one for JD). When you have finished filling in your version of Table 8.1, answer the following questions:

1 Category by category, what are the similarities between the answers given by Ted and JD?

2 What are the differences between the answers given by Ted and JD?

3   Do you think Ted and JD have unbiased answers to the questions being asked?

4   What would you pick out as the three or four key points for the authors' survey?

Exercise 8.4

Since you are the participants in your own course using this book, we will also have you interview each other. Begin by forming pairs. (If you are working alone, simply answer the written questions as though they were asked of you in an interview.) The interviewer should interview the respondent for about 10 minutes; take careful notes on what is said. (Interviewers shouldn't be too shy to ask the respondent to slow down while taking notes.) Then, switch roles and spend another 10 minutes interviewing in the other direction. Each interviewer should use the following questions, which are designed to be parallel (though re-worded to fit you, the students) to those put by the authors to each other:

1   What advantages/disadvantages did you find with the content of this book?

2   What advantages/disadvantages did the teacher find in presenting the content of this book?

3   Which chapter or chapters do you think were most important?

4   Which of the sections (experiencing, compiling, analyzing, designing, interpreting, significance, and reflecting) that are found across all the chapters do you think was the most important for you?

5   What abilities does the book assume on your part as a student?

6   What abilities does the book assume on the part of the teacher?

7   What are your attitudes toward the qualitative research types presented in Chapters 2, 3, and 4 in this book?

8   What are your attitudes toward the quantitative research types presented in Chapters 5, 6, and 7 of this book?

9   Give one possible solution to a problem or issue you raised in the first eight questions above.

10   Give a possible solution to at least one other problem or issue you raised in the first eight questions above.

The purpose of the pair work in Exercise 8.4 was to get answers to the 10 questions in that exercise. However, one additional subordinate, but still important, purpose is to gather information on what issues might be interesting and/or useful to examine more deeply in the evaluation of the book.

Exercise 8.5

In the same pairs you used in Exercise 8.4, work together and list between 5 and 10 issues that came up as important in doing the interviews. (Again, if you are working alone, just jot down any issues that came to mind as you were answering the questions in the previous exercise.)

Exercise 8.6

In groups of four to six people, write at least two Likert-scale questions (of the 1 2 3 4 5, strongly disagree to strongly agree type) and one open-ended question for each of the issues your various pairs isolated in Exercise 8.5. Be sure to write questions that you could administer to the users of the book to find out what their attitudes are toward the book. You may also want to keep handy the guidelines for writing good survey questions provided in Chapter 5, pages 142–5.

Exercise 8.7

Either the teacher or a student should serve as recorder and discussion leader in this exercise. As a class, issue by issue, discuss all the questions that the groups came up with for each issue. Decide on the best two Likert-scale questions and one open-ended question for each of the 10 issues and list them on the board. Be sure to group the Likert-scale questions together in one place and the open-ended questions in another. Don't forget to provide places for any biodata information (for example, gender, years of teaching experience, educational background, etc.) you think you might want to get from each respondent. (If you are working alone, ignore the first two sentences of this paragraph.)

Exercise 8.8

Clean up the book evaluation questionnaire that you have created on the board, so it includes twenty Likert-scale questions (with 1 2 3 4 5, strongly disagree to strongly agree options), those open-ended questions you think are important, and places for any biodata information you think is important. Once the questionnaire is in good shape on the board, either have each student copy the questionnaire so that each one has a copy, or make one copy that is photocopied so that there are enough copies for each student. (For those working alone, in this exercise, you will have to polish up the questionnaire on your own, and in the next exercise, you will then answer it.)

Exercise 8.9

Whichever way you choose to go, all students in the class should now answer the questionnaire that you have created as a group. Also, have the teacher answer the questionnaire from his/her own point of view and copy it to all the students.

Compiling evaluation data

You have already compiled your notes from the Author Interviews in Exercise 8.3 and from your student interviews in Exercise 8.4. Now, it is time to compile the data from your questionnaire.

Exercise 8.10

You may want to divide the tasks up among various groups of students for the sake of efficiency. (Naturally, if you are working alone, you have nothing to compile in this exercise or the next.) You have had enough practice by now at compiling data so you should be able to figure out among yourselves how to divide up the tasks of compiling these data. However you arrange the logistics, as a class, you will need to compile the Likert-scale data like you did in Table 5.1 of Chapter 5 for the four-point Likert-scale *Language Teaching/ Learning Beliefs Questionnaire* (page 123).

Exercise 8.11

You will also need to compile the open-ended questionnaire data so that all the answers to each open-ended question end up in the same place. If there are many answers to these open-ended questions, it may be best to get 10 volunteers, each of whom will type all the answers for one question into a computer file and then print it in enough copies so everyone can have a copy. If there aren't too many such answers, perhaps one volunteer can type the responses to each question on a different page in a word processor and then print out the ten pages in enough copies so that each student in the class can have one. Also, you will need to make enough copies of the teacher's responses so comparisons can be made between the students' and teacher's attitudes toward the book.

Analyzing evaluation data

In this section, we will quickly revisit ways to descriptively analyze quantitative data. Then we will examine ways to use matrices and macro text analysis to analyze the qualitative data in a course book evaluation like this one.

Using descriptive statistics to analyze the Likert-scale questions

Given the explanations in Chapter 5, analyzing the descriptive statistics for your quantitative Likert-scale data should be no problem for you at this point in the book. We suggest you use Table 5.2 in Chapter 5 (page 124) as a guide to analyzing and displaying your results.

Exercise 8.12

(Calculator needed.)

Use whatever strategy you like to organize yourselves and share responsibilities for analyzing the Likert-scale data from your questionnaire. (If you are working alone, you only have one answer to each question (your own), so you can skip this exercise.)

Calculate and display at least the mean, standard deviation, and percentage of respondents who selected 1, 2, 3, 4, and 5. Naturally, you can calculate and display any of the other descriptive statistics (for example, the mode, median, number of responses, high–low, and range) if you would find it useful.

Using matrices to analyze qualitative data

A MATRIX is any array or table, usually in two dimensions, with one set of categories labeled across the top for the columns and another set of categories labeled down the left-hand side for the rows. (Recall that we discussed the use of a matrix for displaying correlation coefficients in Exercise 8.3.) With the data arranged and summarized in columns and rows, you can more easily detect patterns in the data and can more easily present and explain those patterns to readers of the resulting research report. In fact, before settling on a single matrix or set of matrices, you may end up trying more than one. The process may even involve trying different ways of organizing the data, then revising, rearranging, or changing the categories. The goal is to analyze the data and end up with a display that clearly illustrates the patterns or conclusions you have drawn from the data.

If the data are recorded in a paper-and-pencil format, you may choose to use cards for each data entry. Then you can sort them on a large table (or thumb-tacked to a cork board) in columns and rows. Some people prefer to use large pieces of butcher-paper: you might begin by sketching out column and row categories, then enter the data using a pencil to write and erase as necessary for sorting, changing, and rearranging the data within the emerging matrix. If you have access to a computer, you may wish to use a spreadsheet or a database program.

In the previous section, you summarized the data from the interviews of the authors of this book. We called that data display a table, but it could just as well be called a matrix. In Exercise 8.3, we asked you to examine the similarities and differences between the views of Ted and JD. Note how much easier it was to do so looking at the matrix of their answers (the one you created in a matrix like Table 8.1) than it would have been to look at the entire transcript of their data. (See Appendixes 8.1 and 8. 2, pages 280–286.)

A more complex version of a matrix is shown in Lynch's (1992) evaluation study. To understand that matrix, you must first understand that Lynch's study was created to examine:

> …the two major approaches to program evaluation: quantitative, experimental (in the traditional sense of the term) evaluation and qualitative, naturalistic evaluation. The data came from the University of Guadalajara (UdeG)/University of California, Los Angeles (UCLA) Reading English for Science and Technology (REST) Project. (Lynch 1992: 61)

An EFFECTS MATRIX, like the one shown in Table 8.2, is used to describe various effects and processes in the data. The four abbreviations for groups of people used in Table 8.2 are a bit confusing, so we will define them here: (a) *UdeG Coord* is the abbreviation for the University of Guadalajara Co-ordinator, (b) *UdeG T/B Asst's* stands for the University of Guadalajara teaching/research assistants (where the B appears to be a typo), (c) the *UCLA T/Rs* are the University of California, Los Angeles, teacher/researchers, and (d) the four *Ss Groups* are different groups of students at four different levels (B/Beginning, B/Advanced, and A/C Intermediate, and A/C Beginning).

Matrices can take many forms, and as Lynch pointed out, they do 'not come with preordained means for interpretation as the quantitative analyses do' (p. 84). He analyzed the effects matrix in Table 8.2 by examining his data in three categories (Lynch 1992: 84–7): (a) GENERAL PATTERNS, which are overall patterns across all categories on both dimensions of the matrix (for example, counting the numbers of pluses and minuses in the matrix reveals that there are more negative factors in the column for *Process/Methods* than in the column for *Objectives/Goals*; in fact, there is an even higher proportion of negative factors in the column for *Relations/Climate*); (b) SPECIFIC DIFFERENCE PATTERNS, which are detailed responses that are opposite or contradictory (one of the examples given by Lynch was the fact that the UdeG Coordinator listed more positive factors, four to be exact, than did the teacher/researchers, who listed three, in the column for *Process/Methods*. The opposite was true in the column for *Objectives/Goals*, with the coordinator listing only one positive factor and the teacher/researchers listing five.); and (c) SPECIFIC SIMILARITY PATTERNS, which are detailed responses that match or are parallel in one category on one dimension across several categories on the other dimension. (One of the examples given by Lynch was the use of authentic English-language chemical engineering texts in Ss Group B/Beginning

Table 8.2 Example of a matrix used to analyze evaluation data: the effects matrix

As Seen By	Objectives/Goals	Process/Methods	Relations/Climate
UdeG Coord	+ A curriculum framework to improve Ss ability to read EST. − Ss did not 'master' anything just introduced to. − Did *not* convince Ss that they don't need to read word–by–word.	+ Use grammar in context as a strategy for reading. + Use read. strat's., e.g., preview, prediction, skim, scan. + Teach functions of log. Connectors: rhetorical modes. + Use authentic Chem. E. texts, but exclusively.	+ (Coord) overall positive to Project. + T/Ts hard workers − Cultural misunderstandings: T/Rs 'took it personally'. − Ss more demanding than most & 'a few bad apples'. − T/Rs did not get along well as a group.
UdeG T/B Asst's	+ Interesting curric: helpful to Ss.	+ Well supported mat'ls: prep'd well by UCLA − (REST) Too dependent on other Univ. Dept's − Problems w/ classrms and schedules − Tedious classes; too much time spent on some points; excessive repetition − Need to allow more talking & listening in English & expand grammar module.	+ Good attitude—all T/Rs. − Lack of communication: T/R Assts − Lack of understanding (UCLA T/Rs) of Mex. S behavior.
UCLA T/Rs	++ S confidence to 'attach' Engl. Texts + *Signif. improv't in gen. ESL prof., reading & grades in REST* + Ss Chem. E. profs now expect them to read texts in English, w/o translations, and do 'practicas' based on readings. + Basic elements of a curriculum. + Lots of ideas and infor. For a thesis. − Not enough time for research. − Ss will *not* be 'prof. Readers' of EST in 2 years. − 'We didn't do enough for them'. − Not able to give real training to Mexican T/Rs.	+ Using texts as basis for grammar discuss. ++ Give Ss more basic linguistic skills. + Began to use more '4–skills' type activit's for reading. − Lack of mat'ls. − Lack of focus & organization. − Relied too much on theory: didn't know how to implement it. − 'A clump of strat's': did them w/ every text. − T/Rs hindered by need to all do same mat'ls same way, same rate.	++ UCLA support. ++ Some staff members dedicated. − Lack of UdeG admin. Support. − S resentment of Project & T/Rs. − REST staff 'not taken seriously or taken advantage of' ? Lack of cooperation between T/Rs (1 'yes', 2 'no') − Frustration
Ss Group B/ Begin	+ Were able to use some Chem. E. texts (sugg'std by C.E. prof's) in their 'practicas'—helped them. + Now we can use the strategies taught. + Overall, course help us 'bastante'	+ Use of the OHP. − Need a different system for understanding grammar. − At times, too much mat'l too fast: no time to take notes. + Read. strat's do help us w/ reading.	
Ss Group B/ Adv	+ Used texts (Engl.) in our 'practicas'.	+ Use of OHP. − Read. *strat's* approach doesn't work: 'we look at articles but don't read them'. − Need a review of grammar. − Need more participation on part of Ss.	− At times, we feel a little bored.
Ss Group A/ C Int.	+ Now we know how to form/write a sentence in Engl. − Nothing well-defined in the development of the course. − Very little covered first ½ year.	+ More grammar & vocab. (since Feb.) − 'going in circles': same basic activities. − Reading strat's 'a waste of time': already known. − 'Timed' factor on tests unfair.	− 'Boring' − Lack of attend.: because not what expected/wanted; i.e., '4–skills' & bad schedule for Engl. class.
Ss Group A/ C Begin.	+ Did learn something, *not* a waste of time − Didn't learn as much as possible/ hoped − Didn't know where curric. was heading	− Too much grammar: don't understand how logical connect's help us to read − Lack of dynamism in class activities: always T to S − Not enough 'pressure' from Ts	− Lack of motivation − Lack of attendance: due to lack of interest and to bad schedule for English class

(From Lynch 1992)

classes, which was listed as a positive idea by both students and teachers/ researchers in the column for *Objectives/Goals.*)

Exercise 8.13

Break up into groups of 3–5 students to analyze the data from the open-ended questions compiled in Exercise 8.11. (If you are working alone, you will now have the pleasure of analyzing your own answers for interesting patterns.) Then divide up the responsibilities for the analysis so one group analyzes questions 1 and 2, a second group analyzes questions 3 and 4, and so forth (or something similar). Each group should read through the set of data for their questions. You should look for and discuss any patterns that you see emerging from the data. You may want to sort through the data using the cards approach, the butcher-paper approach, or using a computer spreadsheet. If categories for columns and rows do not begin to emerge, try looking for Lynch's general patterns, specific difference patterns, and specific similarity patterns (discussed in the previous paragraph). The result of this analysis should be one or more matrices displaying the data in a way that makes the patterns you have discovered traceable to the matrix data.

Using course book analysis

Course book analysis is loosely related to the sorts of text analysis presented in Chapter 2, the case study of Helen Keller's letters. However, unlike the text analysis dealt with there, in course book analysis we explore text in larger units. Instead of looking at the details of grammar, vocabulary, mechanics, etc., we examine their overall characteristics. A checklist of such characteristics is shown in Table 8.3. Notice that this includes a number of basic categories and some suggestions as to what to look for in the process of evaluating a course book. Other things will occur to you and there is space in the table for you to add your own ideas.

Exercise 8.14

Individually as homework, do a course book analysis by applying the checklist shown in Table 8.3 to this book by writing a sentence or two in reaction to each category in Table 8.3. Add or subtract categories as you think appropriate.

Table 8.3 Checklist for analyzing course books (www)

A Materials background
   1 Author qualifications
   2 Publisher reputation
   3 _____

B Fit to needs
   1 Students' needs
     a Content
     b Learning style
     c _____
   2 Teacher's needs
     a Content
     b Teaching style
     c _____

C Physical characteristics
   1 Organization
     a Logic of organization
     b Table of contents
     c Index
     d Answer keys
     e _____
   2 Physical layout
     a Text layout
     b Spacing
     c Highlighting
     d _____

   3 Physical qualities
     a Cover
     b Paper
     c Binding
     d _____
   4 Editorial qualities
     a Content is accurate and reads well
     b Directions clear and easy to follow
     c Examples clear
     d _____
   5 Writing
     a Readability
     b Interest
     c Logic
     d Comprehensiveness
     e _____

D Logistical characteristics
   1 Availability
   2 Price
   3 _____

(Reworked from Brown 1995b: 161)

Reporting evaluation results

In this section, you should decide how to report course book evaluation studies. We can think of three possibilities: (a) as written studies in the traditional research report format discussed throughout this book, (b) as portfolios replete with your data, results, interpretations, and reflections; or (c) as oral reports to the rest of the class. Decide which of these approaches you wish to use immediately and start putting together a project. You will, however, want to include information that comes later in the chapter too, so you will not be able to complete the project until you have finished reading the chapter.

Regardless of which type of project you decide to do, you will need to include all the information you have gathered, compiled, and analyzed elsewhere in this chapter. Table 8.4 provides a summary of the information which you may have gathered in doing the exercises in this chapter.

Table 8.4 Data to include in the report

Exercise 8.1	Purposes for course evaluation from the student's point of view
Exercise 8.2	Introspective essay on what the student liked and disliked about the textbook, and how those views changed as the course developed

A copy of the Table 8.1 summary of the interviews with Ted and JD

Exercise 8.3	The students' analysis of Table 8.1.
Exercises 8.4 and 8.5	Interview with another student.
Exercise 8.6	Group work Likert-scale questions about the textbook.
Exercise 8.7 and 8.8	Final version of the class questionnaire about the textbook.
Exercise 8.9	A copy of their responses to the questionnaire, and a copy of the teacher's responses to the questionnaire (both Likert-scale and open-ended responses).
Exercise 8.10	A copy of the Likert-scale data compiled from the student responses to the questionnaire.
Exercise 8.11	A copy of the open-ended data compiled from the student responses to the questionnaire.
Exercise 8.12	A copy of the table of descriptive statistics (like those shown in Chapter 5) for all of the Likert-scale questions.
Exercise 8.13	The matrix or matrixes developed by the group in which the student participated.
Exercise 8.14	The student's textbook analysis (based on Table 8.3).

Photocopiable © Oxford University Press

Traditional research report

The first strategy you might want to use is to report the results of your course book evaluation project in the traditional format, which should include at least some parts of the following:

Abstract
I   **Introduction***
    A *Literature Review*—a review of the relevant literature that situates the study within the field
    B *Purpose*—a statement of the purpose of the study including research questions or hypotheses
II   **Methods***
    A *Participants*—a description of how the participants were selected and of their pertinent characteristics
    B *Materials*—a description of any tests, questionnaires, teaching materials, etc. and why they were reliable and valid for use in the study
    C *Procedures*—a step-by-step description of how the materials were used with the participants, how they were scored or coded, and how they were organized
III   **Results***—a straightforward technical report of what the results of the study were in tables and figures of various types as appropriate
IV   **Discussion**—an explanation of the results including direct answers to the research questions
V   **Conclusions**—a discussion of the theoretical and practical implications of the study as well as its limitations, and suggestions for future research
References
Appendices
Tables

If this project is important to your course grade, you will probably want to make all of the sections fairly complete. However, if the project is just a simple chapter exercise, you would probably want to do it in outline form, and perhaps only include the key sections, i.e. the ones with asterisks(*).

Portfolio of data and results

Alternatively, for the purposes of this course book evaluation, you could put together a portfolio of data and results. To do so, consider using the following steps:

1 Students and teacher should discuss what types of exercises, data, and results they want to include in the portfolio. In this case, consider including all the exercises, and including the original data, tables or matrices of results. Also, bear your reader in mind; find a balance between providing too much information, which will swamp the reader, and offering too little, which may weaken your case.

2 Consider including not just the results but also the steps involved in arriving at the results.
3 Each student should write a summary statement that reflects both (a) on what they found in doing the research but also (b) what they learned in putting together the portfolio.
4 Be sure to include a table of contents and a preface that describes the logic of your choices and their organization.

Oral report option

The last option would be for each student (or pairs/groups of students) to make oral reports to the class. Such reports could be used instead of the above two options or to supplement either one. These oral reports could be organized like a traditional research report to explain the research, or could simply be organized to tell the class about the portfolio development process and the research results.

Designing your own evaluation studies

The recent literature on second language research indicates that two different sets of similar issues have arisen for judging the merit of quantitative and qualitative research.

We will first look at quantitative research, which is often judged in terms of:

1 validity
2 reliability and
3 objectivity.

Brown (1997a) defined VALIDITY as 'the degree to which the results can be accurately interpreted and effectively generalized'. We can then divide this in to two parts: the first (i.e. 'the degree to which the results can be accurately interpreted') is commonly labeled INTERNAL VALIDITY; the second (i.e. 'the degree to which the results can be generalized') is commonly called EXTERNAL VALIDITY.

Similarly, RELIABILITY can be defined as the degree to which the results of a study are consistent, a concept that can also be viewed in internal and external terms. INTERNAL RELIABILITY is the degree to which we can expect consistent results if the data for the study were re-analyzed by another researcher. EXTERNAL RELIABILITY is the degree to which we can expect consistent results if the study were replicated (i.e. repeated). To some degree, issues of reliability are addressed by calculating reliability statistics for the measures involved and by examining the probabilities that statistical results occurred by chance alone.

OBJECTIVITY will be defined here as the observation of an object as it actually is rather than as it exists just in the mind of the person making the observations. Objectivity is usually contrasted with subjectivity. However, even objectivity is a relative concept, which depends on the scale of observation. For instance, consider how you see the book in your hand *objectively* and compare that to how a chemist would view the same book objectively as a piece of matter at the molecular level.

Second, let us look at qualitative research. Again the concepts of validity and reliability are viewed as equally valuable here. (See for instance, Davis 1992, 1995; Lazaraton 1995; Lynch 1992, 1997.) However, other terms are used and indeed the concepts are defined somewhat differently. Lincoln and Guba (1985: 145) contend that terminology like internal validity, external validity, reliability, and objectivity used in judging quantitative research should be replaced when judging qualitative research. They suggested analogous terminology: credibility, transferability, dependability, and confirmability.

CREDIBILITY is essentially the believability of the results for a qualitative study, which is roughly analogous to the concept of *internal validity* in quantitative studies. TRANSFERABILITY is the degree to which the results of a qualitative study could be transferred to other settings (particularly the setting of the particular reader), which is loosely analogous to the concept of *external validity* in quantitative studies. DEPENDABILITY is the consistency of the results of a qualitative study or the degree to which they can be trusted, which is roughly analogous to the concept of *reliability* in quantitative studies. CONFIRMABILITY is the degree to which qualitative results are or could be corroborated, which is roughly analogous to objectivity in quantitative studies.

Table 8.5 maps the two sets of terminology onto each other.

Credibility and *transferability* will be enhanced if you have a very clear, complete, and detailed description of the research (sometimes referred to as a 'thick description'). *Credibility* and *dependability* will be improved if you use TRIANGULATION and MEMBER CHECKING (both concepts will be defined and described in a moment). Finally, *confirmability* can be enhanced by using *triangulation* and *member checking* and by making the data available to other researchers (as described in detail in Lincoln and Guba 1985). Other strategies have been worked out for improving the credibility, transferability, dependability, and confirmability of qualitative research. For more details, see Davis 1992, 1995; Lynch 1992, 1997; Brown 2001.

Table 8.5 Quantitative and qualitative research terminology: rough equivalences

Quantitative		Qualitative
Validity	Internal	Credibility
	External	Transferability
Reliability	Internal	Dependability
	External	
Objectivity		Confirmability

Photocopiable © Oxford University Press

Focus on triangulation

TRIANGULATION is a term the social sciences have borrowed, somewhat casually, from the fields of surveying and navigation. In surveying and navigation, one determines the position of an object by measuring the angles of observation to this object from two points of already known positions. In the social sciences, triangulation refers to the attempt to understand some aspect of human behavior by studying it from more than one standpoint, often making use of both quantitative and qualitative data in doing so.

If you can examine your data from at least two points of view, you will maximize the possibility of getting credible findings by cross-validating those findings. Miles and Huberman (1984: 235) said much the same thing when they wrote: 'Stripped to its basics, triangulation is supposed to support a finding by showing that independent measures of it agree with it or, at least, don't contradict it.'

Denzin (1978) listed four kinds of triangulation: 'data triangulation', 'investigator triangulation', 'theory triangulation', and 'methodological triangulation'; Janesick (1994) suggested 'interdisciplinary triangulation' as a fifth type. Freeman (1998) suggested one other type of triangulation, which Brown (2001) divided into what could be considered the sixth and seventh types ('time triangulation' and 'location triangulation'). All of these types of triangulation are listed and defined (with examples) in Table 8.6.

Table 8.6 Summary of seven types of triangulation

DATA TRIANGULATION—using multiple sources of information, usually people with different roles, helps you to understand and moderate the natural biases of those people; e.g. in a language course/program evaluation, you might use students, teachers, and administrators.

INVESTIGATOR TRIANGULATION—using multiple researchers to examine the same data independently helps you to understand and moderate the researchers' biases; e.g. two or three researchers might analyze the same open-response questions on a questionnaire, then compare their conclusions.

THEORY TRIANGULATION—using multiple theoretical frameworks; e.g. you might analyze the open-response questions from a series of interviews based on three theoretical frameworks: error analysis, discourse analysis, and behavioral analysis.

METHODOLOGICAL TRIANGULATION—using multiple data-gathering procedures; e.g. you might choose to use interviews, questionnaires, and classroom observations to gather data.

INTERDISCIPLINARY TRIANGULATION—using the perspectives of several disciplines; e.g. you might use perspectives drawn from second language studies, education, and psychology.

TIME TRIANGULATION—using multiple occasions to gather data; e.g. you might gather data at the beginning, middle, and end of a school term.

LOCATION TRIANGULATION—using multiple sites to gather data; e.g. you might gather data from three different high schools, or from two junior high schools, and two high schools.

Photocopiable © Oxford University Press

Exercise 8.15

Let us say you are attempting to determine, as a teacher, which vocabulary words in your L2 textbook learners will have the hardest time remembering. Below are listed some possible sources of data on L2 vocabulary. In trying to triangulate data that best answer your question, which data sources are you likely to find most useful?

Rank order the data sources as to their usefulness and suggest in a sentence why you think each one would or would not be useful for the purposes of triangulation.

   1   An L1/L2 bilingual dictionary.

   2   Poll of previous text users as to words they found the hardest to remember.

   3   Frequency list of L2 vocabulary words as used in writing by L2 native speakers.

4   Pre-test of new learners to determine which vocabulary items they already know meanings for.

5   Number of repetitions of each vocabulary item in the L2 textbook.

6   A poll of L2 native speakers as to which L2 words they think learners of L2 as a foreign language will have the hardest time remembering.

7   A list of the words which you as an L2 teacher feel that learners have had the most difficulty with in past classes.

8   An ordering of vocabulary items in the L2 textbook in terms of word length.

9   Survey of an issue of an L2 daily newspaper to see which words from the L2 textbook appear in that day's newspaper.

Interpreting evaluation studies

Triangulation in an example evaluation study

While it is usually not feasible (or even desirable) to use all seven types of triangulation, using several can prove helpful. In one recent evaluation study (Brown 2000), Brown was given the daunting task of evaluating the English language teaching, course books, and testing for all public secondary schools in Tunisia. He used three forms of triangulation, the first, fourth, and seventh in the list in Table 8.4 above: data triangulation, methodological triangulation, and location triangulation. Data triangulation was done by gathering information from the coordinators (inspectors, pedagogical advisors, and teacher trainers), teachers, and students. Methodological triangulation was accomplished by using group interviews, observations, and questionnaires with each of these three groups. Location triangulation was achieved by visiting ten different school sites over the course of two weeks including one basic education (grades 7, 8, and 9) and one secondary school (grades 10, 11, 12, and 13) in each of five cities (Tunis, Siliana, Medenine, Sfax, and Sousse). In brief, data were gathered from each of three data groups, using each of three methods in each of ten locations.

An additional qualitative research technique called 'member checking' was used at various points in this study. MEMBER CHECKING entails confirming the data, analyses, interpretations, and conclusions with the respondents themselves. At each stage of this research, member checking was an important factor in developing the questionnaires, in deciding which questions to ask in the group interviews, and in verifying the conclusions as they emerged.

Limitations of the example evaluation study

As with all research (qualitative research in particular), it is important to recognize not only operational strengths in research methodology, like triangulation and member checking, but also on-site, real-time limitations. In this Tunisian evaluation research, at least the following limitations should be recognized:

1 This study was conducted by a JIJOE (Jet In Jet Out Expert), who knew very little about education in Tunisia when he arrived. Note: an evaluation conducted by an outsider can also be viewed as a positive aspect of this study in the sense that a JIJOE has little or no personal or political stake in any aspect of the educational system in Tunisia, and so may arrive with few partisan attitudes toward any aspect of the curriculum. As such, a JIJOE may have little *credibility* initially, though the *objectivity* of such a person may be very high. (See discussions of these terms earlier in this chapter.)

2 All group meetings, observations, and questionnaires were done in the first few weeks of the school year, perhaps before students and teachers were settled into a routine. This certainly all took place before students were used to the new materials and teaching styles they were encountering.

3 As a consequence of number 2, the students and teachers were asked to reflect on 'last year's' course. Naturally, memory of what last year was like may be weaker.

4 Prolonged engagement is one of the primary underpinnings of really solid qualitative research. This study took place over a period of two weeks.

5 Only five sites and ten schools were visited. They may or may not be typical of the 'average' schools in Tunisia. However, it is clear that only urban schools—no rural ones—were visited.

Exercise 8.16

In the Tunisian evaluation study, the researcher used three forms of triangulation: data triangulation, methodological triangulation, and location triangulation (i.e. the first, fourth, and seventh types listed in Table 8.6). Now, we would like you to think about triangulation in terms of your course book evaluation study. The data gathered in this chapter include the following eight items:

1   The author e-mail interview with Ted (Exercise 8.3)

2   The author e-mail interview with JD (Exercise 8.3)

3   Your retrospective essay (Exercise 8.2)

4   The student interviews (Exercise 8.4)

5   The student Likert-scale questionnaire (Exercise 8.9)

6   The student open-ended questionnaire (Exercise 8.9)

7   The teacher Likert-scale questionnaire (Exercise 8.9)

8   The teacher open-ended questionnaire (Exercise 8.9)

9   Course book analysis (Exercise 8.14)

Individually, answer the following questions:

1   How would each of these nine be labeled according to the triangulation categories in Table 8.6?

2   How might they be systematically combined to strengthen the course book evaluation?

3   What are the strengths of your course book evaluation study (especially in terms of triangulation) and its weaknesses?

4   How could the study be improved next time it is done?

Be sure to include these responses as part of your research write-up, portfolio, or oral report for this chapter.

Significance of evaluation studies

We had three reasons for choosing evaluation research as the topic of this final chapter. One was the general importance of educational evaluation studies in terms of money and energy invested in them over the years. The second reason was the way evaluation research today requires the use of both qualitative and quantitative research tools and typically combines several of the research types presented in this book. This chapter thus provides a review of the course. The third reason was that evaluation has direct relevance to your professional life. Let's consider each of these issues separately.

The general importance of evaluation studies

Evaluation has long been an important component of educational planning and funding. Millions of dollars have been at stake annually in such efforts in the United States alone. In education circles, at least four major approaches to program evaluation have been advocated over the years. (For further elaboration, see Brown 1995a.)

1   *Product-oriented approaches* simply focused on evaluating the degree to which the instructional objectives of a program have been achieved. (See, for example, Tyler 1942, 1951; or Metfessel and Michael 1967.)

2   *Static-characteristic approaches* evaluated program effectiveness by having outside experts inspect a program's static characteristics such as the number of library books, student-to-teacher ratio, parking facilities, accounting practices, etc., usually for purposes of institutional accreditation, a

process whereby an association of institutions sets up evaluation procedures to decide whether individual institutions should be certified, or accredited, as members. (For more on this, see Popham 1975: 25.)

3 *Process-oriented approaches* were based on the realization that evaluation should examine the degree to which an institution is meeting program objectives, but should also facilitate curriculum revision, change, and improvement. (See, for example, Scriven 1967 on 'goal-free evaluation'; or Stake 1967, on his 'countenance model'.)

4 *Decision-facilitation approaches* attempt to avoid evaluator judgments, favoring instead the gathering of information to help the faculty and administrators arrive at their own assessments, judgments, and decisions. (Examples are provided by Alkin 1969 and the 'CSE model', named after the Center for the Study of Evaluation at UCLA; Provus 1971 and the 'Discrepancy model'; and Stufflebeam 1974 and the 'CIPP model', an acronym for Context Input Process and Product.)

The notions of program development and program evaluation have also evolved from systems approaches to the design of (a) business products and marketing strategies, (b) government programs like weapons systems, and (c) training programs for business and government (as described in Dick and Carey 1985). These approaches presumed a linear sequence of events comprising formulation of objectives, selection of content, task analysis, design of learning activities, definition of behavioral outcomes and evaluation measures for determining the achievement or non-achievement of planned outcomes. As we pointed out earlier, such linear thinking appears to have become outmoded for some types of research even within the hard sciences from which it emerged. This situation has left program evaluation in somewhat of a quandary. On the one hand, educational funding agencies are asking for 'competency-based' analysis of supported educational programs of the Dick and Carey type. On the other hand, the evaluators themselves are looking for more situational, more qualitative, more interactive models of program evaluation. You are an active contributor to the current dialog as you take part in this course and in the decisions you exercise after you have completed it. You are part of the action.

Combining quantitative and qualitative research tools

The second reason we chose evaluation research for this final chapter is because evaluation demands the use of a variety of research tools, such as those presented in this text, including both quantitative and qualitative research methods. To review briefly, Brown (1989) defines quantitative data as information 'gathered using those measures which lend themselves to being turned into numbers and statistics. Examples might include test scores, student rankings within a class, or simply the number of males and females in a program' (Brown 1989: 231). However, Rodgers (1986) foresaw the changes in the wind when he wrote, 'the recent history of science has … cut the ground out from those in evaluation who sought to apply the methods of science to the practices of education. Evaluators like philosophers of science are experimenting with new paradigms or are doing without' (Rodgers 1986: 114).

One such new paradigm included both quantitative and qualitative data collection and analysis techniques. Lynch (1992, 1997) provided excellent examples of how quantitative data in the form of test scores can be used in an evaluation study. However, more importantly he shows how qualitative data can be used. Qualitative data will be defined here as information gathered using techniques that do not necessarily lend themselves to being turned into numbers and statistics. Examples might include meetings, interviews, open-ended questionnaire items, observations, etc. In the Lynch study, he used interview transcripts, observation notes, journal entries, and corres- pondence. He analyzed those qualitative data using different types of displays 'to reduce and interpret the data' (Lynch 1997: 62).

Beretta (1990) provides another good example of how useful qualitative data (in the form of teachers' accounts of the implementation process in a program) can be. Ross (1992: 169) similarly proposed that, 'both qualitative and quantitative types of evaluation can be utilized with a view to defining a program' and added that using both qualitative and quantitative methods may provide alternative views of the same classroom phenomena'.

However, Lynch realistically finds that qualitative data are 'incredibly time- consuming to collect and analyze' (Lynch 1992: 93). Alderson and Scott (1992: 53–4) further point out that quantitative data are 'both easier to gather, and more amenable to analysis and summary' and add that 'although responses to the more qualitative methods were good, their open-ended nature made it more difficult to compare reports of discussions and interviews …'. The solutions found in the literature include the following:

1 'always have an explicit purpose in mind for any data that are collected' (Alderson and Scott 1992: 93),
2 'make sure that anyone asked to collect those data know the purpose for doing so' (Alderson and Scott 1992: 93),
3 'focus on answerable questions' (Beretta 1992: 19), and
4 'make the best of whatever tools are available' (Beretta 1992: 19).

In any case, by his example, Lynch (1992, 1997) has clearly shown that both quantitative and qualitative research methods can be effectively combined in doing program evaluation, and his study illustrates how well that can be done. Indeed, in doing the exercises in this chapter, you have demonstrated the same thing.

Exercise 8.17

Look back at the nine items of course book evaluation data gathered in this chapter listed in Exercise 8.16. Think about how you compiled and analyzed each type of data. Then, decide which of them would most appropriately be classified as quantitative data and which as qualitative data. Write your classification lists. Then answer the following questions:

1   What did you learn from the qualitative data that you couldn't learn from the quantitative data?

2   What did you learn from the quantitative data that you couldn't learn from the qualitative data?

3   How did using both types of data strengthen your course book evaluation study?

Direct relevance to your professional life

We are assuming that many of you are taking this course as part of a graduate program in language education, primarily teacher education. Like other educational programs, it requires competent program evaluation to make it optimally effective—maybe even more so than most. Yet meta-analyses of such evaluations have consistently characterized them as 'orphans' or have commented on the lines that 'Much has been written about program evaluation in many other fields, but little has been written about it in teacher education' (Galluzzo 1995). This is an area that is crying out for professional attention (such as you might offer). Your evaluation project in this chapter is one step in the direction of evaluating at least the course book part of such a teacher-training program. Naturally, the techniques and skills that you have learned in this chapter, indeed in this book, could be turned to evaluating other aspects of your teacher-training program. The next move is yours.

Reflecting on evaluation research

As we mentioned at the top of this chapter, this evaluation could have been expanded to include evaluations of the teacher's performance, classroom dynamics, students' performances, available resources, etc.

Exercise 8.18

In groups of 3–5 people, if possible, consider the following questions:

1   What other types of data would you have to gather to perform a more inclusive evaluation research project examining the whole course?

2   Would classroom observations help?

3   What types of information would you be looking for in such observations?

4   How would you collect, compile, analyze, and report such classroom observations?

5   How would text analysis fit into the analysis of data for this broader evaluation project?

We have commented previously that one pervasive contemporary view in our field is that there is no right way to teach, though there may be a variety of wrong ways. Teachers with widely different personalities and approaches to teaching have become very effective. Good teaching then appears to be a mix—largely indeterminate—of intuition and knowledge, magic and science. Pennington (1989) postulates a continuum, represented diagrammatically as shown in Figure 8.1.

Figure 8.1 Teaching as a continuum from magic to science

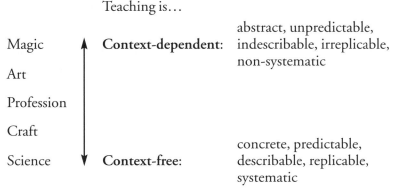

Teaching is…

Magic	↑	**Context-dependent:**	abstract, unpredictable, indescribable, irreplicable, non-systematic
Art			
Profession			
Craft			
Science	↓	**Context-free:**	concrete, predictable, describable, replicable, systematic

(From Pennington 1989: 97)

The range of views runs the gamut from those who see teaching as a spontaneous, idiosyncratic, even innately determined (magic) activity to those who see teaching as susceptible to comprehensive analysis and full description, an activity that is thus fully trainable to a universal standard (science).

Exercise 8.19

Answer the following questions:

1   What is your own view of teaching?

2   Describe an instance in your own teaching or learning experience that is particularly memorable.

3   Where on the magic-to-science continuum would you put this example? Why?

Then, as a class, discuss your differing views on whether teaching is magic or science. Make two lists: one for the ways teaching can be viewed as magic and one for the ways it can be viewed as science. Is there any middle ground? Is there a way of combining the two views of teaching?

Scriven, a well-known figure in educational program evaluation, provides an overview of the broader field of *applied evaluation*:

> While most of program and personnel evaluation is heavily dependent on the social sciences and capable of a high degree of objectivity and utility, others vary independently on these dimensions. Some come close to being pseudo-evaluative (for example, wine tasting, art criticism), some are partially valid (architectural criticism, portfolio management, literary criticism), and some support highly valid evaluations but are not dependent on the social sciences (for example, the reviews done by appellate courts, the evaluations of claimed proofs of Fermat's Theorem in mathematical journals). (Scriven 1999: 1)

Scriven has sketched some fields of applied evaluation covering a range that looks somewhat like Pennington's magic to science continuum. Given your experience in this chapter, where on the magic-to-science continuum would you place program evaluation?

Exercise 8.20

Consider the links between Pennington's magic-to-science continuum and Scriven's range of evaluation fields. Try to decide whether you feel program evaluation is a fully rational, well-structured, scientific process or is a process heavily dependent on the researcher's personality, happenstance, and the *art* of research. What aspects of evaluation strike you as *science* and what parts strike you as *art*?

Exercise 8.21

Table 8.7 (from Rodgers 1986: 117) shows a matrix similar in form to the Lynch (1992) matrix in Table 8.2, but quite different in function. While the Lynch matrix provides the effects or results of a qualitative analysis for the REST program, the Rodgers matrix shows the design for the evaluation of the Hawaii English Program (HEP). Notice in Table 8.7 that the columns represent different points in time for the evaluation activities and that the categories labeled A, B, C, and D in the rows are different groups of people, under each of which are the various numbered evaluation activities. Examine Table 8.7, then answer the following questions and record your answers, if you can, in pairs:

1   What are the many different types of research that contribute to the total HEP evaluation? List at least one example from Table 8.7 for each of the following five types of research: comparative test measures, classroom observations, interviews, questionnaires, and introspections.

2   What likely dimensions in this design could be laid out in a matrix in reporting the results? What would at least one such matrix look like? Prepare a draft matrix awaiting data (with rows and columns labeled).

Exercise 8.22

As homework, look back at the short retrospective essay you wrote in Exercise 8.2 about what you liked and disliked about this course book and about how your views of this course book have changed as the course developed, and answer the following questions:

1   How have your views changed since you wrote that retrospective essay? Write a list of the ways your views have changed.

2   To what degree are the changes in your views (the ones you listed in Question 1) based on the processes that you have experienced in this chapter?

3   How have the various types of data you have gathered, compiled, and analyzed in this chapter affected your views? Next to each change in your list in Question 1, jot down the data source(s) that helped to bring about the change.

4   Consider the following research types taken from the table of contents of this book:
    Case study research
    Introspection research
    Classroom research
    Descriptive statistics research
    Correlational research
    Quasi-experimental research

Table 8.7 Hawaii English Program, secondary evaluation testing instrument

I At the beginning of the year	II At the beginning of the unit	III. During the unit	IV. At the end of the unit	V. At the end of the year
A Student (about two English periods)	A Student (about one English period)	A Student (part of English program)	A Student (about one English period)	A Student (about two English periods)
1 Performance in English test	1 Student unit performance test	1 Student assessment of activity and components in unit questionnaire (optional)	1 Student unit performance test	1 Performance in English test
2 Survey of reading and writing habits	2 Student attitude toward unit or areas covered by unit questionnaire (optional)		2 Student attitude toward unit questionnaire (optional)	2 Survey of reading and writing habits
3 Attitude toward the study of English questionnaire			3 Student attitude toward subprogram (optional)	3 Attitude toward the study of English questionnaire
4 Attitude toward self as a learner questionnaire				4 Attitude toward self as a learner questionnaire
5 Esteem for language tests				5 Esteem for language tests
B Teacher (about two preparation periods)	B Teacher (about one preparation period)	B Teacher (about 10–20 minutes per assessment period)	B Teacher (about two preparation periods)	B Teacher (about two preparation periods)
1 Teacher assessment of HEP Part I	1 Delivery of testing materials: teacher assessment	1 Unit activities: teacher assessment (to be specified by each subprogram)	1 Removal of testing materials: teacher assessment	1 Teacher assessment of HEP Parts II.A, II.B
2 Teacher self-assessment		2 Unit components: teacher assessment	2 Teacher assessment of units	2 Teacher self-assessment of some language arts teaching methods Part II
		3 Teacher citation of offensive references flag sheet	3 Teacher assessment of subprogram	3 Teacher English curriculum assessment scales
			4 General teacher's manual: teacher assessment	
			5 Unit teacher's manual: teacher assessment	

C Test administrator (teacher or evaluator)
1 HEP program tests: test administrator's assessment

C Evaluator
1 Unit test: evaluator assessment

C Evaluator (periodic visit to the classroom)
1 Classroom observation record: evaluator assessment of implementation of unit/subprogram
2 Materials observation record: assessment of suitability of curriculum for classroom use
3 Field test support: evaluator interview with teacher

D Visitor
1 Visitor assessment of HEP classroom

C Test administrator (teacher or evaluator)
1 Unit test: test administrator assessment

C Test administrator (teacher or evaluator)
1 HEP program tests: test administrator's assessment

D Parents
1 HEP parent questionnaire

(From Rodgers 1986: 117)

Briefly, list one way each of those six research types could be incorporated into a program evaluation (for example, an evaluation of this book).

Summary

This chapter began with definitions of the discipline of evaluation, the concept of evaluation itself, and the notion of language program evaluation. You also looked at reasons why teachers and administrators do evaluations of this kind and you started thinking about your evaluation of this book. The next step in doing an evaluation involved deciding on the purpose of the evaluation and figuring out what issues are involved. You then found a set of interview questions for the authors of this book along with their answers, and you did a tentative analysis of their answers.

After assembling the Likert-scale and open-ended data into a useable form, you (a) used descriptive statistics to analyze the Likert-scale data, (b) looked for patterns in the open-ended data using the matrix technique, and (c) used the course book analysis technique. Next, you looked at three different ways to report your course book evaluation: the traditional research-report format, a portfolio of your data and results, and/or an oral report. Next, there was a discussion of how quantitative research is often judged in terms of validity (both internal and external), reliability (including both internal and external), and objectivity. You then saw how qualitative research is often judged by analogous concepts of credibility, transferability, dependability, and confirmability, especially using techniques like triangulation and member checking. Next, an example of triangulation in an evaluation study in Tunisia was presented along with a discussion of the limitations of that study. Finally, you had an opportunity to compare briefly some case study evaluation designs with your own study design for this book.

ANSWER KEYS

Exercise 2.5

Our analysis of noun changes in the Helen Keller letters:

	Proper nouns	Simple nouns	Plural nouns	Conjoined nouns	Pronouns	Noun phrases
Letter 1	helen, anna, george	Apple, bird, medicine, mother	0	0	0	stick of candy, new dress
Letter 2	Helen, helen, mildred	papa, swing, lemonade, dog	0	0	0	0
Letter 3	Helen, Mildred, mildred, boston	gun, water, mouth	girls, ducks	prince and jumbo, jumbo and mamie	0	blind girls
Letter 4	memphis, mildred, memphis, huntsville	mother	Apples	mother and mildred, dress and hat	I, it, me, he	a letter, a pretty new dress and hat
Letter 5	Mr.Anagnos, Boston, June Miss Betty, Christmas-tree	Father	gloves, cuffs, scholars, presents	→	I, me, her, it	This morning, nice collar, Miss Betty and her scholars, many pretty presents
Letter 6	Lucien Thompson, Adeline Moses, New York	→	violets (etc.), eyes, arms	violets and crocuses and jonquils	me, Her, She, their	a beautiful bouquet of v & c & j, a lovely doll, a pretty red dress, Nancy's sister

Exercise 2.19

The rank of items given by Nunan's language teacher participants to the Category Three question were:

1 Talking to L1 speakers
2 Pictures, films, videos
3 Learning by doing
4 Talking to friends
5 Practicing out of class

6 Watching television
7 Small group work
8 In-class conversation
9 Having a coursebook
10 Learning by hearing

(Nunan 1991: 154)

Exercise 5.8

mean = 338/11 = 30.7272 ≈ 30.73
mode = trimodal 27, 29, and 31
median = 30

Exercise 6.8

Name	NEPE $(X) - M_X$	$= X–M_X$	MTELP $(Y) - M_Y$	$= Y–M_Y$	$(X–M_X)(Y–M_Y)$
Fahtima	100 − 78.11	= 21.89	9 − 77.00	= 21.00	459.67
Jose	94 − 78.11	= 15.89	9 − 77.00	= 15.00	238.83
Maria	86 − 78.11	= 7.89	8 − 77.00	= 12.00	94.67
Jaime	89 − 78.11	= 10.89	8 − 77.00	= 9.00	98.00
Abdullah	78 − 78.11	= −0.11	7 − 77.00	= −2.00	0.22
Noriko	76 − 78.11	= −2.11	7 − 77.00	= 2.00	-4.22
Hans	64 − 78.11	= −14.11	6 − 77.00	= −8.00	112.89
Tatania	61 − 78.11	= −17.11	5 − 77.00	= −23.00	393.56
Jürgen	55 − 78.11	= −23.11	5 − 77.00	= −26.00	600.69
Mean	78.11		77.00		= 1994.00 $= \Sigma(X–M_X)(Y–M_Y)$
SD	14.69		15.52		

$$r = \frac{\Sigma(X-M_x)(Y-M_y)}{NS_xS_y} = \frac{1994.00}{9(14.69)(15.52)} = \frac{1994.00}{2051.8992} = .9717826 \approx .97$$

Exercise 6.10

$$\Phi = \frac{BC - AD}{\sqrt{(A+B)(C+D)(A+C)(B+D)}} = \frac{(12 \times 16) - (5 \times 6)}{\sqrt{(5+12)(16+6)(5+16)(12+6)}} = \frac{192 - 30}{\sqrt{(17)(22)(21)(18)}}$$

$$= \frac{162}{\sqrt{141,372}} = \frac{162}{375.99} = .4308625 \approx .43$$

This correlation shows only a weak relationship between country of training and preference for teaching English using the grammar-translation method.

Exercise 6.13

Pearson r critical would be .2540; since the observed r is .31, which is greater than the critical value, it is *significant* at .01 (i.e. $p < .01$) with 102 students, non-directional.

Exercise 6.14

Pearson r critical value would be .3233; since the observed r is .31, which is less than the critical value, the observed r is *not significant* at .05 (i.e. $p > .05$) with 102 students, non-directional.

Exercise 6.15

Spearman ρ critical would be .714; since the observed r is .65, which is less than the critical value, the observed ρ is *not significant* at .05 (i.e. $p > .05$) with 7 pairs of ranks, directional.

Exercise 6.16

$$\Phi_{critical\,(.01)} = \frac{1.960}{\sqrt{N}} = \frac{1.960}{\sqrt{57}} = \frac{1.960}{7.5498} = .2596 \approx .26$$

Since the observed r is .30, which is higher than the critical value, the observed Φ *is significant* at .05 (i.e. $p < .05$) with 57 data points in the contingency table.

Exercise 7.2

Experiment E

No.	Spanish word	Translation
1	Caracol	*Snail*
2	Barro	*Mud*
3	Toalla	*Towel*
4	Vientre	*Belly*
5	Carpa	*Tent*
6	Comedor	*Dining room*
7	Tailarin	*Noodle*
8	Corazon	*Heart*
9	Prado	*Meadow*
10	Parabrisas	*Windshield*
11	Sabor	*Taste*
12	Pollo	*Chicken*
13	Sabio	*Scholar*
14	Herida	*Wound*
15	Lata	*Tin can*
16	Jefe	*Boss*
17	Polvo	*Dust*
18	Espaldas	*Back*
19	Helado	*Ice cream*
20	Viajero	*Traveler*

Exercise 7.3

Experiment F

No.	Spanish word	Translation
1	Tarde	*Afternoon*
2	Cama	*Bed*
3	Fondo	*Bottom*
4	Ciudad	*City*
5	Payaso	*Clown*
6	Postre	*Dessert*
7	Muneca	*Doll*
8	Huevo	*Egg*
9	Bombero	*Fireman*
10	Piso	*Floor*
11	Saltamontes	*Grasshopper*
12	Ayuda	*Help*
13	Pulgado	*Inch*
14	Bolsillo	*Pocket*
15	Arroz	*Rice*
16	Arena	*Sand*
17	Sabana	*Sheet*
18	Guerra	*War*
19	Mujer	*Woman*
20	Gusano	*Worm*

Exercise 7.12

The following are short quotes from an article by Atkinson (1975). For more detailed answers to these questions and research references, see the original article.

Question 1: Does pre-training of participants in use of the keyword technique increase their scores on recall of vocabulary words using the keyword technique? Your hypothesis?

> 'Instruction in the keyword method is helpful.' (Atkinson 1975: 824)

Question 2: Is it better if the experimenter invents the keyword and gives it to participants or is it better if participants invent their own keywords?

> 'Our results indicate that providing a keyword for subjects is best.' (Atkinson 1975: 824)

However:

> 'Subjects appear to be less effective when they must generate their own keywords: but results from the free-choice procedure indicate that keywords need only be supplied when requested by the subject.' (Atkinson 1975: 825)

Question 3: Is it better if the experimenter provides the image link (say, in the form of a cartoon) to participants or is it better if participants invent their own imagery links?

> 'It is better to have the subject generate his own image linking the keyword to the English translation.' (Atkinson 1975: 825)

Question 4: Is providing a sentence link as effective as providing an imagery link? For example, instead of imagining a picture of a duck with a pot on its head to help in the association of *pato* (Spanish) = *duck* (English), the participant creates/hears a sentence such as 'When the farmer put a pot on its head, the *pato* quacked'.

> 'Imagery instructions have a significant advantage over sentence generation instructions when using the keyword method.' (Atkinson 1975: 825)

Question 5: The keyword technique may facilitate the learning of vocabulary items in the direction of Given L2 word → Recall L1 word, but does it help in the learning of vocabulary in the direction Given L1 word → Recall L2 word?

> Even though the forward associations (Given L2 word → Recall L1 word) had been learned to the same criterion, the keyword group was significantly better on backward associations (Given L1 word → Recall L2 word).' (Atkinson 1975: 825)

Question 6: Are some keywords better than other keywords?

> 'Data on individual items learned by the keyword method indicate that some keywords are clearly better than others.' (Atkinson 1975: 825)

Question 7: The keyword techniques may prove useful in laboratory learning, but is it of any use in real, regular classroom situations?

> 'The first large-scale application of the keyword method [in regular Russian classes] proved to be encouraging and was well-received by the Slavic language faculty.' (Atkinson 1975: 827)

Question 8: Does use of the keyword technique, because of its several steps, slow the speed of recall or impede the fluency of use of L2 in conversation?

> 'What evidence we have indicates that the keyword method does not slow down or otherwise interfere with the retrieval process.' (Atkinson 1975: 827)

APPENDICES

Appendix 3.1

The Lady of the Moon

Instructions: This is a 'think-aloud' exercise. We are asking you to read the following short story and to let us know what you are thinking about as you read the story. Every line or two there is a box □ in the lines of the story. When you come to a box, stop reading, don't look forward or backward, and say *aloud* whatever you are thinking right then. The box is a sign for you speak your thoughts and put them 'in the box', so to speak. If you are curious, happy, sad, confused, informed by what you just read, think of the box as a signal for you to express these feelings.

The first line is the title of the story. Stop at the box after you have read the title and say what thoughts you have, just having read the title of the story.

The Lady of the Moon □

'You look carefully,' said Old Mother, 'you look carefully
at the moon and you will see a woman. □ She's the lady of the moon.
She washes her hair in the water of a stream, then dries it, and
sticks a jade comb in it. □ A comb of real jade – not like
mine, which has only a small pin-head of jade.' And she good-
humoredly removed the jade pin from the knot of hair at the
back of her head to show the children. □
    Michelle giggled, clapped her hands to her mouth, looked
10 at her mother and giggled again. □ Then she listened
intently to her grandmother. She liked listening to stories. Every
day in school she asked her teachers for stories. □
    'The lady of the moon combs her hair and sings. She is
tired of her jade comb. She wants another one—a gold one. □
15 And she invites the man on the other side of the moon to come.
If he wants to marry her, he must bring a gold comb. That will
make her very happy.' □
    'Are there really people on the moon?' asked Michelle.
    'The lady of the moon—last time you told us she tried to
20 cross a river on her small feet and she drowned,' said Michael.
    'The moon's an uninhabited planet. □ It's waterless.
The conditions there are not fit for human habitation. Nobody can
live there,' said Mark. □ He hated to see his younger

brother and sister listen to nonsense and superstition.

25 'The lady of the moon drowned because, with her small feet, she couldn't cross the bridge over the river,' said Old Mother. 'But the man on the other side of the moon sent a big band of silk with many colors: silver, pink, purple. □ The lady clung to the silk and was saved.'

30 'How can she cling to the silk if she's drowned?' asked Michelle.

'She came to life, when she saw the band of silk,' said Michael. □

'The man on the other side of the moon gave her not one gold comb, but two—the second one was actually silver,

35 washed in gold like Grandma's belt. It looks like gold, but actually it's only silver, washed in gold.'

Old Mother laughed. □ She touched Michael on the cheek and laughed again.

'There was an old man. He lived in a temple on the top of

40 a mountain,' said Old Mother. □

'Another story—good,' said Michelle, hugging her knees.

'An old man with skin like yellow paper and teeth yellower than mine,' and Old Mother showed her teeth, brown stumps where they were not gold. □

45 Michael laughed and said, 'Aiya, Grandma. You are funny!'

(Introspective reading activity adapted from Johar (1996: 165–168)
(Story adapted from *The Serpent's Tooth* by Catherine Lim) □

Appendix 3.2

Participant no. 1 – Passage 6B

1   *The title of the is passage is 'The Lady of the Moon'.. what does the mean the lady of the moon means.. is it shows that there's a lady in the moon or whether a girl name.. Moon.. I find out after reading the passage.*

2   'You look carefully,' said Old Mother, 'you look carefully at the moon and you will see a woman.'

3   *Oh now from this sentence I know that ... this title means there's a lady in the moon ... so I continue and find out what happen.*

4   'She's the lady of the moon.

5   She washes her hair in the water of a stream, then dries it, and sticks a jade comb in it.'

6   *Why the lady have to wash her hair... (5 sec.) in the water of the stream.. is there a stream in the moon.. how does it look like.. does the moon look like the same as the Earth like the normal as we look at the stream.. maybe.. we'll find out after continuing.*

7   'A comb of real jade – not like mine, which has only a small pinhead of jade.'

8   'And she good-humoredly removed the jade pin from the knot of hair at the back of her head to show the children.'

9   *What does the meaning mean she had to remove the jade pin from the knot of hair and show it to the children.. is there any children in the moon ... (5 sec.) maybe there is some children in the moon.. who are the children.. is it her child or.. some other people.. we'll find out after.. we read .. some more.*

10   'Michelle giggled, clapped her hands to her mouth, looked at her mother and giggled again.'

11   *Who is Michelle.. is it the lady of the moon or either the writer.. and why is she giggling at her mother again and again .. does she find something funny or she.. she feel happy seeing the moon.. we'll find out after reading it.*

12   'Then she listened intently to her grandmother.'

13   'She liked listening to stories.'

14   'Every day in school she asked her teachers for stories.'

15   *On why Michelle always like to listen to story ... does she always have to listen to one story once a day ... every time in school she asked her teacher for story.. what type of story does she like.. do she like the fairy tale or some horrible stories ... we'll find out afterward.*

16   'The lady of the moon combs her hair and sings.'

17   'She is tired of her jade comb.'

18   'She wants another one—a gold one.'

19   *W-Why why she tired of her jade comb and want wanted a gold.. is it the jade is a false jade ... no I think it's real jade and why wanted a gold one.. is she not happy with the present one had.. so we'll continue after we find out more.*

Appendix 3.3
Checklist for critiquing introspective studies

1 Review the criteria for undertaking useful introspective studies from this section and from previous sections, especially Section 2.
2 Create your own checklist of features for an introspective study report. Some suggestions for checklist items are included below. Your checklist might begin as follows:

CHECKLIST FOR CRITIQUING INTROSPECTIVE STUDIES

Name of Study:

Author:

Source:

Type of Study:

	Explicit/ clear	Partial/ not clear	No	Can't tell
1 Has explicit model of mental processes stated				
2 Introspections immediately accompany task				
3 Has adequate warm-up for participant introspections				
4 Coding clear and consistent				
5				
6				

7				
8				
9				
10				

Some possible critiquing checklist criteria
Is nature of study clear?
Sufficient overview provided?
Research question(s) clear?
Citation of previous studies appropriate?
Good instructions?
Good procedure?
Based on clear mental model?
Clear coding system for data?
Results clear from abstract?
Useful for your own inquiries?

Appendix 3.4
A think-aloud study of L2 output monitoring

In producing the target language, learners may encounter a linguistic problem leading them to notice what they do not know, or know only partially. In other words, the activity of producing the target language may prompt second language learners to consciously recognize some of their linguistic problems; it may make them aware of something they need to find out about their L2.

To test this hypothesis, one would need to demonstrate that learners may, on occasion, notice a problem (even without external cueing) through, for example, implicit or explicit feedback provided from an interlocutor about problems in the learners' output. It seems to me that there is ample evidence from the communication strategy literature (for example, Tarone 1977; Færch and Kasper 1983; Bialystok 1990; Kellerman 1991) that learners do notice problems as they speak, and do try to do something about them. But what do they do when they notice a problem? Do they focus on morphology and syntax? Do they engage in cognitive processes related to second language learning?

In a recent study (Swain and Lapkin 1994), we attempted to examine directly the cognitive processes that are activated as a result of noticing a problem—as directly, that is, as current research methods allow. The participants in the study were grade-eight early French-immersion students (average age thirteen). The students were individually trained to use think-aloud procedures, and were then asked to think aloud while writing an article for a newspaper about an environmental problem. Students were prompted with 'What are you thinking?' if they stopped talking for very long, or if they made a change to their text without commenting on it. Students were advised that they could not have access to a dictionary or any other aid, and that the researcher would not be able to help either. These last conditions were imposed because we were interested in seeing what students would do without further input from external sources; whether they would try to work out solutions on their own.

From the think-aloud protocols, we abstracted what we have termed language-related episodes. These language-related episodes were any segment of the protocol in which a learner either spoke about a language problem he or she encountered while writing, and solved it either correctly or incorrectly; or simply solved it (again, either correctly or incorrectly) without having explicitly identified it as a problem. These episodes were categorized according to the mental processes we thought were reflected in the changes the students made to their output. Overall, in about 40% of these episodes, students paid attention to grammatical form.

The results demonstrate quite clearly that even second language learners as young as these students do indeed, as they produce their L2, notice gaps in their linguistic knowledge. Output led to noticing. Furthermore, when these learners encounter difficulties in producing the target language, they do engage in thought processes of a sort which may play a role in second language learning (see also Cumming 1990; Wood 1994). The cognitive processes identified represent processes hypothesized to be involved in second language learning: extending first language knowledge to second language contexts; extending second language knowledge to new target language contexts; and formulating and testing hypotheses about linguistic forms and functions. (See, for example, Selinker 1972; Corder 1981; Kellerman and Sharwood Smith 1986; McLaughlin 1987.)

It is our conclusion that this evidence supports the hypothesis that output can stimulate noticing; that it raises learners' awareness of gaps in their knowledge; in short, that it plays a consciousness-raising role. Furthermore, noticing can trigger cognitive processes that have been implicated in second language learning, cognitive processes that generate linguistic knowledge that is new for learners, or that consolidate their existing knowledge.

(Swain 1995: 127–8)

Appendix 4.1

Characterization of the four teachers in the Nystrom study

Nystrom does not discuss the experience, age, or educational background of her four (female) subject teachers. She does discuss in considerable detail their assignment responsibilities and how the teacher subjects interpreted these responsibilities. A brief sketch of these (adapted from Nystrom 1983: 174, 178) follows:

Teacher A1: The official 'bilingual' teacher at her school. Taught Spanish-speaking children in all grades, kindergarten to 5th grade, for at least an hour a day in situations in which they were 'pulled out' of their regular classes. Used a variety of oral activities and worked with the children in small groups with the help of a Spanish-speaking aide.

Teacher B1: The English reading teacher in her school. Spent all her observed time in reading aloud activities. Errors observed were thus fewer, occurring only between reading groups or during discussion of a story. Her classes were of mixed Spanish and English dominance, and of the 29 errors she identified 83% were English-dominant dialect errors. She did not consider non-standard dialect as erroneous language (despite her citing of 83% of the errors in this category) and did not see her role as a 'correcting machine'.

Teacher A2: The 'regular' classroom teacher for a group of 27 students with approximately equal numbers of Spanish-dominant and English-dominant students. Activities were typically whole class or interaction with individual students. Individual interactions were principally of the 'language experience' type in which students dictated sentences for the teacher to write on the board. She herself was a native speaker of Spanish and often cued or encouraged the Spanish speakers (all gathered at two tables in the back of the room) using Spanish.

Teacher B2: Taught Spanish reading to a class of Mexican-American students of a wide range of language dominance. Children sat on the floor and were encouraged to participate in discussion of visuals shown or drawn by her. This teacher corrected 30% of errors of form using one technique or another but indicated her major concern was oral production, not error correction.

Appendix 4.2

Extract from a lesson recorded at Essex University, England, February 1975

176	T	I started at Essex on the fifth of October. When did you start? (Nominates by gesture)
	S4	I start in in Excess since the eleventh of January.
	T	When did you arrive? You arrived on the eleventh of January, did you? You must have started the next day, did you?
180	S2	(the eleventh of January
	S5	(the twelfth
	S5	No, I we start at thirteenth
	T	on the thirteenth of January
		When did you start at Essex? (Nominates by gesture)
185	S1	I start at Essex on the thirteenth of January
	T	On the thirteenth of January.
	S1	Yes
	T	Again.
	S1	I start at Essex on the thirteenth of January
190	T	Eulyces (pause)
		I started
	S2	I stotted
	T	(started
	S1	(start
195	S2	I... ( ) Aside to S1 in Spanish
		I start on on Essess eh fourteen January.
	T	I
	S2	Fourteenth January
	T	I started at Essex on the thirteenth of January.
200		All right, Eulyces: on the thirteenth of January
	S2	On the th
	T	Thirteenth
	S2	on the fourteenth of January
	T	of January
205	S2	of January.
	T	on the thirteenth of January.
	S2	On the fourteenth of January
	T	All together. .... (on the thirteenth of January
	SSS	on the thirteenth of January
210		on the thirteenth of January
	T	All right. I started at Essex. (Gesture for choral response)
	SSS	I started at Essex on the thirteenth of January.
	T	Good. Good
		Were you at University before?

Author's Notes on Transcript

Line	
177	Many errors – relatively weak learner chosen
178	Above errors ignored, except for error against truth concerning data
180–2	Learners sorting out truth. Errors of pronunciation, person and tense form ignored subsequently.
183	T models full correct date phrase
185	Tense form error
186	T confirms correct phrase, ignores tense form error.
188	T requests repeat
189	Tense form error again
190	T ignores above error and renominates
191	S2 hesitates, T models start of utterance
192	Pronunciation error
192–3	T remodels but so does S1, repeating own tense form error
195–6	S2 seeks S1's help, in Spanish, then copies S1 rather than T
198	S2 spontaneously self-corrects 'fourteen' to 'fourteenth'
199	T remodels full correct utterance. No emphasis on factual error
200	T acknowledge S2's difficulties, and remodels final phrase
201	S2 pauses after 'th'
203	S2 repeats factual error
204	T ignores factual error, repeats what S2 got right
206	T remodels correct phrase
207	S2 repeats factual error, omits 'the'
208	T transfers treatment to whole class
213–4	T praises satisfactory choral responses and changes subtopic.

(from Allwright 1975)

Appendix 4.3

There are four picture sets given here. The pictures in each set are labeled alphabetically for identification. Alphabetic labeling has nothing to do with the final sequence.

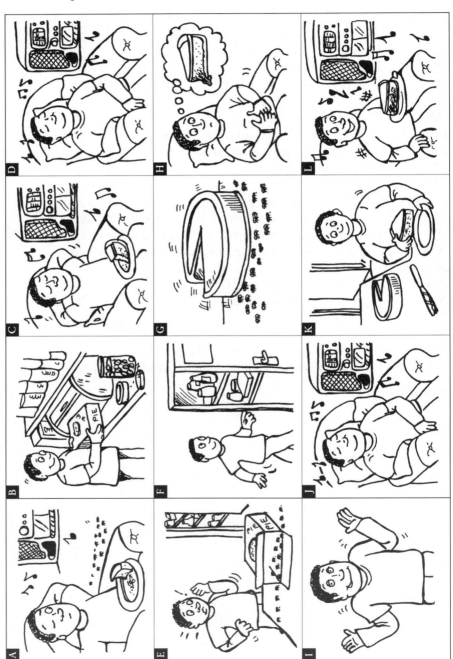

Picture set 1: A piece of pie

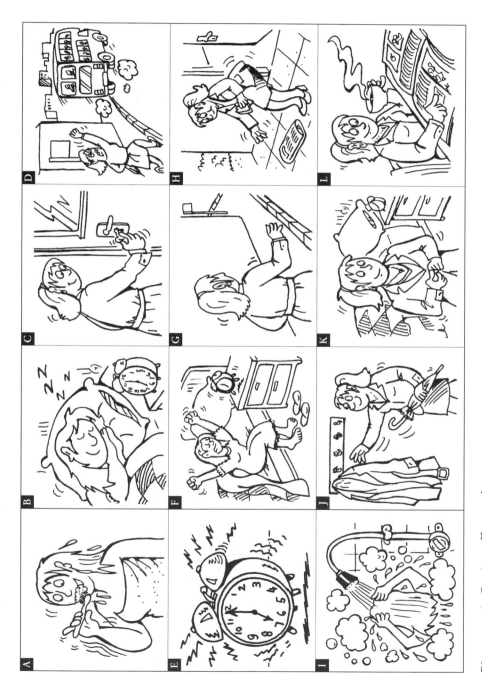

Picture set 2: Getting off to work

Picture set 3: Late for class

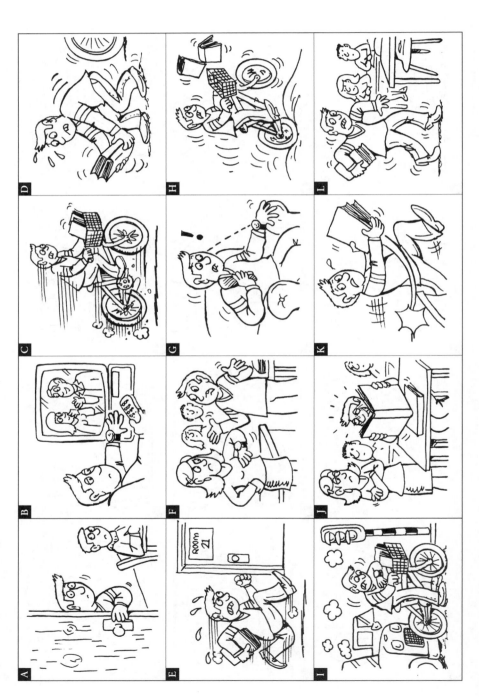

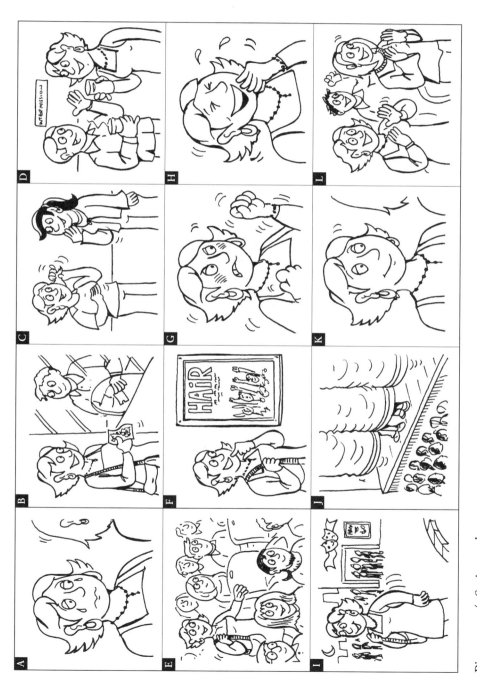

Picture set 4: Seeing a play

Appendix 7.1

List E: Words to Recall

No	Spanish word	Translation
Practice		
a	Domingo	Sunday
b	Trigo	Wheat
c	Faena	Task
d	Cubeta	Pail
Learning Trial		
1	Barro	Mud
2	Helado	Ice cream
3	Corazón	Heart
4	Espaldas	Back
5	Comedor	Dining room
6	Lata	Tin can
7	Jefe	Boss
8	Pollo	Chicken
9	Tallarín	Noodle
10	Toalla	Towel
11	Carpa	Tent
12	Polvo	Dust
13	Prado	Meadow
14	Viajero	Traveler
15	Herida	Wound
16	Sabor	Taste
17	Caracol	Snail
18	Vientre	Belly
19	Parabrisas	Windshield
20	Sabio	Scholar

Appendix 7.2

List F: More Words to Recall

No	Spanish word	Key word	Translation
Practice			
a	Pato	[pot]	Duck
b	Butaca	[boot]	Armchair
c	Cordero	[cord]	Lamb
d	Jabon	[bone]	Soap
Learning Trial			
1	Huevo	[wave]	Egg
2	Mujer	[hair]	Woman
3	Postre	[post]	Dessert
4	Guerra	[garlic]	War
5	Pulgado	[pool]	Inch
6	Tarde	[tar]	Afternoon
7	Saltamontes	[salt]	Grasshopper
8	Cama	[comma]	Bed
9	Arena	[rain]	Sand
10	Bombero	[bomb]	Fireman
11	Fondo	[phone]	Bottom
12	Payaso	[pie]	Clown
13	Piso	[pea]	Floor
14	Muñeca	[moon]	Doll
15	Sábana	[sob]	Sheet
16	Arroz	[a rose]	Rice
17	Bolsillo	[bowl]	Pocket
18	Ciudad	[see you, dad]	City
19	Gusano	[goose]	Worm
20	Ayuda	[I/you]	Help

Appendix 8.1

Author questionnaire
Ted Rodgers' responses

1 *What problems do you think students might have with the content of your book?*
The design of the book seems to me more problematical than the content which, in the large, is like other books with similar intent and audience. The interleaving of exercises with text (as opposed to parking a few questions at chapter-end) and the highly hands-on nature of the presentation (doing rather than describing) will be unfamiliar to some instructors and, perhaps, students. I wonder if there is the will among teachers and students to really immerse themselves in some of the processes of research?

2 *What problems do you think teachers might have with presenting the content of this book?*
See above. Also teachers may have to pick and choose among exercises and themes to tailor the text to the course time available. Will take a fairly thorough 'knowing' of the text to do this effectively.

3 *Which chapter or chapters do you think are most important?*
I'm not sure how I would measure 'importance'. I think the content least well-covered by existing texts is that dealing with introspective techniques in research. I think this is a re-emerging area in educational—especially second language educational—research and deserves an adequate treatment as a research option. I think we gave it that.

4 *Which of the sections (experiencing, compiling, analyzing, designing, interpreting, significance, and reflecting) that are found across all the chapters do you think are the most important?*
Again, I would probably have to define 'important'. Here, perhaps, as 'unique'. Obviously the experiencing section is critical to the whole thrust of the book. It is central to the book design and thus the least expendable of the sections. I think the significance section where we try to look at the big picture and tie this kind of research to a larger sense of inquiry is also unique and important to second language researchers who tend, like other specialists, to get locked into their own specialties.

5 *What abilities does the book assume on the part of students?*
There is a good deal of student self-direction assumed. Almost all of the many exercises are mental rather than mechanical and require an ability (and willingness) to think through a topic. It anticipates a curiosity among students and a willingness to 'discover' the topic rather than to have the topic laid on with examples from other people's data. It assumes a disposition to cooperate with partners and larger groups of classmates to carry out required tasks.

6 *What abilities does the book assume on the part of the teacher?*

Again, I think the teacher will have to know the text pretty well in order to facilitate activities, make priorities among exercises and to encourage reflection on the part of students as they identify key themes. A lot of this will require some standing back and letting students struggle a bit with what will seem, occasionally, like pretty daunting material.

7 *What are your attitudes toward the qualitative research types presented in Chapters 2, 3, and 4 in this book?*

I don't have a particular attitude towards the qualitative versus quantitative research types presented in the course text. I know that most of my students who shied away from anything 'quantitative' in their own thesis work, wound up doing quite a bit of 'counting' in analyzing data from surveys, questionnaires, interviews, etc., which they had chosen as exemplary of qualitative approaches. So I think our approach which uses the qualitative – quantitative cline as an organizational structure but emphasizes the interweaving of qualitative and quantitative techniques throughout fairly represents what really goes on in SLA research.

8 *What are your attitudes toward the quantitative research types presented in Chapters 5, 6, and 7 of this book?*

Obviously the answer here follows that of Question 7. The quantitative chapters presented a bit more of a quandary as to how much analytical accompaniment should go in the text—tables, formulae, technical explanations, etc. We had to take some shortcuts to keep the book from becoming too bulky and too technical. Sometimes I think there may still be too much technical material in these chapters and that we should have cross-referenced the technical material to an alternative text where the quantitative support pieces are central to that alternative text. This meant a required 'two-text' course, however, which we wanted to avoid if possible to minimize the weight of our users' book bags.

9 *Give one solution to a problem or issue you raised in the first eight questions above.*

Re Question 2, it might be useful to have a teacher's 'road-map' for each chapter identifying, from the authors' perspective, places 'not to be missed' versus 'for particular interests' or 'a great stop if you have time' locations.

10 *Give a solution to at least one other problem or issue you raised in the first eight questions above.*

Re Questions 7 and 8, the chapters, by design, are largely self-contained. Where material is required from another chapter, this is pretty well sign-posted. There is not a strong assumption that users should start at the beginning of the text and work their way through to the end. We might think of some alternative course sequences which would juxtapose research types in different ways – maybe suggesting pairs of chapters which would interestingly contrast two styles of research but which would nevertheless have some interesting commonalities. For example, Chapters 4 and 5 both deal with 'beliefs' and the role of beliefs in teaching and in doing research. This might be an interesting focal point for pairing these two chapters.

Appendix 8.2

Author questionnaire
J D Brown's responses

1 *What problems do you think students might have with the content of your book?*

If they are coming directly out of undergraduate studies, students might have trouble with being responsible for their own learning and with learning deductively. In this book, we ask them to do various things that involve higher order cognitive skills. Instead of the simple comprehension and memorization of facts that they may be used to, we are constantly asking students to apply concepts, analyze things, synthesize, and critically evaluate. In my experience, many graduate students are not accustomed to taking such an active role in their own learning. Yet, if as rumored, there is life after university, those are exactly the sorts of skills that will help make them successful in their professional lives.

2 *What problems do you think teachers might have with presenting the content of this book?*

Most teachers I know are very accustomed to a teacher-centered approach: the teacher lectures, the students take notes. The teacher gives the students a midterm and final test or examination, the teacher requires a term project, the teacher this, the teacher that. I think at least some teachers could have trouble turning the learning process over to the students.

Also, this book has many more activities than can be covered in any real course. We provided an overabundance of activities so there would be plenty of different ways to experience research, but that throws a responsibility on the teacher to pick and choose those activities that will work best with the unique group of students involved in a particular course.

I guess the answer to this question is that this book will work best for a teacher who can select from among the many exercises in this book and orchestrate activities for the students without the teacher feeling useless and left out just because the students are doing everything. That could be a problem for any teachers who lack the experience or confidence to turn things over to the students.

3 *Which chapter or chapters do you think are most important?*

Personally, I think I like the first and last chapters best as they are shaping up now.

The first chapter sort of opens up the area of language learning research to students who may never have thought much about it before. Once they see that it is not necessarily experimental with lots of statistics and mathematics, language teachers in training may find research much more interesting than they would ever have thought. I also like the way the first chapter legitimizes the wide variety of research types and shows students the many ways they might want to head in their own research.

The last chapter summarizes the book by tying together the various strands of research covered in the other chapters and relates research to something they themselves have been experiencing in going through this book. In this sense, the last chapter is consonant with the ideas of periodic reflection in developing course portfolios and the ideas of reflective teaching in that it helps students reflect on what they have learned in the course, and even perhaps on what they have not learned.

4 *Which of the sections (experiencing, compiling, analyzing, designing, interpreting, significance, and reflecting) that are found across all the chapters do you think are the most important?*
I like the way we pull them right into the research experience in the introducing and experiencing sections. That was Ted's idea when he first proposed the book, and I think it is a good one. I also like the way all the other sections tend to make the students do things with the information we give them.

5 *What abilities does the book assume on the part of students?*
If the students don't already have them when they start the book, they need to develop the abilities to analyze, synthesize, and critically evaluate. I hope the various hands-on exercises will lead to their acquiring such skills. Now, I feel like I'm beginning to harp a little on this topic. So I'll stop.

Maybe there is one other ability that the students need to bring to this book that worries me a little: the ability to apply what they learn in this book to their own research.

6 *What abilities does the book assume on the part of the teacher?*
As I mentioned in Question 2 above, the teacher will need the ability to be selective in deciding which exercises to do, and will need to be a facilitator for the various classroom activities that he or she does choose (that is, be willing to let go of the teacher-centered stance and settle into the role of facilitator). The teacher will also need to know the material covered in the book well enough to explain any concepts the students do not understand on their own and to supplement with explanations of concepts that students bring up along the way, some of which may be only tangentially related to the content of this book.

7 *What are your attitudes toward the qualitative research types presented in Chapters 2, 3, and 4 in this book?*
I think I have very positive attitudes toward all kinds of research. I know enough about quantitative research methods to know that they are very often misapplied in language teaching and learning research. I also know that many

language teachers are uncomfortable with mathematics and statistics. So I welcome other research traditions, where at least some language teachers may work more comfortably. What I would really like to see is high quality research being produced in a variety of research traditions, rather than a lot of statistical studies of marginal quality.

8 *What are your attitudes toward the quantitative research types presented in Chapters 5, 6, and 7 of this book?*

One of my colleagues in the Psychology department at the University of Hawaii talks about how social sciences seem to suffer from '*p* value envy'. What I think he means is that we wish we could produce the *p* values and apparent precision of findings in the hard sciences. That attitude reveals two things: a tremendous naïveté about the precision of scientific findings and a lack of understanding about the complexity of what we are trying to study in language learning and teaching. The results of pure science are not nearly as precise as we would like to think. That is why such care is taken to control all but one variable at a time, why replication of results is so important, why scientists are not satisfied until they understand the mechanisms underlying their findings, why knowledge in science is usually built through gradual consensus, and so forth. Those are not characteristics of even our best quantitative research. We cannot control all but one variable, period. We do not replicate, even when the research is designed by a 'big name' to push that big name's own theories. Would we trust the tobacco companies in that way? We do not understand any of the mechanisms underlying what we are studying. And so forth.

Now, I've started to ramble. But what I'm getting at is that many aspects of our subject matter may simply be far too complex for the linear quantitative research methods we tend to use, and hence, in some cases, other research methods not involving any *p* values may be more appropriate.

9 *Give one solution to a problem or issue you raised in the first eight questions above.*

I think the book itself offers one solution to the problem raised in Question 8 above. By offering an overview of research that is not restricted to any particular tradition, the book encourages students to find the type or types of research that best fit their working methods and ways of thinking, and perhaps even the types of questions they would like to address in doing research on language learning and teaching.

10 *Give a solution to at least one other problem or issue you raised in the first eight questions above.*

I am concerned with the potential problem that I raised in Question 5, which was concerned with the students' ability to apply what they learn in this book to their own research. This is an area where the teacher will be crucial. While students are working through this book, they should probably be encouraged to think of ways to apply what they are learning to answering questions that are directly relevant to their professional lives and (future) teaching situations. In fact, if the students are required to do a personal project for the course, the teacher will probably have to spend several one-on-one conferences with each student or group doing a project to guide the research in a useful direction and answer questions as they arise. So, you see, the teacher is as important as ever.

GLOSSARY

This glossary contains definitions of the terms printed in SMALL CAPITALS throughout the body of the book. The definitions are of the terms *as used in the book*.

ABSTRACT: The opening section of a research report which briefly (+/– 150 words) states the research question, the research method, and the results. (22)

ACTION RESEARCH: A small-scale intervention in the real world (for example, a classroom) and close observation of the results of this intervention. (99)

ALTERNATIVE HYPOTHESIS: A competing hypothesis to a stated NULL HYPOTHESIS. (216)

ALTERNATIVE TYPE RESPONSE: A response in which a participant pronounces a letter sequence while trying to solve an anagram, in an attempt to find a sound–syllable match in lexical memory. Compare with CONSTRAINT TYPE RESPONSE. (66)

ASSUMPTIONS: Preconditions that must be checked in advance so a researcher can accurately and responsibly apply a particular method of data collection and analysis. (182)

AVERAGE: See MEAN.

BELL CURVE: See NORMAL DISTRIBUTION.

BIMODAL: Two MODES in a set of numbers. (128)

CASE STUDY: Observation of the characteristics of an individual unit such as a person, a social group, a class, a school or a community. (21)

CATEGORICAL SCALE: A scale that organizes data into unique, non-overlapping categories or groups. Also called 'nominal scale'. (168)

CATEGORY SYSTEM: Recording procedure in analyzing classroom interaction where a specific behavior is noted on each appearance. (94)

CENTRAL TENDENCY: The propensity of a set of numbers to cluster around a particular middle value; typically estimated using the MEAN, MODE, and MEDIAN. (128)

CLASSROOM: Term covering a wide range of learning contexts such as classes in schools, multi-media labs, distance learning situations, one-to-one tutoring, on-the-job training, computer-based instruction, and so on. (79)

CLOSED-RESPONSE ITEM: Item in which responses must be from a set pre-selected by the researcher. Compare with OPEN-RESPONSE ITEM. (142)

COEFFICIENT OF DETERMINATION: A value calculated by squaring the PEARSON PRODUCT-MOMENT CORRELATION COEFFICIENT; represents the proportion of shared variance between the two sets of numbers. (190)

CONFIRMABILITY: The degree to which QUALITATIVE results are or could be corroborated, roughly analogous to OBJECTIVITY in a QUANTITATIVE study. (242)

CONSTRAINT TYPE RESPONSE: In anagram solution studies, a response in which the participant uses her knowledge of possible letter sequences in English as a guide for constructing longer sequences, for rejecting a test sequence as 'un-English', etc. Compare with ALTERNATIVE TYPE RESPONSE. (66)

CONTINUOUS SCALE: Any scale that shows the order of a set of values and the distances between the values. (168)

CORRELATION: The mutual relationship of two or more data sets. (158)

CORRELATION COEFFICIENT: A statistic that represents the degree of relationship, or ratio of go-togetherness, between two or more numerical data sets. (166)

CORRELATIONAL RESEARCH: Studies that measure the relationship between two or more variables by calculating a statistic called a CORRELATION COEFFICIENT. (157, 166)

CREDIBILITY: The believability of the results for a QUALITATIVE study, which is roughly analogous to the concept of INTERNAL VALIDITY in a QUANTITATIVE study. (242)

DEGREES OF FREEDOM (df): A value calculated by subtracting one from the number of participants in one or more groups involved in calculating a particular statistic; used in the *t*-TEST, CORRELATION COEFFICIENT, etc. (205)

DEPENDABILITY: The consistency of the results of a QUALITATIVE study or the degree to which they can be trusted, roughly analogous to the concept of RELIABILITY in a QUANTITATIVE study. (242)

DESCRIPTIVE RESEARCH: Research that describes group characteristics or behaviors in numerical terms. (12)

DESCRIPTIVE STATISTICS: Those statistics used to analyze descriptive research data, usually in terms of CENTRAL TENDENCY and DISPERSION. (122)

DESCRIPTIVE STATISTICS RESEARCH: See DESCRIPTIVE RESEARCH and DESCRIPTIVE STATISTICS.

DEVELOPMENTAL STUDIES: Research studies which involve following changes in language use of an individual or small group of individuals over time. (21)

DISCOURSE: A continuous piece of written or spoken language; generally speaking, a linguistic unit longer than a sentence. (27, 82)

DISPERSION: The degree to which the individual numbers in a set vary away from the CENTRAL TENDENCY; typically estimated using the RANGE, LOW-HIGH, and STANDARD DEVIATION. (131)

EFFECTS MATRIX: A MATRIX used to display various outcomes and processes in the data. (235)

EVALUATION: The process of seeking to establish the value of something for some purpose. (227)

EXPERIMENTAL RESEARCH: Studies that compare group behavior in PROBABILISTIC terms under controlled conditions using RANDOM ASSIGNMENT to groups. (12, 195)

EXPLORATORY RESEARCH: Studies that, in one way or another, examine relationships among variables. (12)

EXTENSIVE RESPONSE: In reading response research, a response in which the reader attempts to deal explicitly with the message conveyed by the author rather than relating the text to themselves. Compare with REFLEXIVE RESPONSE. (64)

EXTERNAL RELIABILITY: The degree to which we can expect consistent results if a particular study were replicated. (241)

EXTERNAL VALIDITY: The degree to which results can be generalized beyond the study itself. (45, 241)

FREQUENCIES: Counts or 'tallies' of the number of things or people in different categories. (125)

GENERAL PATTERNS: Overall patterns across all categories on both dimensions of a MATRIX. (235)

HISTOGRAM: A graphical display where each numerical possibility in a set of data is indicated along the horizontal axis and frequency is indicated on the vertical axis. The frequency of each number in the data can be represented by stacks of Xs, asterisks, etc. in columns. (126)

INDEPENDENCE ASSUMPTION: An ASSUMPTION of the PEARSON r and some other statistics that the pairs of numbers within a data set are independent of one another. (182)

INTACT GROUP: A set of research subjects pre-existing as a group (such as a class of students) prior to the research study. (12, 212)

INTERACTION: A term used with a variety of different senses, used primarily to refer to language exchanges between two or more individuals. (79)

INTERNAL RELIABILITY: The degree to which we can expect consistent results if the data for the study were re-analyzed by another researcher. (241)

INTERNAL VALIDITY: The degree to which the researchers have observed what they set out to observe and have reported all the critical observational data. (44, 241)

INTERVIEW: A SURVEY done orally in a face-to-face format, on the telephone, or in groups. (142)

INTERVIEW SCHEDULE: A list of questions or prompts (sometimes with follow-up questions and prompts) for the interviewer to use when conducting an interview. (142)

LANGUAGE PROGRAM EVALUATION: The systematic collection and analysis of all relevant information necessary to assess the effectiveness and efficiency of a curriculum and to promote its improvement. (227)

LIBRARY RESEARCH: Any research based solely on a study of the relevant research literature in a particular field. See also SECONDARY RESEARCH. (10)

LIKERT SCALE: Type of survey item where respondents are asked to register their reactions to statements or questions on, for example, a strongly agree to strongly disagree, 4 3 2 1, scale. (120)

LINEARITY ASSUMPTION: An ASSUMPTION of the PEARSON *r* and some other statistics that two sets of numbers, if plotted on a SCATTERPLOT, should be more or less in a line. (182)

LITERATURE REVIEW: A written summary and analysis of research precedents to a particular new research study. Also the labeled section of a research paper or academic thesis devoted to such summary and analysis. See also SECONDARY RESEARCH. (10, 22, 36)

LOW–HIGH: The lowest value and the highest value in a set of numbers. (131)

MATRIX: Any array or table, usually in two dimensions, with one set of categories labeled across the top for the columns and another set of categories labeled down the left-hand side for the rows. (234)

MEAN: The sum of all the values in a distribution divided by the number of values, also called 'average'. See also CENTRAL TENDENCY, MODE, MEDIAN. (128)

MEDIAN: The point in the distribution below which 50% of the values lie and above which 50% lie. (128)

MEMBER CHECKING: Confirming the data, analyses, interpretations, and conclusions with research respondents themselves. (242, 245)

METHOD-COMPARISON STUDIES: Large-scale experimental studies which try to establish which of two or more 'methods' is best for teaching languages. (214)

MODE: That value in a set of numbers that occurs most frequently. See also CENTRAL TENDENCY, MEAN, MEDIAN. (128)

MORPHOLOGY/MORPHOLOGICAL: (Relating to) the meaningful units (morphemes) that form the structure words. (27, 82)

NEGATIVE CODES: Coding for two-person communication in which response of one subject to the other is non-supportive and unexplained. See also POSITIVE CODES, NEUTRAL CODES. (85, 106)

NEUTRAL CODES: Coding for two-person communication in which response of one subject to the other is factual or peripheral, neither supportive nor non-supportive. See also POSITIVE CODES, NEGATIVE CODES. (85)

NOMINAL SCALE: See CATEGORICAL SCALE.

NORMAL DISTRIBUTION: A set of numbers distributed symmetrically around a MEAN. Also known as a 'bell curve'. (136)

NORMALITY ASSUMPTION: An ASSUMPTION of the PEARSON *r* and many other statistics that the distributions involved must be NORMAL DISTRIBUTIONS. (182)

NULL HYPOTHESIS: A hypothesis that states that no statistically significant result is expected. For instance, the null hypothesis might be that no correlation significantly different from zero is expected. (216)

OBJECTIVITY: Observations based on facts, free from personal feelings or prejudice. (242)

OPEN-RESPONSE ITEM: An item in a QUESTIONNAIRE that requires participants to fill in an answer or provide a short answer in their own words. Compare with CLOSED-RESPONSE ITEM. (120, 142)

ORDINAL SCALE: See RANK-ORDERED SCALE.

PEARSON PRODUCT-MOMENT CORRELATION COEFFICIENT: A means to estimate the degree of relationship between two sets of CONTINUOUS SCALE data. More simply known as PEARSON *r*, or *r*. (170)

PEARSON *r*: see PEARSON PRODUCT-MOMENT CORRELATION COEFFICIENT.

PERCENTAGES: Values calculated by dividing the total number in one category by the total number in all categories and multiplying the result by 100. (125)

PHI COEFFICIENT: A means to estimate the degree of relationship between two categorical variables with two possibilities each. (178)

PHONOLOGY/PHONOLOGICAL: (Relating to) the nature of language sounds (phonemes). (27, 82)

PICTURE SEQUENCING: A task involving a set of randomly presented pictures which must be sorted to represent a logical sequence. (85)

PIE CHART: A graph in the form of a circle that shows the proportions or percentages of subcategories of a whole in proportionally sized wedges. (119)

POSITIVE CODES: Coding for two-person communication in which the response of one subject to the other is reasoned and/or supportive. See also NEGATIVE CODES, NEUTRAL CODES. (85, 106)

PRIMARY RESEARCH: Research based on original data. Compare with LIBRARY RESEARCH. (10)

PROBABILISTIC: Anything having to do with odds, likelihood, or chances. (12)

QUALITATIVE RESEARCH: Any research based predominantly on non-numerical data. (12)

QUALITATIVE RESEARCH TECHNIQUES: Procedures for doing QUALITATIVE RESEARCH such as observations/field notes, case studies, diaries, etc. (12)

QUANTITATIVE RESEARCH (METHODS): Investigative procedures used to describe in numerical terms a setting and the things going on in it. (15, 118)

QUASI-EXPERIMENTAL RESEARCH: Studies that compare group behavior in PROBABILISTIC terms under controlled conditions using INTACT GROUPS. Compare with TRUE EXPERIMENTAL STUDIES. (12, 212)

QUESTIONNAIRE: A written survey administered to individuals containing CLOSED-RESPONSE and/or OPEN-RESPONSE items. (142)

QUESTIONNAIRE RESEARCH: Any study employing data collected using a QUESTIONNAIRE.

r: See PEARSON PRODUCT-MOMENT CORRELATION COEFFICIENT.

RANDOM ASSIGNMENT: Placement of participants into a study or into two or more groups using a 'chance' selection mechanism. (12)

RANGE: The highest value minus the lowest value plus one. (131)

RANK-ORDERED SCALE: Any scale that arranges or sorts the values according to order. Also called 'ordinal scale'. (168)

RAW FREQUENCIES: The actual counts or tallies as compared to PERCENTAGES. (125)

REFLEXIVE RESPONSE: In reading research, a subject response which is directed away from the text and towards one's own experience, thoughts or feelings. Compare with EXTENSIVE RESPONSE. (64)

RELIABILITY: The degree to which the results of a measure or study are consistent. (73, 241)

RESEARCH HYPOTHESIS: Any claim that you believe an experimental study might support (or perhaps refute). (215)

RESEARCH QUESTION: A question that you will try to answer in a study. (215)

RETROSPECTIVE STUDIES: Those studies in which responses to given stimuli are given after considerable time has elapsed since exposure to the stimuli. (56)

ROUNDING ERROR: A small error which is the result of rounding a series of figures or values up or down to the nearest whole numbers. (125)

SCALES ASSUMPTION: An ASSUMPTION of the PEARSON r and some other STATISTICS that each set of numbers must be a CONTINUOUS SCALE. (182)

SCATTERPLOT: A graphical display in which possible values for one variable (typically labeled X) are represented along the horizontal axis and possible values for a second variable (typically labeled Y) are represented along the vertical axis such that each participant's scores on X and Y can simultaneously be represented by a single X, asterisk, etc. (182)

SECONDARY RESEARCH: Any research based on secondary sources, especially other researchers' books and articles. Compare with PRIMARY RESEARCH. See also LITERATURE REVIEW, LIBRARY RESEARCH. (10)

SELECTED-RESPONSE ITEMS: Items in a questionnaire that must be answered by selecting from among alternatives, for example, circling or checking choices. (120)

SIGN SYSTEM: Recording procedure in analyzing classroom interaction where all behaviors which occur within a specified time period are noted. (94)

SIGNIFICANCE: See STATISTICAL SIGNIFICANCE. (186)

SIMULATED CLASSROOM DATA: Data collected from artificial re-creation of actual classrooms, usually employed where location and/or observation of actual classrooms is impractical. (100)

SLA: Second language acquisition. (47)

SPEARMAN RANK-ORDER CORRELATION COEFFICIENT: A means to estimate the degree of relationship between two sets of RANK-ORDERED data. More simply known as SPEARMAN RHO. (170)

SPEARMAN RHO: see SPEARMAN RANK-ORDER CORRELATION COEFFICIENT.

SPECIFIC DIFFERENCE PATTERNS: Detailed responses that are opposite or contradictory in a MATRIX. (235)

SPECIFIC SIMILARITY PATTERNS: Detailed responses that match or are parallel in one category on one dimension across several categories on the other dimension in a MATRIX. (235)

STANDARD DEVIATION: 'A sort of average of the differences of all scores from the mean.' (Brown, see Chapter 5.) (131)

STANDARD FORM: The customary sections and organization of a formal research report. (33)

STATISTICAL RESEARCH: Any research based predominantly on numerical data and consequently often referred to as QUANTITATIVE RESEARCH. Compare with QUALITATIVE RESEARCH. See also DESCRIPTIVE RESEARCH, EXPLORATORY RESEARCH, QUASI-EXPERIMENTAL RESEARCH, EXPERIMENTAL RESEARCH. (12)

STATISTICAL SIGNIFICANCE: The probability that a particular statistical result could have occurred by chance alone; for example, $p < .01$ indicates that there is less than a one percent probability that a particular statistical result (CORRELATION COEFFICIENT, *t*-TEST, etc.) could have occurred by chance alone. (189)

STIMULATED RECALL: Technique in which the researcher records and transcribes parts of a lesson and then gets the teacher (and where possible, the learners) to comment on what was happening at the time that the observed teaching and learning took place. (100)

SURVEY: Procedures used to gather and describe the characteristics, attitudes, views, opinions, and so forth of students, teachers, administrators, or any other people who are important to a study. (12, 142)

SURVEY RESEARCH: Studies using INTERVIEWS and/or QUESTIONNAIRES. (117)

SYNTAX/SYNTACTIC: (Relating to) the organization of words and phrases into sentences. (27, 82)

t-TEST: The most frequently used statistic in second language research when comparing mean scores for two groups for statistical significance. (205)

TALK-ALOUDS: Those studies in which oral responses to a stimulus are concurrent with exposure to the stimulus and for which the information is already linguistically encoded and can be directly stated. Compare with THINK-ALOUDS. (55)

TALLY: See FREQUENCIES.

TESTING: A means of gauging learning outcomes. Compare with EVALUATION. (227)

THINK-ALOUDS: Those studies in which oral responses to stimuli are concurrent with exposure to the stimuli but for which information is not already linguistically encoded and thus requires linguistic encoding for verbalization. Compare with TALK-ALOUDS. (55)

TRANSFERABILITY: The degree to which the results of QUALITATIVE research could be applied to other settings; loosely analogous to the concept of EXTERNAL VALIDITY in QUANTITATIVE research. (242)

TRIANGULATION: A variety of techniques for viewing the same phenomena from multiple perspectives. (242)

TRIMODAL: Three MODES in a set of numbers. (128)

TRUE EXPERIMENTAL STUDY: A study that compares behavior in two groups of participants who have been randomly selected and assigned to control and treatment groups and then given control and experimental treatments. Change in behavior is measured by pre- and post-tests on both groups. Compare with QUASI-EXPERIMENTAL RESEARCH. (211)

VALIDITY: The degree to which the results of a study can be accurately interpreted and effectively generalized. (241)

BIBLIOGRAPHY

Alderson, J. C. 1986. 'The nature of the beast' in A. Wangsotorn, A. Maurice, K. Prapphal and B. Kenny (eds.): *Trends in Language Programme Evaluation*. Bangkok: Chulalongkorn University.

Alderson, J. C. and **M. Scott.** 1992. 'Insiders, outsiders and participatory evaluation' in J.C. Alderson and A. Beretta (eds.): *Evaluating Second Language Education*. Cambridge: Cambridge University Press. pp. 25–58.

Alkin, M. C. 1969. 'Evaluation theory development.' *Evaluation Comment* 2/1.

Allwright, D. 1975. 'Problems in the study of teachers' treatment of learner error' in M. Burt and H. Dulay (eds.): *On TESOL '75: New Directions in Second Language Learning, Teaching and Bilingual Education*. Washington, D.C.: TESOL.

Allwright, D. 1988. *Observation in the Language Classroom*. London: Longman.

American Psychological Association. 1994. *Publication Manual of the American Psychological Association* (4th edn.). Washington, D.C.: American Psychological Association.

Anderson, B. F. 1969. *The Psychological Experiment*. Belmont, Ca.: Brooks/Cole.

Anderson, R. W. 1976. 'The impoverished state of cross-sectional morpheme acquisition/accuracy methodology (or: The leftovers are more nourishing than the main course).' *Working Papers in Bilingualism* 4: 47–82.

Atkinson, R. C. 1975. 'Mnemotechnics in second language learning.' *American Psychologist* 30/8: 821–8.

Bailey, K. 1983. 'Competitiveness and anxiety in adult second language learning: looking at and through the diary studies' in H. Seliger and M. Long (eds.): *Classroom Oriented Research in Second Language Acquisition*. Rowley, Mass.: Newbury House. pp. 123–35.

Bailey, K. 1991. 'Diary studies of classroom language learning: the doubting game and the believing game' in E. Sadtono (ed.): *Language Acquisition and the Second/Foreign Language Classroom*. Singapore: SEAMEO Language Centre. pp. 60–102.

Bailey, K. M. and **D. Allwright.** 1991. *Focus on the Language Classroom*. Cambridge: Cambridge University Press.

Bailey, K. M. and **J. D. Brown.** 1996. 'Language testing courses: what are they?' in A. Cumming and R. Berwick (eds.): *Validation in Language Testing*. Clevedon, U.K.: Multilingual Matters. pp. 236–56.

Beretta, A. 1990. 'Implementation of the Bangalore project.' *Applied Linguistics* 11/4: 321–40.

Beretta, A. 1992. 'Evaluation of language education: an overview' in J.C. Alderson and A. Beretta (eds.): *Evaluating Second Language Education.* Cambridge: Cambridge University Press. pp. 5–24.

Best, J. and **J. Kahn.** 1989. *Research in Education.* Englewood Cliffs, N.J.: Prentice-Hall.

Bialystok, E. 1990. *Communication Strategies.* Oxford: Basil Blackwell.

Block, E. 1986. 'The comprehension strategies of second language readers.' *TESOL Quarterly* 20: 463–84.

Boring, E. G. 1953. 'A history of introspection.' *Psychological Bulletin* 50: 169–89.

Brindley, G. 1984. *Needs Analysis and Objectives Setting in the Adult Migrant Education Program.* Sydney: NSW Adult Migrant Education Service.

Brock, C. 1986. 'The effects of referential questions on ESL classroom discourse.' *TESOL Quarterly* 20: 47–8.

Brown, C. S. and **S. L. Lytle.** 1988. 'Merging assessment and instruction: protocols in the classroom' in S. M. Glazer (ed): *Reexamining Reading Diagnosis: New Trends and Procedures.* Newark, Del.: International Reading Association.

Brown, H. D. 1994. *Principles of Language Learning and Teaching.* Englewood Cliffs, N.J.: Prentice-Hall Regents.

Brown, J. D. 1983. 'An exploration of morpheme-group interactions' in K. B. Bailey, M. H. Long, and S. Peck (eds.): *Second Language Acquisition Studies* Rowley, Mass.: Newbury House. pp. 25–40.

Brown, J. D. 1988. *Understanding Research in Second Language.* Cambridge: Cambridge University Press.

Brown, J. D. 1989. 'Language program evaluation: a synthesis of existing possibilities' in K. Johnson (ed.): *The Second Language Curriculum.* Cambridge: Cambridge University Press. pp. 222–41.

Brown, J. D. 1992a. 'Statistics as a foreign language, Part 2: more things to look for in reading statistical language studies.' *TESOL Quarterly* 26/4: 629–64.

Brown, J. D. 1992b. 'What is research?' *TESOL Matters* 2/5: 10.

Brown, J. D. 1995a. 'Language program evaluation: problems and solutions.' *Annual Review of Applied Linguistics* 15: 227–48.

Brown, J. D. 1995b. *The Elements of Language Curriculum: A Systematic Approach to Program Development.* New York: Heinle and Heinle.

Brown, J. D. 1997a. 'Designing a language study' in D. Nunan and D. Griffee (eds.): *Classroom Teachers and Classroom Research.* Tokyo: Japan Association for Language Teaching. pp. 109–21.

Brown, J. D. 1997b. 'Designing surveys for language programs' in D. Nunan and D. Griffee (eds.): *Classroom Teachers and Classroom Research.* Tokyo: Japan Association for Language Teaching. pp. 55–70.

Brown, J. D. 2000. *An Evaluation of the Basic-education and Secondary English Language Curricula in Tunisia.* Tunis, Tunisia: Ministry of Education.

Brown, J. D. 2001. *Using Surveys in Language Programs.* Cambridge: Cambridge University Press.

Brown, J. D., M. Knowles, D. Murray, J. Neu, and E. Violand-Hainer. 1992. 'TESOL Research Task Force report to the TESOL Executive Board'. Unpublished manuscript. Alexandria, Va.: TESOL.

Brown, R. 1973. *A First Language: The Early Stages.* Cambridge, Mass: Harvard University Press.

Buteau, M. F. 1970. 'Students' errors in the beginning of French as a second language.' *IRAL* 7/2: 133–46.

Butler, C. 1985. *Statistics in Linguistics.* Oxford: Blackwell.

Campbell, D. T. and J. C. Stanley. 1963. *Experimental and Quasi-experimental Designs for Research.* Chicago: Rand McNally.

Candlin, C., J. Leather, and C. Bruton. 1978. *Doctor Patient Communication Skills.* Chelmsford, U.K.: Graves Audio-Visual Medical Foundation.

Carr, W. and S. Kemmis. 1985. *Becoming Critical: Knowing Through Action Research.* Geelong, Australia: Deakin University Press.

Cavalcanti, M. C. 1987. 'Investigating foreign language reading performance through pause protocols' in C. Færch and G. Kasper (eds.): *Introspection in Second Language Research.* Clevedon, U.K.: Multilingual Matters. pp. 230–50.

Chamot, A. 1999. *Teaching Learning Strategies to Language Students. ERIC DOC ED 433719.* Washington, D.C.: ERIC Clearinghouse.

Chaudron, C. 1988. *Second Language Classroom: Research on Teaching and Learning.* Cambridge: Cambridge University Press.

Cohen, A. 1987. 'Student processing of feedback on their compositions' in A. Wenden and J. Rubin (eds.): *Learner Strategies in Language Learning.* Englewood Cliffs, N.J.: Prentice-Hall. pp. 123–34.

Corder, S. P. 1974. 'Techniques in applied linguistics' in J. P. B. Allen and S. Pit Corder (eds.): *Edinburgh Course in Applied Linguistics* (3rd edn.). Oxford: Oxford University Press.

Corder, S. P. 1981. *Error Analysis and Interlanguage.* Oxford: Oxford University Press.

Coulthard, R. M. 1985. *Introduction to Discourse Analysis.* London: Longman.

Cousins, N. 1989. *Healing and Belief.* N.Y.: W. W. Norton.

Cumming, A. 1990. 'Metalinguistic and ideational thinking in second language composing.' *Written Communication* 7: 482–511.

Davis, K. A. 1992. 'Validity and reliability in qualitative research on second language acquisition and teaching: another researcher comments.' *TESOL Quarterly* 26: 605–8.

Davis, K. A. 1995. 'Qualitative theory and methods in applied linguistics research.' *TESOL Quarterly* 29: 427–53.

Day, R. 1984. 'Student participation in the ESL classroom, or some imperfections of practice.' *Language Learning* 34: 69–102.

Day, R. 1990. 'Teacher observation in second language teacher education' in J. Richards and D. Nunan (eds.): *Second Language Teacher Education.* Cambridge: Cambridge University Press.

Denzin, N. K. 1978. *The Research Act: A Theoretical Introduction to Sociological Methods* (2nd edn.). New York: McGraw-Hill.

Dewey, J. 1933. 'How we think', reprinted in W. B. Kolesnick (ed.): *Mental Discipline in Modern Education.* Madison, Wis.: University of Wisconsin Press.

Dick, W. and **L. Carey.** 1985. *The Systematic Design of Instruction* (2nd edn.). Glenview, Ill.: Scott Foresman.

Dixon, W. J. and **F. J. Massey Jr.** 1951. *Introduction to Statistical Analysis.* New York: McGraw-Hill.

Dörnyei, Z. and **R. Schmidt.** (eds.). 2001. *Motivation and Second Language Acquisition.* Honolulu, Hawaii: Second Language Teaching and Curriculum Center, University of Hawaii Press.

Ellis, R. 1994. *The Study of Second Language Acquisition.* Oxford: Oxford University Press.

Ellis, R. 1999. *Learning a second language through interaction.* Studies in Bilingualism 17.

Ericsson, K. A. and **H. A. Simon.** 1987. 'Verbal reports on thinking' in C. Færch and G. Kasper (eds.): *Introspection in Second Language Research.* Clevedon, U.K.: Multilingual Matters. pp. 24–53.

Ericsson, K. A. and **H. A. Simon.** 1993. *Protocol Analysis.* Cambridge, Mass.: Bradford/MIT Press. (First edition 1984.)

Ervin-Tripp, S. M. 1974. 'Is second language learning like the first?', *TESOL Quarterly* 8/2: 124.

Færch, C. and **G. Kasper.** 1983. *Strategies in Interlanguage Communication.* London: Longman.

Færch, C. and **G. Kasper** (eds.). 1987. *Introspection in Second Language Research.* Clevedon, U.K.: Multilingual Matters.

Fisher, R. A. and **F. Yates.** 1963. *Statistical Tables for Biological, Agricultural, and Medical Research.* London: Longman.

Freeman, D. 1998. *Doing Teacher Research: From Inquiry to Understanding.* Boston, Mass.: Heinle and Heinle.

Fries, C. C. 1957. *The Structure of English: An Introduction to the Construction of English Sentences.* New York: Harcourt Brace Jovanovich.

Galluzzo, G. R. 1995. 'Evaluation of teacher education programs' in L. W. Anderson (ed.): *International Encyclopedia of Teaching and Teacher Education.* Terryton, N.J.: Elsevier Science. pp. 552–6.

Gersten, R. and **S. Baker.** 2000. 'What we know about effective instructional practices for English-language learners.' *Exceptional Children* 66/4: 454–70.

Gould, S. J. 1981. *The Mismeasure of Man.* New York: Norton.

Gow, L. and **D. Kember.** 1993. 'Conceptions of teaching and their relationship to student learning.' *British Journal of Educational Psychology* 63: 20–33.

Grabe, W. 1988. 'Reassessing the term "interactive"' in P. Carrell, J. Devine and D. Eskey (eds.): *Interactive Approaches to Second Language Reading.* Cambridge: Cambridge University Press.

Green, A. 1998. *Verbal Protocol Analysis in Language Testing Research: A Handbook.* Cambridge: Cambridge University Press.

Grotjahn, R. 1987. 'On the methodological basis of introspective methods' in C. Færch and G. Kasper (eds.): *Introspection in Second Language Research.* Clevedon, U.K.: Multilingual Matters.

Guilford, J. P. and **B. Fruchter.** 1973. *Fundamental Statistics in Psychology and Education.* New York: McGraw-Hill.

Halliday, M. A. K. 1975. *Learning How to Mean: Explorations in the Development of Language.* London: Edward Arnold.

Hammersley, M. 1986. *Controversies in Classroom Research.* Milton Keynes: Open University Press.

Hansen-Bede, L. A. 1975. 'A child's creation of a second language.' *Working Papers in Bilingualism* 7: 2–9.

Hatch, E. (ed.). 1978. *Second Language Acquisition.* Rowley, Mass.: Newbury House.

Hatch, E. and **H. Farhady.** 1982. *Research Design and Statistics for Applied Linguistics.* Rowley, Mass.: Newbury House.

Hatch, E. and **A. Lazaraton.** 1991. *The Research Manual: Design and Statistics for Applied Linguistics.* Rowley, Mass.: Newbury House.

Holley, F. M. and **J. K. King.** 1971. 'Imitation and correction in foreign language learning.' *Modern Language Journal* 55/8: 494–8.

Horwitz, E. K. 1985. 'Using student beliefs about language learning and teaching in the foreign language methods course.' *Foreign Language Annals* 18/4: 333–40.

Horwitz, E. K. 1988. 'Beliefs about language learning of beginning university foreign language students.' *Modern Language Journal* 72/3: 283–94.

Hymes, D. 1971. *On Communicative Competence.* Philadelphia, Pa.: University of Pennsylvania Press.

Jacobs, G. M. 1997. 'Can learner strategy instruction succeed? The case of higher order questions and elaborated responses.' *System* 25/4: 561–70.

Jakobson, R. 1960. 'Concluding statement: linguistics and poetics' in T. Sebeok (ed.): *Style in Language.* Cambridge: The Technology Press.

James, W. 1890. *The Principles of Psychology.* New York: Holt.

Janesick, V. J. 1994. 'The dance of qualitative research design: metaphor, methodology, and meaning' in N. K. Denzin and Y. S. Lincoln (eds.): *Handbook of Qualitative Research.* Thousand Oaks, Ca.: Sage. pp. 209–19.

Johar, N. 1996. 'Reading strategies used by good and poor readers in narrative texts: an exploratory study.' Unpublished masters degree dissertation. National University of Singapore.

Johns, A. M. 1981. 'Necessary English: a faculty survey.' *TESOL Quarterly* 15: 51–7.

Johnson, D. M. 1992. *Approaches to Research in Second Language Learning.* N.Y.: Longman.

Johnson, K. 1995. *Understanding Communication in Second Language Classrooms.* Cambridge: Cambridge University Press.

Joyce, J. 1998. *Ulysses.* Oxford. Oxford University Press. (First published 1922.)

Kagan, S. 1995. *Cooperative Learning.* Los Angeles: Kagan Publishing.

Kasper, G. 2000. 'Verbal Protocols' in G. Kasper and K. Rose (eds.): *Research Methods in Interlanguage Pragmatics.* Mahwah: Erlbaum.

Keller, Helen. 1954. *The Story of My Life.* New York: Doubleday & Co. (First published 1903.)

Kellerman, E. 1991. 'Compensatory strategies in second language research: a critique, a revision, and some (non-)implications for the classroom' in R. Phillipson, E. Kellerman, L. Selinker, M. Sharwood Smith, and M. Swain (eds.): *Foreign/Second Language Pedagogy Research.* Clevedon, U.K.: Multilingual Matters.

Kellerman, E. and **M. Sharwood Smith.** (eds.). 1986. *Cross-linguistic Influence in Second Language Acquisition.* Oxford: Pergammon.

Kemmis, S. and **R. McTaggart.** (eds.). 1988. *The Action Research Planner* (3rd edn.). Geelong, Australia: Deakin University Press.

Krashen, S. 1977. 'Some issues relating to the monitor model.' *On TESOL '77. Selected papers from the 11th annual TESOL convention, Miami.* Washington, D.C.: TESOL.

Labov, W. and **D. Fanshel.** 1977. *Therapeutic Discourse: Psychotherapy as Conversation.* New York: Academic Press.

Lado, R. 1957. *Linguistics Across Cultures: Applied Linguistics for Language Teachers.* Ann Arbor: University of Michigan Press.

Larsen-Freeman, D. 2000. *Techniques and Principles in Language Teaching.* Oxford: Oxford University Press.

Laufer, B. and **J. Hulstijn.** 2001. 'Incidental vocabulary acquisition in a second language: the construct of task-induced involvement.' *Applied Linguistics* 22/1: 1–26.

Lazaraton, A. 1995. 'Qualitative research in applied linguistics: a progress report.' *TESOL Quarterly* 29/3: 455–72.

Lennon, P. 1989. 'Introspection and intentionality in advanced second-language acquisition.' *Language Learning* 39: 375–96.

Leopold, W. 1939–49. *Speech Development of a Bilingual Child: A Linguist's Record* (Volumes 1–4). Evanston, Ill.: Northwestern University Press.

Leopold, W. 1978. 'A child's learning of two languages' in E. Hatch (ed.): *Second Language Acquisition.* Rowley, Mass.: Newbury House. pp. 23–32.

Levin, J. R. and **M. Pessley.** 1985. 'Mnemonic vocabulary acquisition: what's fact, what's fiction?' in R. F. Dillon (ed.): *Individual Differences in Cognition* (Volume 2). Orlando, Fl.: Academic Press. pp. 145–72.

Lightbown, P. and **N. Spada.** 1999. *How Languages are Learned* (2nd edn.). Oxford: Oxford University Press.

Lim, W. L. 2000. 'An analysis of students' dyadic interaction on a dictogloss task.' Unpublished dissertation submitted for the Degree of Master of Arts in Applied Linguistics, National University of Singapore.

Lincoln, Y. and **E. Guba.** 1985. *Naturalistic Inquiry.* Beverly Hills, Ca.: Sage.

Long, M. 1983. 'Does second language instruction make a difference? a review of the research.' *TESOL Quarterly* 17: 359–82.

Long, M. 1984. 'Process and product in ESL program evaluation.' *TESOL Quarterly* 18/3: 409–25.

Long, M. and **C. Sato.** 1983. 'Classroom foreigner talk discourse: forms and functions of teachers' questions' in H. Seliger and M. Long (eds.): *Classroom-oriented Research on Second Language Acquisition.* Rowley, Mass.: Newbury House.

Lotz, J. 1963. 'On speech.' *Word* 6/1–2: 17–27.

Lynch, B. 1992. 'Evaluating a program inside and out' in J. C. Alderson and A. Beretta (eds.): *Evaluating Second Language Education.* Cambridge: Cambridge University Press.

Lynch, B. 1997. *Language Program Evaluation: Theory and Practice.* Cambridge: Cambridge University Press.

Lytle, S. L. 1982. 'Exploring comprehension style: A study of twelfth-graders' transactions with text.' PhD dissertation, University of Pennyslvania.

Madigan, R., S. Johnson, and **P. Linton.** 1995. 'The language of psychology: APA style as epistemology.' *American Psychologist* 50/6: 428–36.

McLaughlin, B. 1987. *Theories of Second Language Learning.* London: Edward Arnold.

McNamara, J. 1973. 'Nurseries, streets and classrooms: some comparisons and deductions.' *Modern Language Journal* 57: 250–5.

Meighan, R. and **J. Meighan.** 1990. 'Alternative roles for learners with particular reference to learners as democratic explorers in teacher education courses.' *The School Field* 1/1: 61–77.

Metfessel, N. S. and **W. B. Michael.** 1967. 'A paradigm involving multiple criterion measures for the evaluation of the effectiveness of school programs.' *Educational and Psychological Measurement* 27: 931–43.

Miles, M. B. and **A. M. Huberman.** 1984. *Qualitative Data Analysis: A Sourcebook of New Methods.* Beverly Hills, Ca.: Sage.

Naiman, N., M. Fröhlich, H. H. Stern, and **A. Todesco.** 1978. *The Good Language Learner. Research in Education Series No. 7.* Toronto: Modern Language Centre, OISE.

Nespor, J. 1987. 'The role of beliefs in the practice of teaching.' *Journal of Curriculum Studies* 19/4: 317–28.

Nisbett, R. and **T. Wilson.** 1977. 'Telling more than you can know: verbal reports on mental processes.' *Psychological Review* 84: 231–59.

Nunan, D. 1989. *Understanding Language Classrooms.* London: Prentice-Hall.

Nunan, D. 1991. *The Learner-centred Curriculum.* Cambridge: Cambridge University Press.

Nunan, D. 1992. *Research Methods in Language Learning.* Cambridge: Cambridge University Press.

Nystrom, N. 1983. 'Teacher-student interaction in bilingual classrooms: four approaches to error feedback' in H. Seliger and M. Long (eds.): *Classroom-oriented Research in Second Language Acquisition.* Rowley, Mass.: Newbury House. pp. 169–88.

Ochsner, R. 1980. 'Job-related aspects of the M.A. in TESOL degree.' *TESOL Quarterly* 14/2: 199–207.

Oller Jr., J. W. and **P. A. Richard-Amato** (eds.). (1983). *Methods that Work: Ideas for Literacy and Language Teachers* (2nd edn.). Cambridge, Mass.: Newbury House.

Olsen, R. and **S. Kagan.** 1992. 'About cooperative learning' in C. Kessler (ed.): *Cooperative Language Learning.* Englewood Cliffs, N.J.: Prentice-Hall. pp. 1–30.

O'Malley, M. and **A. Chamot.** 1990. *Learning Strategies in Second Language Acquistion.* Cambridge: Cambridge University Press.

Oxford, R. L. 1990. *Language Learning Strategies: What Every Teacher Should Know.* Rowley, Mass.: Newbury House.

Pajares, M. G. 1992. 'Teachers' beliefs and educational research: clearing up a messy construct.' *Review of Educational Research*, 62/3: 307–32.

Pennington, M. 1989. 'Faculty development for language programs' in R. K. Johnson (ed.): *The Second Language Curriculum.* Cambridge: Cambridge University Press. pp. 91–110.

Pienemann, M. 1985. 'Learnability and syllabus construction' in K. Hyltenstam and M. Pienemann (eds.): *Modelling and Assessing Second Language Acquisition.* Clevedon, U.K.: Multilingual Matters.

Popham, W. J. 1975. *Educational Evaluation.* Englewood Cliffs, N.J.: Prentice-Hall.

Pressley, M. and **P. Afflerbach.** 1995. *Verbal Protocols of Reading.* Hillsdale, N.J.: Erlbaum.

Provus, M. M. 1971. *Discrepancy Evaluation.* Berkeley, Ca.: McCutchan.

Raugh, M. R. and **R. C. Atkinson.** 1975. 'A mnemonic method for learning a second-language vocabulary.' *Journal of Educational Psychology* 67/1: 1–16.

Ravem, R. 1974. 'Second language acquisition: a study of two Norwegian children's acquisition of English syntax in a naturalistic setting.' Unpublished Ph.D. thesis, University of Essex.

Richards, J. C. 1974. *Error Analysis.* London: Longman.

Richards, J. C. 1998. *Beyond Training: Perspectives on Teacher Education.* Cambridge: Cambridge University Press.

Richards, J. C. and **T. S. Rodgers.** 2001. *Approaches and Methods in Language Teaching* (2nd edn.). Cambridge: Cambridge University Press.

Rivers, W. 1979. 'Learning a sixth language: an adult learner's daily diary.' *Canadian Modern Language Review* 36/1: 67–82.

Rodgers, T. S. 1979. 'Teacher training: in progress' in *Developments in the Training of Teachers of English.* London: The British Council, ETIC Publications. pp. 84–98.

Rodgers, T. S. 1986. 'Changing models of language program evaluation: a case study' in A. Wangsotorn, A. Maurice, K. Prapphal, and B. Kenny (eds.): *Trends in Language Programme Evaluation*. Bangkok: Chulalongkorn University.

Rodgers, T. S. 1989. 'After Methods? What?' in S. Anivan (ed.): *Language Teaching Methodology*. Singapore: Regional English Language Centre. pp. 1–15.

Rodgers, T. S. 2000. 'Assessing learner problem-solving strategies through introspection.' Unpublished paper given at Third International Conference on Language Teaching, Middle Eastern Technical University, Ankara, Turkey.

Rosenshine, B. and **N. Furst.** 1973. 'Teacher behavior and student attitudes revisited.' *Journal of Educational Psychology* 65/2: 177–80.

Ross, S. 1992. 'Program-defining evaluation in a decade of eclecticism' in J.C. Alderson and A. Beretta (eds.): *Evaluating Second Language Education*. Cambridge: Cambridge University Press. pp. 167–95.

Rossett, A. 1982. 'A typology for generating needs assessments.' *Journal of Instructional Development* 6/1: 28–33.

Rubin, J. 1975. 'What the "good language learner" can teach us.' *TESOL Quarterly* 9: 41–51.

Rubin, J. and **I. Thompson.** 1983. *How to be a More Successful Language Learner*. New York: Heinle and Heinle.

Schmidt, R. 1983. 'Interaction, acculturation and the acquisition of communicative competence: a case study of an adult' in N. Wolfson and E. Judd (eds.): *Sociolinguistics and Language Acquisition*. Rowley, Mass.: Newbury House.

Schmidt, R. 2002. 'Theories, evidence, and practice in foreign language teaching'. Unpublished handout from paper presented at the Conference of Nordic Languages as Second and Foreign Languages, Reykjavik, Iceland.

Schmidt, R. and **S. Frota.** 1986. 'Developing basic conversational ability in a second language: a case study of an adult learner of Portuguese' in R. Day (ed.): *Talking to Learn: Conversation in Second Language Acquisition*. Rowley, Mass.: Newbury House. pp. 237–326.

Schumann, F. and **J. Schumann.** 1977. 'Diary of a language learner: an introspective study of second language learning' in H. D. Brown, C. A. Yorio, and R. C. Crymes (eds.): *On TESOL '77: Teaching and Learning English as a Second Language: Trends in Research and Practice*. Washington, D.C.: TESOL. pp. 241–9.

Schwartz, B. 1986. 'The epistemological status of second language acquisition.' *Second Language Research* 2: 120–59.

Scriven, M. 1967. 'The methodology of evaluation' in R. E. Stake (ed.): *Curriculum Evaluation*. Chicago: Rand-McNally.

Scriven, M. 1999. *The Nature of Evaluation. Part I: Relation to Psychology. ERIC/AE Digest. EED435710.* Washington, D.C.: ERIC Clearinghouse on Assessment and Evaluation.

Seliger, H. 1977. 'Does practice make perfect? A study of the interaction patterns and L2 competence.' *Language Learning* 27: 263–78.

Seliger, H. and **E. Shohamy.** 1989. *Second Language Research Methods.* Oxford: Oxford University Press.

Selinker, L. 1972. 'Interlanguage.' *International Review of Applied Linguistics* 10: 209–31.

Shavelson, R. and **P. Stern.** 1981. 'Research on teachers' pedagogical thoughts, judgements, decisions and behavior.' *Review of Educational Research* 51/4: 455–98.

Simon, H. 1979. *Models of thought.* New Haven: Yale University Press.

Sinclair, J. M. and **R. M. Coulthard.** (1975). *Towards an Analysis of Discourse.* Oxford: Oxford University Press.

Skehan, P. 1997. 'Task-based instruction.' *Annual Review of Applied Linguistics* 18: 268–86.

Snow, C. and **M. Hoefnagel-Hohle.** 1978. 'Age differences in second language acquisition' in E. Hatch (ed.): *Second Language Acquisition.* Rowley, Mass.: Newbury House. p. 335.

Stahl, R. J. 1995. 'Cooperative learning: a language arts context and an overview' in R. J. Stahl (ed.): *Cooperative Learning in Language Arts.* Menlo Park, Ca.: Addison-Wesley. pp. 1–16.

Stake, R. E. 1967. 'The countenance of educational evaluation.' *Teachers College Record* 68/7: 523–40.

Stockwell, R., J. D. Bowen, and **J. W. Martin.** 1965. *The Grammatical Structures of English and Spanish.* Chicago: University of Chicago Press.

Stubbs, M. 1975. 'Teaching and talking: a sociolinguistic approach to classroom interaction' in G. Chanan and S. Delamont (eds.): *Frontiers of Classroom Research.* Slough, U.K.: National Foundation for Educational Research.

Stubbs, M. 1981. 'Scratching the surface: linguistic data in educational research' in C. Adelman (ed.): *Uttering, Muttering.* London: Grant McIntyre. 114–33. Reprinted in M. Hammersley. 1986. *Controversies in Classroom Research.* Milton Keynes: Open University Press. pp. 62–78.

Stufflebeam, D. L. 1974. 'Alternative approaches to educational evaluation' in W. J. Popham (ed.): *Evaluation in Education: Current Applications.* Berkeley, Ca.: McCutchan.

Swain, M. 1995. 'Three functions of output in second language learning' in G. Cook and B. Seidlhofer (eds): *Principles and Practice in Applied Linguistics: Studies in Honour of H.G. Widdowson.* Oxford: Oxford University Press. pp. 125–44.

Swain, M. and **S. Lapkin.** 1994. 'Problems in output and the cognitive processes they generate: a step towards second language learning.' Unpublished manuscript. Toronto: Modern Language Centre, OISE.

Tarone, E. 1977. 'Conscious communication strategies in interlanguage' in H. D. Brown, C. A. Yorio, and R. C. Crymes (eds.): *On TESOL '77: Teaching and Learning English as a Second Language: Trends in Research and Practice.* Washington, D.C.: TESOL.

Titchener, E. B. 1912. 'Prolegomena to a study of introspection.' *American Journal of Psychology* 23: 427–48.

Tyler, R. W. 1942. 'General statement on evaluation.' *Journal of Educational Research* 35: 492–501.

Tyler, R. W. 1951. 'The functions of measurement in improving instruction' in E. F. Lindquist (ed.): *Educational Measurement.* Washington, D.C.: American Council on Education.

van Lier, L. 1988. *The Classroom and the Language Learner.* London: Longman.

Vygotsky, L. 1988. *Mind in Society: the Development of Higher Psychological Processes.* Cambridge, Mass.: Harvard University Press.

Wardhaugh, R. 1974. *Topics in Applied Linguistics.* Rowley, Mass.: Newbury House.

Watson, J. B. 1913. 'Psychology as the behaviorist sees it.' *Psychological Review* 20: 158–77.

Weinstein, C. S. 1989. 'Teacher education: Students' preconceptions of teaching.' *Journal of Teacher Education* 40/2: 53–60.

Weir, R. 1962. *Language in the Crib.* The Hague: Mouton.

White, L. 1991. 'Adverb placement in second language acquisition: some effects of positive and negative evidence in the classroom.' *Second Language Research* 7: 133–61.

Williams, M. and **R. L. Burden.** 1997. *Psychology for Language Teachers: A Social Constructivist Approach.* Cambridge: Cambridge University Press.

Willing, K. 1988. *Learning Styles in Adult Migrant Education.* Adelaide, Australia: National Centre for English Language Teaching and Research, Macquarie University.

Wode, H. 1978. 'Developmental sequences in naturalistic L2 acquisition' in E. Hatch (ed.): *Second Language Acquisition.* Rowley, Mass.: Newbury House. pp. 101–17.

Wood, D. 1994. 'Output unbound: making a case for the role of output in adult learners' acquisition of Japanese as a foreign language'. Unpublished Master's research paper. Toronto: Modern Language Centre, OISE.

Woods, A., P. Fletcher, and **A. Hughes.** 1986. *Statistics in Language Studies.* Cambridge: Cambridge University Press.

Yucel, S. 2000. 'Snapshots of classroom interaction: teacher questioning behavior and error correction strategies' in S. Tuzel-Koymen, and E. Kortan (eds.): *Interaction on the Threshold of a New Millennium.* Ankara: Middle Eastern Technical University. pp. 144–54.

INDEX